SELECTED PROSE OF

T. S. ELIOT

SELECTED PROSE OF

T. S. ELIOT

Edited with an Introduction by
FRANK KERMODE

Harcourt Brace Jovanovich
Farrar, Straus and Giroux
New York

Literary criticism is a distinctive activity of the civilized mind.

T. S. ELIOT, 1961

CONTENTS

9

II

SOCIAL AND RELIGIOUS CRITICISM

INTRODUCTION

In 'To Criticize the Critic', a lecture delivered at Leeds University in 1961, Eliot looked back over his own career as a critic and sought to draw from it 'some plausible generalizations of wider validity'. He distinguished several categories – Professional Critics, Critics with Gusto (who call attention to neglected writers), Academic and Theoretical Critics – but the category in which he placed himself was that of the critic whose criticism is a by-product of his creative activity, and 'particularly, the critic who is also a poet'. (Other critics of this kind are Johnson, Coleridge, Dryden, Racine and Matthew Arnold.[1]) Eliot's critical writings are diverse and extensive, but it is not to be doubted that he put himself into the right group. His readers (and, of course, his editor) must always be mindful of this, and of certain other admonitions in the same retrospective survey.

As he reviewed his work Eliot, in tones of amused severity, observed in it certain faults: 'the occasional note of arrogance, of vehemence, of cocksureness or rudeness, the braggadocio of the mild-mannered man safely entrenched behind his typewriter'. By way of excuse he urged upon all who cite his work the need to reflect that it is not a single seamless garment or premeditated system, but a series of essays belonging to different dates and different stages of his life. He maintained that his early criticism achieved its success partly because of its dogmatic manner and because it was, inexplicitly, a defence of the poetic practice of his friends and himself. Later readers enjoy the tones of warm advocacy even though they do not understand exactly what the author was reacting against; and so this early work is more appealing than the more 'detached' and 'judicial' pieces he wrote later.

To get his work into perspective, Eliot proposed to divide it into three periods. During the first he was writing for the *Egoist*, in which appeared what is arguably his most influential single essay, 'Tradition and the Individual Talent'. The main influences

---

[1] The footnotes to this Introduction are at the end of the Introduction on p. 23.

on his work at this time were Ezra Pound (and through him Remy de Gourmont and Henry James) and Irving Babbitt, who at Harvard introduced Eliot to the philosophy of Humanism, and whose traditionalist doctrines were reinforced, a little later, by the ideas of T. E. Hulme and Charles Maurras.[2]

The second period, from 1918 to about 1930, was primarily one of regular contributions to the *Athenaeum*, edited by Middleton Murry, and the *Times Literary Supplement*, edited by Bruce Richmond; and the third primarily one of lectures and addresses.

Throughout, he believed, there was 'an important line of demarcation' between 'essays of generalization' and 'appreciations of individual authors'; and he thought the second class the more likely to retain a value for future readers. Without wholly accepting that judgment, I have, in this selection, adopted the classification Eliot proposed, dividing the work into three periods, and, within those periods, into 'essays of generalization' and 'appreciations of individual authors'. (They overlap, of course; the generalizations are founded on appreciations, and the appreciations require, for reasons explored below, to be set in a context of generalization. And there are anomalies: I hope nobody will complain that Marie Lloyd is not exactly an 'individual author'.)

The scheme of this book therefore complies, as far as possible, with Eliot's own prescription, and in the matter of selection it also follows his lead. I shall not embark on a general defence of my selections; no two editors would fill the available space with identical choices, though there would be agreement about six or eight essays. A word, however, should be said concerning the policy of choosing – with two exceptions – only what has appeared in collections made by the poet himself. There is a large body of criticism by Eliot that has never been collected; some of it is of high interest, and it is greatly to be hoped that it will one day be published. But given the exigencies of space, an editor ought, I think, to respect the initial act of selection made by the critic himself. The exceptions to this rule are early essays on James and Joyce, which are not only celebrated but have, with Eliot's consent, appeared in anthologies.

I may here note one further restriction on my choice. I emphasize the literary, at the expense of the ecclesiastical, the political and the social criticism, which, in the course of time, came to constitute a considerable proportion of Eliot's prose, and which not only has its own importance but often illuminates both the literary criticism and the poetry. I have tried to give some notion of its tone and range, but the disproportion should be borne in mind. The short bibliography in Appendix B (p. 313) shows where the missing material is to be sought, and mentions one or two of the better studies of it.

Eliot was clearly right in supposing that the most influential of his essays were among the earliest (though I believe he under-estimated the degree to which later work reinforced them and ensured that they should be read with unusual attention). The works in question are 'essays of generalization'; but despite their superstructure of system and theory such essays as 'Tradition and the Individual Talent', 'The Metaphysical Poets', and *'Hamlet'* all have their origins in his own creative reading of past poetry, and in his programme for new poetry, his own and others', about the time of *Gerontion* and *The Waste Land*.

In May 1935, long after these seminal essays were written, Eliot wrote a remarkable letter to Stephen Spender. He was com-menting on Spender's critical book, *The Destructive Element*, but also on his own experience. 'You don't,' he said, 'really criticize any author to whom you have never surrendered yourself. . . . Even just the bewildering minute counts; you have to give your-self up, and then recover yourself, and the third moment is having something to say, before you have wholly forgotten both sur-render and recovery. Of course the self recovered is never the same as the self before it was given.'[3]

'The bewildering minute' is a quotation from *The Revenger's Tragedy*; Eliot had used it both in 'Tradition and the Individual Talent' and in the essay on Tourneur of 1931:

> *Are lordships sold to maintain ladyships*
> *For the poor benefit of a bewildering minute?*

He gave himself up to these lines, and by the same act possessed them; it is a characteristic 'surrender'. We are here, I think, contemplating an aspect not only of Eliot's critical, but of his poetic genius. The passage by Tourneur – or, as many now believe, by Middleton – celebrates a peculiar blend of fascination and disgust, a mortuary eroticism balancing on the moment of simultaneous enchantment and loss, the sexual surrender. We encountered a version of it in *The Waste Land*:

> *. . . blood shaking my heart*
> *The awful daring of a moment's surrender . . .*

and, negatively, in the seductions of the typist and the Thames-daughters. We recognize it even in accounts of failure, of the

13

withholding of the self: 'I could not / Speak, and my eyes failed' –
and in the prayer of the Hollow Men; transformed, it becomes in
Ash-Wednesday 'The infirm glory of the positive hour'. The
experience of the bewildering minute in poetry is powerfully
described in the essay on Dante: 'It is very much like our intenser
experiences of other human beings. There is a first, or an early
moment which is unique, of shock and surprise, even of terror
(*Ego dominus tuus*); a moment which can never be forgotten, but
which is never repeated integrally; and yet which would become
destitute of significance if it did not survive in a larger whole of
experience; which survives inside a deeper and calmer feeling.'

We remember that in the *Vita Nuova* it is Love who says *Ego
dominus tuus*, and Love is 'of terrible aspect' – he makes Beatrice
eat Dante's heart, and the dream, which leaves the poet sad,
represents an unrepeatable, irreversible and fearful experience
of a kind that may be associated both with love and with poetry.
Dante, speaking of his first seeing Beatrice, explains that the
whole spirit of the man or poet responds to this overwhelming
experience; the mind reacts as to beatitude, the body knows that
henceforth it will know perturbation and sorrow. Eliot himself,
in the essay on Dante, is clear that Dante is speaking of something
that happened to him: a sexual experience remarkable only in that
one would expect it to have happened before the age of nine, and
of course in its intensity: 'I cannot find it incredible that what has
happened to others should have happened to Dante with much
greater intensity.'[4]

In the letter to Spender Eliot is describing the originating
movement of his own most important criticism: a surrender, made
in all probability before the poetry that induces it is fully understood; an excitement later to be integrated with 'a larger whole of
experience'. The second moment, of recovery, is perhaps the
moment when such a line as Tourneur's settles into the mind
it will henceforth inhabit as part of a different complex of
experience. The third, 'having something to say', requires
speculation and systematization, perhaps historical and perhaps
theoretical – faithful to the experience but providing it with an
intellectual vehicle.

The first two stages occur in the poetic as well as the critical
process; the third, for the poet, may be that 'workshop criticism'
of which Eliot speaks in 'The Frontiers of Criticism',[5] and which
was strikingly exemplified in the reworking, by Pound and the
author, of the *Waste Land* drafts. For the critic the third stage is
not so much creative as speculative; he must place his 'impression'
within an intellectual structure; his task is 'to analyse and construct', to '*ériger en lois ses impressions personnelles*', as Eliot puts it

in 'The Perfect Critic', an essay here included as the fullest statement of Eliot's early position on the place of the intellect in
criticism; one understands his admiration for the scientific critics
Aristotle and Remy de Gourmont, here quoted.[6]

Again and again one sees this third moment in the making, for
example in the Marston essay of 1934. The first moment is the
possession of a few beautifully observed lines; the last a general
doctrine of 'double reality' in poetic drama, of 'a pattern behind
the pattern . . . the kind of pattern which we perceive in our own
lives only at rare moments of inattention and detachment.' We
may then go on to observe the meaning of this doctrine in relation
to the poet's own drama, that still lay in the future, and even in
the most recent of his poetry, *Ash-Wednesday*.[7]

The construction of such contexts must, of course, follow the
surrender. In the letter to Spender Eliot warns against doing it
the other way round – constructing a system and bringing it to the
'object' under discussion – reading to prove one's point. That is
not surrender but conquest – an objection which contributes to
Eliot's evident discontent with the use other critics have made of
his own tentative and tertiary theoretical constructions. Without
the first moment there is nothing worth having. When we observe
Eliot in the Dante essay patiently point to passages which, since
they once possessed him, he now possesses; and when we find in
his own poetry signs that its foundations consist in part of matter
similarly achieved by surrender and meditation on surrender, we
have some idea of what he meant when he spoke of the creative
element in criticism. We should reflect further that what began
as a private motion of his sensibility has become part of the
common stock of educated feeling; the lines from *The Revenger's
Tragedy*, fragments of Dante,[8] the objects of a unique creative
impulse, are now of the material of our minds, and from that we
may judge the depth and quality of the initial surrender.

The first moment, then, is one of emotional rather than
intellectual engagement, and here the critic resembles the poet.
He is not thinking; like the poet he 'starts from his own emotions',
as Eliot argued in a striking passage in 'Shakespeare and the
Stoicism of Seneca' (1927).[9] Later there comes the necessity of
'great intellectual power', necessary to the expression of 'precise
emotion'. Just so the critic, most of all in the third phase of the
operation, stands in need of intellect. That is what Eliot meant by
saying that 'the only method is to be very intelligent'. The critic
starts from his own emotions, but 'having something to say' calls
for intellect.

So, in 'Tradition and the Individual Talent', we hear of the
need to *articulate* the emotion we have felt in reading: to have

something to say about the surrender, to understand and speak of an intemporal experience in temporal discourse. For such is the hypothesis: that the moments of our possession occur in the ordinary course of time but give access to something beyond time, to a tradition which conflates past and present and gives to 'the whole of the literature of Europe' simultaneous existence and simultaneous order.

Eliot's idea of tradition implicitly rejects the schismatic, *anti-passéiste* positions of such avant-garde movements as Futurism and Dada; yet he was, on his own admission, campaigning for an avant-garde, and he proposed a view of the past which, though far from abolitionist, was not at all conventional. The work of the poet will, under certain conditions, join that which exists outside time, and speak with that voice rather than with the voice of his immediate predecessors. History is flawed by disaster; the 'dissociation of sensibility' which occurred, according to Eliot, in the seventeenth century – the hypothesis had as its immediate stimulus the need to 'say something' to explain the superiority of the metaphysical poets over Milton – did not prevent access, by dint of much labour, to poetry which did not divide thought and feeling; for that poetry is not borne away by time. The effort of the true poet must be, simply and enormously, to know 'the mind of Europe' – to hold it, changing as it is in time, in a single thought of the permanence that underlies all change and without which we should be unable to apprehend change.[10] This is a way of thinking that issues from some deep place in Eliot's mind, and is registered in his later political and ecclesiastical writings, as well as in his poetry.

Equally profound, and also given later expression in thinking on a more extensive scale, is Eliot's account of the means by which the poet achieves access to the tradition; he does so by 'a continual surrender of himself', by 'a continual self-sacrifice, a continual extinction of personality'. In this way a doctrine of 'impersonality' is associated with the doctrine of tradition; and together they imply a third, imperfectly expressed by the formula 'objective correlative'.

It is unlucky, I think, that this important element in Eliot's theorizing about poetry was stated so briefly, and in one of his least impressive essays, '*Hamlet*'.[11] It suffers from imperfect articulation, and of all the 'notorious phrases' that, as Eliot remarked with amusement, 'have had a truly embarrassing success in the world', this is the one he was least concerned to defend.[12] Yet the objective correlative has its importance, especially in relation to Eliot's own poetry. It is a clumsy expression, first used, as has several times been pointed out, by the American artist

Washington Allston in the mid-nineteenth century; but Allston meant something different.[13] Perhaps the expression stemmed from a remote memory of Santayana's 'object correlative'. The difficulty arises from the fact that what the object is correlative with is the emotion of the poet; and this correlation was, in Eliot's own opinion, the least interesting thing about it to anybody except the poet himself. For although every poet starts from his own emotions, his struggle must be 'to transmute his personal and private agonies into something rich and strange, something universal and impersonal'.[14] Purged of naïve expressiveness, as of all relation to 'the logic of concepts', the poem achieves an impersonality which established its relation to the tradition at the expense of its correlation with the suffering of its author. In short, its objectivity, accomplished at the *expense* of its correlativity, is the measure of the poet's success, his surrender to the tradition. An adequate objective correlative would be the most effective mask of its relation to the originating emotion; and of course it is an inadequacy in this regard that Eliot complains of in *Hamlet*. In later years he sometimes referred to the personal nature of *The Waste Land*, but by then he could do so without harming the good reader's reaction to that work precisely because of the effectiveness of the mask; nor does information posthumously made available concerning the composition of that poem, and Eliot's emotional disturbances at the time, affect the situation. The great poet, as Eliot went on to say in the Seneca essay, 'writes his time', not himself. He was to remark of his poem that 'to me it was only the relief of a personal and wholly insignificant grouse against life . . . just a piece of rhythmical grumbling';[15] but the important words in that sentence are *to me*.

In 'The Three Voices of Poetry', a lecture delivered in 1953, Eliot commended Gottfried Benn's *Probleme der Lyrik* for its understanding of his 'first voice', which is 'the voice of the poet talking to himself – or to nobody'. Benn explains that poetry of this sort begins with 'an inert embryo or "creative germ" (*ein dumpfer schöpferischer Keim*) and, on the other hand, the Language, the resources of the words at the poet's command. He has something germinating in him for which he must find words; but he cannot know what words he wants until he has found the words; he cannot identify this embryo until it has been transformed into an arrangement of the right words in the right order. When you have the words for it, the "thing" for which the words had to be found has disappeared, replaced by a poem.' The process is painful. 'When the words are finally arranged in the right way – or in what he comes to accept as the best arrangement he can find – [the poet] may experience a moment of exhaustion, of appeasement, of absolution, and of something very near annihilation, which is in itself indescribable. And then he can say to the poem: "Go away! Find a place for yourself in a book – and don't expect *me* to take any further interest in you." '16

This passage seems to account more satisfactorily for the process by which the surrender of the personality produces the impersonal objective correlative, and to emphasize the importance of the idea for a certain kind of poetry. The argument seems to owe something to Mallarmé's sonnet '*Don du poème*'. There needs only a reminder that the birth of such an impersonal poem requires a submission to something outside oneself; and to make such a submission implies the existence of external authority. The reward for such submission is great, and not only in the making of poems; and we shall see that Eliot began to develop more than the merely aesthetic implications of this fact.

'The Function of Criticism' restates the need for sacrifice to something outside oneself, and expresses in consequence a preference for the classic over the romantic, for external 'Catholic' authority over the 'inner voice', for tradition over self-sufficient novelty. And the role of the critic is to contribute to 'the common pursuit of true judgment', a task undertaken with the 'possibility of arriving at something outside of ourselves, which may provisionally be called the truth'.

Clearly that 'surrender' to a line or a poem, which is the first moment of both poetry and criticism, and the construction of a 'generalization' – the having something to say about one's 'contact with the individual object' – are both essential constituents of the act of criticism. That is why the dividing line between 'generalizations' and 'appreciations' is so vague; and though Eliot himself thought the latter would survive longer, the former are just as surely based, in so far as they are valuable, upon an initial encounter with a line, a stanza, a poem, or an *œuvre*.

It is in the earliest works that the relation between the emotional stimulus and the act of intelligence is closest. Later the manner grows more discursive, and this is partly a consequence of the demand for longer pieces – the eight or so thousand words of a lecture, or the substantial contribution to some collection of essays. Many of these works are retrospective in character, as if to recall a time when the critic's relation to poetry was more spontaneous and more engaged. For the commitment to external authority, when, in 1927, it took a more intelligibly doctrinal form ('The general point of view may be described as classicist in

18

literature, royalist in politics, and anglo-catholic in religion')[17] could hardly be made without some reduction in spontaneity – which is not at all to say that the general pattern of Eliot's critical activity was altered.

What is surprising – especially to readers who erroneously suppose that a conversion is not founded in a habit of mind, a temperament already established – is that this change is not accompanied by any marked discontinuity of literary interest or method (the Dante essay, arguably the centre of Eliot's critical work, recapitulates in many respects his earlier criticism, and carefully refrains from insisting on a political and theological context, as it might easily, and without palpable loss, have done).[18] Perhaps the opening words of 'Religion and Literature' (1935) could not have been written very much earlier: 'Literary criticism should be completed by criticism from a definite ethical and theological standpoint.' A critic so early committed to external authority against the inner voice; to the surrender of self to something greater; to permanence as the opposite and measure of change; to the intemporal as opposed to merely sequential time and history – such a critic, as 'The Function of Criticism' suggests, would almost necessarily be drawn to a religion, an ethic, a politics that accorded with such convictions. The classicist in literature might, for a time, rest content with the traditionalist, even élitist humanism of Babbitt; but there was an element of mysticism also, and a scholastic sense of the complexities of time and eternity, that impelled him to a Catholic Christianity and a conservative-imperialist politics.

Having seen the individual poet as subordinate to a time-transcending tradition, Eliot extended the idea of submission and became a citizen of that Empire which constituted the political aspect of the mind of Europe and of the Church which represented its spiritual being. It need not surprise us that he chose the variants proper to his province; he had always seen the historical necessity of accepting the Empire in the divided form time had imposed upon it, and a vernacular church as similarly entailed; though he once said that England was a Latin country, it had not a Latin language or a Latin church. Appropriately he announced his conversion in a book called *For Lancelot Andrewes* (1928). Andrewes he took to be the greatest of the early Anglican bishops, and he gave reasons why we should admire both the Elizabethan episcopate and the accuracy and force of Andrewes's vernacular style.

Henceforth, perhaps, there could be no denying that poetry, though still in some senses what he called 'a superior amusement', nevertheless 'certainly has something to do with morals, and with religion, and even with politics perhaps, though we cannot say what.'[19] Some hardening of this formula is visible in *After Strange Gods* (1934) in which Eliot was willing to call certain of his contemporaries, Pound and Lawrence included, heretical – not in the sense that they expressed unacceptable doctrine – Marlowe, he said in 1927, was 'the most blasphemous (and therefore, probably, the most Christian) of his contemporaries'[20] – but because of a heterodoxy of sensibility.

The Dante essay is not concerned with censures of this kind, but gives most satisfactory expression to the relation between poetry and those other matters from which it cannot ultimately be separated. Obviously it has many affinities with the earlier work, for Dante was always important to Eliot, and had provided many bewildering minutes; but he was also the poet of the catholic, the imperial, and the illustrious vernacular. He could communicate, as good poetry can, before he was well understood; but the language in which he did so was the *volgare illustre*, which inherited the universality of Latin. His Tuscan had a quality Eliot valued above all others; though founded in the common speech, it possessed an extreme poetic lucidity, and was versatile enough to encompass the whole range of human experience. This range and lucidity make him the most important model of all European poets; and Eliot himself was engaged throughout his poetic career in emulating them.

He spoke, in an unpublished lecture at New Haven in 1933, of his long ambition to 'write poetry which should be essentially poetry, with nothing poetic about it, poetry standing naked in its bare bones, or poetry so transparent that we should not see the poetry, but that which we are meant to see through the poetry.... To get *beyond poetry*, as Beethoven, in his later works, strove to *get beyond* music. . . .' And he goes on to speak of the 'forty or fifty original lines' he has written which approach this condition.[21] He was probably, as Matthiessen remarks, thinking of part of the last section of *The Waste Land*, which he elsewhere singles out in the same way.[22]

This was a Dantesque enterprise, and it continued throughout his subsequent poetry. 'The kind of debt that I owe to Dante is the kind that goes on accumulating, the kind which is not the debt of one period or another of one's life . . . The whole study and practice of Dante seems to me to teach that the poet should be the servant of his language, rather than the master of it . . . Dante is, beyond all other poets of our continent, the most *European*. He is the least provincial . . . The Italian of Dante is somehow *our* language from the moment we begin to try to read it; and the lessons of craft, of speech and of exploration of sensibility, are lessons which any European can take to heart and try to apply in his own tongue.'[23]

The perfection of Dante's language is not independent of his exemplary Europeanism, his faith in the Empire. Eliot's emphasis on the need for modern men to be members of a larger polity than that of their own province – to accept their nationality yet aspire to membership of a more abstract empire[24] embodied in Latin Europe – is borne out by his long labours on the *Criterion*. In practice obedience to Empire must, in a nation state, take the form of Royalism; hence Eliot chose also the Catholicism of the English province, accepting (as he was to explain in *Notes towards the Definition of Culture*) the measure of provincialism that this entailed, but without scandal to the universality of a Church beset, in the modern age, by heresy, standing against the corruption called, in 'Religion and Literature', secularism, in later writings liberalism.

The implications, then, of the mature positions adumbrated in the Dante essay are not confined to poetry but extend into ethics, politics and religion. In later, more generalizing performances, Eliot was able to make clear how this was so. Thus his lecture on 'What is a Classic?', and the supporting talk on 'Virgil and the Christian World'[25] explain why the Roman Empire and its principal poet are central to our conceptions of civility and poetry, and why these are providentially linked to the truths of religion. And it is obvious that such implications, less explicitly stated, had been present in much earlier writings.

Dante remained the chief exemplar long after the other stimulants of the early poetry had lost their effect. The last major poem, *Little Gidding*, contains a brilliant imitation of a canto from the *Commedia*. Honouring Yeats after his death, Eliot found in him a Dantesque impersonality – 'that of the poet who, out of intense and personal experience, is able to express a general truth; retaining all the particularity of his experience, to make of it a general symbol'.

Eliot's mind was both exploratory and retentive; it turned to new themes but was always loyal to its past. Thus Babbitt and Bradley continued to engage his thought, even as it engaged the old problems in new and shifting forms; thus early essays, the immaturity and even the arrogance of which he himself was the first to detect and deprecate, are seen to be continuous with the later thought. As he remarked, his work is not a seamless web; but certain deep preoccupations endure and may be observed in this selection, and more at large in the collections he made himself, in such books as *Notes towards the Definition of Culture*, in the Commentaries he contributed over the years to *Criterion*. However remote we may seem to be from those early literary formulations – in the fields of education and politics, in the advocacy of stable class systems or of asceticism as a remedy for social chaos – we cannot escape the consistency any more than we can evade the deliberate clarity of his thought. It is a final tribute to that clarity, and to the delicacy with which certain discriminations are made, that Eliot profoundly changed our thinking about poetry and criticism without trying to impose as a condition of his gift the acceptance of consequences which, for him, followed as a matter of reason, as well as of belief and personal vocation.

NOTES

1. Published in *To Criticize the Critic*, 1965, 11–26. Eliot always believed, though he expressed the belief less dogmatically as time went on, in the superiority of practitioners as critics. (See 'The Function of Criticism'.) In the early days he thought of his own criticism no part of his work as poet: 'The poetic critic is criticizing poetry in order to create poetry.' See 'Imperfect Critics' in *The Sacred Wood*, 1920.

2. Eliot says this period ended in 1918 after the demise of the *Egoist*; in fact that journal lasted longer, and 'Tradition and the Individual Talent' appeared in it in September and December 1919. He always dated his essays when he collected them; 1917, the date he gives for 'Tradition' is wrong.

3. 'Remembering Eliot', in *T. S. Eliot: The Man and his Work*, edited by Allen Tate, 1966, 55–6.

4. *Selected Essays*, 1932, 3rd ed., 1951, 273.

5. *On Poetry and Poets*, 1957, 107.

6. On the other hand, 'there is no method except to be very intelligent.' Eliot strives to distinguish between Symons's 'impressionism' and his own 'surrender'; the difference lies in the ability to elevate impressions into rules, though without ceasing to be intelligent. 'The point is that you never rest at the pure feeling.'

7. *Selected Essays*, 221–33.

8. See, for example, the passage on p. 213, where he speaks of the Brunetto and Ulysses episodes of the *Inferno* as among those 'for which I was unprepared by quotation or allusion'. Because both of these passages possessed Eliot they became parts of the traditional knowledge of readers of poetry.

9. He goes on to say that poets express belief only incidentally, or even accidentally. 'The poet makes poetry, the metaphysician makes metaphysics, the bee makes honey, the spider secretes a filament; you can hardly say that any of these agents believes: he merely does' (*Selected Essays*, 137–8). What is called 'the problem of belief' – in this essay described by Eliot as 'very complicated and probably insoluble' – continued to engage him, especially because of the contemporary investigations of I. A. Richards, whom he tackles directly in a Note to Section II (here

omitted) of his 'Dante' and in *The Use of Poetry and the Use of Criticism*. In the Note Eliot expressly denies 'that the reader must share the beliefs of the poet in order to enjoy the poetry fully'; to maintain the converse is to deny poetry. On the other hand it is clear to him that 'full understanding' (he confesses that the word *full* is obscure) will terminate in belief: thus increased understanding of Dante's *la sua voluntate è nostra pace* brings him to the point of recognizing it as '*literally true*'. He came to believe that there was, in some extended sense of the word, an *orthodoxy* in poetry, and that this distinguished the best of the 'tradition'. This view made him unhappy about much contemporary literature, as he explains in *After Strange Gods* (1933) and in 'Religion and Literature'; the same strain of thought continues in *The Idea of a Christian Society* and *Notes Towards the Definition of Culture*.

It is important, however, not to confuse this notion of orthodoxy with a requirement that poetry should have a specific Christian *meaning*. The Dante essay distinguishes between poetic and intellectual lucidity; *The Use of Poetry* explains that 'what a poem means is as much what is means to others as what it means to the author,' calls meaning the meat the burglar brings along to quiet the housedog, and insists that poetry originates in the depths of feeling, where 'certain images recur, charged with emotion' – emotion, not meaning.

On the whole it is reasonable to say that Eliot continued faithful to the distinction he drew on the concluding page of his Dante essay: 'The English reader needs to remember that even had Dante not been a good Catholic, even had he treated Aristotle or Thomas with sceptical indifference, his mind would still be no easier to understand; the forms of imagination, phantasmagoria, and sensibility would be just as strange to us. We have to learn to accept these forms: and this *acceptance* is more important than anything that can be called belief' (*Selected Essays*, 277). A year or so earlier, feeling towards this position in the Preface to the 1928 edition of *The Sacred Wood*, he had written: '. . . certainly poetry is not the inculcation of morals, or the direction of politics; and no more is it religion or an equivalent of religion. . . . And certainly poetry is something over and above, and something quite different from, a collection of psychological data about the minds of poets, or about the history of an epoch. . . .' For later observations see the remarks on Shelley below, pp. 81ff., and *The Use of Poetry*, 87–102.

10. As to the critic, his business is to see literature '*not* as consecrated by time, but to see it beyond time' (Introduction to *The Sacred Wood*, 1920). On Eliot's commitment to *permanence* see a revealing letter to Bonamy Dobrée, dated 12 November 1927: 'I should say

that it was at any rate essential for Religion that we should have the conception of an immutable object or Reality the knowledge of which shall be the final object of the will; and there can be no permanent reality if there is no permanent truth. I am of course quite ready to admit that human apprehension of truth varies, changes and perhaps develops, but that is a property of human imperfection rather than of truth. You cannot conceive of truth at all, the word has no meaning, except by conceiving of it as something permanent. And that is really assumed even by those who deny it. For you cannot even say it changes except in reference to something which does not change; the idea of change is impossible without the idea of permanence.' ('T. S. Eliot: A Personal Reminiscence', in Allen Tate, ed., *T. S. Eliot: The Man and His Work*, 1966, 75).

11. It crops up again in the Tourneur essay of 1931: 'The cynicism, the loathing and disgust of humanity, expressed consummately in *The Revenger's Tragedy*, are immature in the respect that they exceed the object. Their objective equivalents are characters practising the grossest vices; characters which seem merely to be spectres projected from the poet's inner world of nightmare, some horror beyond words.' The whole passage is interesting, and I have sometimes suspected that it is a covert self-critique of *The Waste Land*. See *Selected Essays*, 189–90.

12. 'The Frontiers of Criticism', 1956, in *On Poetry and Poets*, 1957, 103–18. In 'To Criticize the Critic' he says it 'may stand for my bias towards the more mature plays of Shakespeare', just as the 'dissociation of sensibility' represented his devotion to Donne and his reaction against Milton (19–20). But this latter idea is, though qualified, defended in 'Milton II', whereas the 'objective correlative' gets no explicit support in the later work.

13. In 1955 Eliot told an Indian enquirer that he thought he had coined it, adding that he was no longer 'quite sure of what I meant 35 years ago'. In a Preface to the Harvest paperback *Essays on Elizabethan Drama* (1955) he says, speaking of 'objective correlative' in the course of explaining why he excludes '*Hamlet*' from the collection, that the 'phrase, I am now told, is not even my own but was first used by Washington Alston (*sic*)'.

14. 'Shakespeare and the Stoicism of Seneca', *Selected Essays*, 137. Compare: 'one is prepared for art when one has ceased to be interested in one's own emotions and experiences except as material' (Introduction to Paul Valéry, *Le Serpent*, 1924, 12).

15. *The Waste Land: A Facsimile and Transcript of the Original Drafts* . . . ed. Valerie Eliot, 1971, p. 1. Eliot's words in 'Thoughts After Lambeth' may seem to suggest that he was not 'writing his time', at any rate as his time thought he was: '. . . when I wrote a poem

called *The Waste Land* some of the more approving critics said that I had expressed the "disillusionment of a generation", which is nonsense. I may have expressed for them their own illusion of being disillusioned, but that did not form part of my intention.' (*Selected Essays*, 368.) Usually he disavowed the author's intentional control, as in his argument with Richards in *The Use of Poetry*. Of course to express unintentionally an illusion of being disillusioned may be to 'write one's time'. See below, p. 243.

16. *On Poetry and Poets*, 106–7. There is, of course, no inconsistency in holding these views and also being interested in the process of composition. The essay on Pascal (see the extract below) is an indication of such interest; it may reflect the poet's own experience in writing the last section of *The Waste Land*; see Mrs. Eliot's edition, p. 129, n. 1 to p. 71. In an unpublished lecture on *Ulysses*, given in 1933, he said that 'in some minds certain memories, both from reading and life, become charged with emotional significance. All these are used, so that intensity is gained at the expense of clarity' (quoted by F. O. Matthiessen, *The Achievement of T. S. Eliot*, 3rd edition, paperback, 56). In *The Use of Poetry*, delivered in the same year, he specifies (see below, pp. 89–90) some of his own memories of this kind, clearly intending to distinguish between the proper use of such memories and that condemned by Hulme in the passage quoted immediately afterwards. See also 'The Perfect Critic', in which he refers again to the process by which such memories are made into poems: 'In an artist . . . suggestions made by a work of art, which are purely personal, become fused with a multitude of other suggestions from multitudinous experience, and result in the production of a new object which is no longer purely personal, because it is a work of art itself.'

17. Preface to *For Lancelot Andrewes*, 1928. Later, Eliot was to regret the emphasis of this remark, but not, of course, to deny its authority.

18. Thus Eliot rightly remarked, in his Preface to the 1928 edition of *The Sacred Wood*, that he had discovered, on contemplating a revision of the contents of that book, 'that what had happened in my own mind . . . was not so much a change or reversal of opinions, as an expansion or development of interests'.

19. 1928 Preface to *The Sacred Wood*, viii, x.

20. 'Shakespeare and the Stoicism of Seneca', *Selected Essays*, 133.

21. Matthiessen, 90. This may be the second of his recorded remarks on his desire to emulate Beethoven. See also a letter of 28 March 1931 to Spender about the Beethoven A minor Quartet: 'I should like to get something of that into verse before I die' (Tate, ed., *T. S. Eliot, The Man and his Work*, 54). Later, when the Quartets

were written, he spoke at more length on the subject in 'The Music of Poetry' (1942).

22. In letters to Bertrand Russell and Ford Madox Ford; the latter specifies 'the 29 lines of the water-dripping song'. See Mrs. Eliot's edition of the *Waste Land* manuscripts, 129.

23. 'What Dante Means to Me' (1950), in *To Criticize the Critic*, 125–35.

24. Commending Kipling's imperialism he speaks of a vision 'almost that of an empire laid up in heaven' (*On Poetry and Poets*, 245) – recalling a passage in Plato's *Republic* ix which evidently meant much to him.

25. *On Poetry and Poets*, 135–48.

PART ONE

LITERARY CRITICISM

REFLECTIONS ON *VERS LIBRE*[1]

Ceux qui possèdent leur *vers libre y tiennent:*
on n'abandonne que le *vers libre.*
DUHAMEL ET VILDRAC.

A lady, renowned in her small circle for the accuracy of her stop-press information of literature, complains to me of a growing pococurantism. 'Since the Russians came in I can read nothing else. I have finished Dostoevski, and I do not know what to do.' I suggested that the great Russian was an admirer of Dickens, and that she also might find that author readable. 'But Dickens is a sentimentalist; Dostoevski is a realist.' I reflected on the amours of Sonia and Rashkolnikov, but forbore to press the point, and I proposed *It Is Never too Late to Mend.* 'But one cannot read the Victorians at all!' While I was extracting the virtues of the pro-position that Dostoevski is a Christian, while Charles Reade is merely pious, she added that she could not longer read any verse but *vers libre.*

It is assumed that *vers libre* exists. It is assumed that *vers libre* is a school; that it consists of certain theories; that its group or groups of theorists will either revolutionize or demoralize poetry if their attack upon the iambic pentameter meets with any success. *Vers libre* does not exist, and it is time that this preposterous fiction followed the *élan vital* and the eighty thousand Russians into oblivion.

When a theory of art passes it is usually found that a groat's worth of art has been bought with a million of advertisement. The theory which sold the wares may be quite false, or it may be con-fused and incapable of elucidation, or it may never have existed. A mythical revolution will have taken place and produced a few works of art which perhaps would be even better if still less of the

[1] This article appeared in the *New Statesman*, March 3rd, 1917.

revolutionary theories clung to them. In modern society such revolutions are almost inevitable. An artist, happens upon a method, perhaps quite unreflectingly, which is new in the sense that it is essentially different from that of the second-rate people about him, and different in everything but essentials from that of any of his great predecessors. The novelty meets with neglect; neglect provokes attack; and attack demands a theory. In an ideal state of society one might imagine the good New growing naturally out of the good Old, without the need for polemic and theory; this would be a society with a living tradition. In a sluggish society, as actual societies are, tradition is ever lapsing into superstition, and the violent stimulus of novelty is required. This is bad for the artist and his school, who may become circumscribed by their theory and narrowed by their polemic; but the artist can always console himself for his errors in his old age by considering that if he had not fought nothing would have been accomplished.

Vers libre has not even the excuse of a polemic; it is a battle-cry of freedom, and there is no freedom in art. And as the so-called *vers libre* which is good is anything but 'free', it can better be defended under some other label. Particular types of *vers libre* may be supported on the choice of content, or on the method of handling the content. I am aware that many writers of *vers libre* have introduced such innovations, and that the novelty of their choice and manipulation of material is confused – if not in their own minds, in the minds of many of their readers – with the novelty of the form. But I am not here concerned with imagism, which is a theory about the use of material; I am only concerned with the theory of the verse-form in which imagism is cast. If *vers libre* is a genuine verse-form it will have a positive definition. And I can define it only in negatives: (1) absence of pattern, (2) absence of rhyme, (3) absence of metre.

The third of these qualities is easily disposed of. What sort of a line that would be which would not scan at all I cannot say. Even in the popular American magazines, whose verse columns are now largely given over to *vers libre*, the lines are usually explicable in terms of prosody. Any line can be divided into feet and accents. The simpler metres are a repetition of one combination, perhaps a long and a short, or a short and a long syllable, five times repeated. There is, however, no reason why, within the single line, there should be any repetition; why there should not be lines (as there are) divisible only into feet of different types. How can the grammatical exercise of scansion make a line of this sort more intelligible? Only by isolating elements which occur in other lines, and the sole purpose of doing this is the production of a similar effect elsewhere. But repetition of effect is a question of pattern.

Scansion tells us very little. It is probable that there is not much to be gained by an elaborate system of prosody, but the erudite complexities of Swinburnian metre. With Swinburne, once the trick is perceived and the scholarship appreciated, the effect is somewhat diminished. When the unexpectedness, due to the unfamiliarity of the metres to English ears, wears off and is understood, one ceases to look for what one does not find in Swinburne; the inexplicable line with the music which can never be recaptured in other words. Swinburne mastered his technique, which is a great deal, but he did not master it to the extent of being able to take liberties with it, which is everything. If anything promising for English poetry is hidden in the metres of Swinburne, it probably lies far beyond the point to which Swinburne has developed them. But the most interesting verse which has yet been written in our language has been done either by taking a very simple form, like the iambic pentameter, and constantly withdrawing from it, or taking no form at all, and constantly approximating to a very simple one. It is this contrast between fixity and flux, this unperceived evasion of monotony, which is the very life of verse.

I have in mind two passages of contemporary verse which would be called *vers libre*. Both of them I quote because of their beauty:

> *Once, in finesse of fiddles found I ecstasy,*
> *In the flash of gold heels on the hard pavement.*
> *Now see I*
> *That warmth's the very stuff of poesy.*
> *Oh, God, make small*
> *The old star-eaten blanket of the sky,*
> *That I may fold it round me and in comfort lie.*

This is a complete poem. The other is part of a much longer poem:

> *There shut up in his castle, Tairiran's,*
> *She who had nor ears nor tongue save in her hands,*
> *Gone – ah, gone – untouched, unreachable –*
> *She who could never live save through one person,*
> *She who could never speak save to one person,*
> *And all the rest of her a shifting change,*
> *A broken bundle of mirrors . . . –*

It is obvious that the charm of these lines could not be, without the constant suggestion and the skilful evasion of iambic pentameter.

At the beginning of the seventeenth century, and especially in the verse of John Webster, who was in some ways a more cunning technician than Shakespeare, one finds the same constant evasion and recognition of regularity. Webster is much freer than Shakespeare, and that his fault is not negligence is evidenced by the fact that it is often at moments of the highest intensity that his verse acquires this freedom. That there is also carelessness I do not deny, but the irregularity of carelessness can be at once detected from the irregularity of deliberation. (In *The White Devil* Brachiano dying, and Cornelia mad, deliberately rupture the bonds of pentameter.)

> *I recover, like a spent taper, for a flash*
> *and instantly go out.*

> *Cover her face; mine eyes dazzle; she died young.*

> *You have cause to love me, I did enter you in my heart*
> *Before you would vouchsafe to call for the keys.*

> *This is a vain poetry: but I pray you tell me*
> *If there were proposed me, wisdom, riches, and beauty,*
> *In three several young men, which should I choose?*

These are not lines of carelessness. The irregularity is further enhanced by the use of short lines and the breaking up of lines in dialogue, which alters the quantities. And there are many lines in the drama of this time which are spoilt by regular accentuation.

> *I loved this woman in spite of my heart.* (The Changeling)
> *I would have these herbs grow up in his grave.* (The White
>   Devil)
> *Whether the spirit of greatness or of woman* . . . (The
>   Duchess of Malfi)

The general charge of decadence cannot be preferred. Tourneur and Shirley, who I think will be conceded to have touched nearly the bottom of the decline of tragedy, are much more regular than Webster or Middleton. Tourneur will polish off a fair line of iambics even at the cost of amputating a preposition from its substantive, and in the *Atheist's Tragedy* he has a final 'of' in two lines out of five together.

We may therefore formulate as follows: the ghost of some simple metre should lurk behind the arras in even the 'freest' verse; to advance menacingly as we doze, and withdraw as we

34

rouse. Or, freedom is only truly freedom when it appears against the background of an artificial limitation.

Not to have perceived the simple truth that *some* artificial limitation is necessary except in moments of the first intensity is, I believe, a capital error of even so distinguished a talent as that of Mr. E. L. Masters. The *Spoon River Anthology* is not material of the first intensity; it is reflective, not immediate; its author is a moralist, rather than an observer. His material is so near to the material of Crabbe that one wonders why he should have used a different form. Crabbe is, on the whole, the more intense of the two; he is keen, direct, and unsparing. His material is prosaic, not in the sense that it would have been better done in prose, but in the sense of requiring a simple and rather rigid verse-form and this Crabbe has given it. Mr. Masters requires a more rigid verse-form than either of the two contemporary poets quoted above, and his epitaphs suffer from the lack of it.

So much for metre. There is no escape from metre; there is only mastery. But while there obviously is escape from rhyme, the *vers librists* are by no means the first out of the cave.

> The boughs of the trees
> Are twisted
> By many bafflings;
> Twisted are
> The small-leafed boughs.
> But the shadow of them
> Is not the shadow of the mast head
> Nor of the torn sails.

> When the white dawn first
> Through the rough fir-planks
> Of my hut, by the chestnuts,
> Up at the valley-head,
> Came breaking, Goddess,
> I sprang up, I threw round me
> My dappled fawn-skin . . .

Except for the more human touch in the second of these extracts a hasty observer would hardly realize that the first is by a contemporary, and the second by Matthew Arnold.

I do not minimize the services of modern poets in exploiting the possibilities of rhymeless verse. They prove the strength of a Movement, the utility of a Theory. What neither Blake nor Arnold could do alone is being done in our time. 'Blank verse' is the only accepted rhymeless verse in English – the inevitable

35

iambic pentameter. The English ear is (or was) more sensitive to the music of the verse and less dependent upon the recurrence of identical sounds in this metre than in any other. There is no campaign against rhyme. But it is possible that excessive devotion to rhyme has thickened the modern ear. The rejection of rhyme is not a leap at facility; on the contrary, it imposes a much severer strain upon the language. When the comforting echo of rhyme is removed, success or failure in the choice of words, in the sentence structure, in the order, is at once more apparent. Rhyme removed, the poet is at once held up to the standards of prose. Rhyme removed, much ethereal music leaps up from the word, music which has hitherto chirped unnoticed in the expanse of prose. Any rhyme forbidden, many Shagpats were unwigged.

And this liberation from rhyme might be as well a liberation *of* rhyme. Freed from its exacting task of supporting lame verse, it could be applied with greater effect where it is most needed. There are often passages in an unrhymed poem where rhyme is wanted for some special effect, for a sudden tightening-up, for a cumulative insistence, or for an abrupt change of mood. But formal rhymed verse will certainly not lose its place. We only need the coming of a Satirist – no man of genius is rarer – to prove that the heroic couplet has lost none of its edge since Dryden and Pope laid it down. As for the sonnet I am not so sure. But the decay of intricate formal patterns has nothing to do with the advent of *vers libre*. It had set in long before. Only in a closely-knit and homogeneous society, where many men are at work on the same problems, such a society as those which produced the Greek chorus, the Elizabethan lyric, and the Troubadour canzone, will the development of such forms ever be carried to perfection. And as for *vers libre*, we conclude that it is not defined by absence of pattern or absence of rhyme, for other verse is without these; that it is not defined by non-existence of metre, since even the *worst* verse can be scanned; and we conclude that the division between Conservative Verse and *vers libre* does not exist, for there is only good verse, bad verse, and chaos.

TRADITION AND THE INDIVIDUAL TALENT

I

In English writing we seldom speak of tradition, though we occasionally apply its name in deploring its absence. We cannot refer to 'the tradition' or to 'a tradition'; at most, we employ the adjective in saying that the poetry of So-and-so is 'traditional' or even 'too traditional'. Seldom, perhaps, does the word appear except in a phrase of censure. If otherwise, it is vaguely approbative, with the implication, as to the work approved, of some pleasing archaeological reconstruction. You can hardly make the word agreeable to English ears without this comfortable reference to the reassuring science of archaeology.

Certainly the word is not likely to appear in our appreciations of living or dead writers. Every nation, every race, has not only its own creative, but its own critical turn of mind; and is even more oblivious of the shortcomings and limitations of its critical habits than of those of its creative genius. We know, or think we know, from the enormous mass of critical writing that has appeared in the French language the critical method or habit of the French; we only conclude (we are such unconscious people) that the French are 'more critical' than we, and sometimes even plume ourselves a little with the fact, as if the French were the less spontaneous. Perhaps they are; but we might remind ourselves that criticism is as inevitable as breathing, and that we should be none the worse for articulating what passes in our minds when we read a book and feel an emotion about it, for criticizing our own minds in their work of criticism. One of the facts that might come to light in this process is our tendency to insist, when we praise a poet, upon those aspects of his work in which he least resembles anyone else. In these aspects or parts of his work we pretend to find what is individual, what is the peculiar essence of the man.

37

We dwell with satisfaction upon the poet's difference from his predecessors, especially his immediate predecessors; we endeavour to find something that can be isolated in order to be enjoyed. Whereas if we approach a poet without this prejudice we shall often find that not only the best, but the most individual parts of his work may be those in which the dead poets, his ancestors, assert their immortality most vigorously. And I do not mean the impressionable period of adolescence, but the period of full maturity.

Yet if the only form of tradition, of handing down, consisted in following the ways of the immediate generation before us in a blind or timid adherence to its successes, 'tradition' should positively be discouraged. We have seen many such simple currents soon lost in the sand; and novelty is better than repetition. Tradition is a matter of much wider significance. It cannot be inherited, and if you want it you must obtain it by great labour. It involves, in the first place, the historical sense, which we may call nearly indispensable to anyone who would continue to be a poet beyond his twenty-fifth year; and the historical sense involves a perception, not only of the pastness of the past, but of its presence; the historical sense compels a man to write not merely with his own generation in his bones, but with a feeling that the whole of the literature of Europe from Homer and within it the whole of the literature of his own country has a simultaneous existence and composes a simultaneous order. This historical sense, which is a sense of the timeless as well as of the temporal and of the timeless and of the temporal together, is what makes a writer traditional. And it is at the same time what makes a writer most acutely conscious of his place in time, of his own contemporaneity.

No poet, no artist of any art, has his complete meaning alone. His significance, his appreciation is the appreciation of his relation to the dead poets and artists. You cannot value him alone; you must set him, for contrast and comparison, among the dead. I mean this as a principle of aesthetic, not merely historical, criticism. The necessity that he shall conform, that he shall cohere, is not onesided; what happens when a new work of art is created is something that happens simultaneously to all the works of art which preceded it. The existing monuments form an ideal order among themselves, which is modified by the introduction of the new (the really new) work of art among them. The existing order is complete before the new work arrives; for order to persist after the supervention of novelty, the *whole* existing order must be, if ever so slightly, altered; and so the relations, proportions, values of each work of art toward the whole are readjusted; and
38

this is conformity between the old and the new. Whoever has approved this idea of order, of the form of European, of English literature will not find it preposterous that the past should be altered by the present as much as the present is directed by the past. And the poet who is aware of this will be aware of great difficulties and responsibilities.

In a peculiar sense he will be aware also that he must inevitably be judged by the standards of the past. I say judged, not amputated, by them; not judged to be as good as, or worse or better than, the dead; and certainly not judged by the canons of dead critics. It is a judgment, a comparison, in which two things are measured by each other. To conform merely would be for the new work not really to conform at all; it would not be new, and would therefore not be a work of art. And we do not quite say that the new is more valuable because it fits in; but its fitting in is a test of its value – a test, it is true, which can only be slowly and cautiously applied, for we are none of us infallible judges of conformity. We say: it appears to conform, and is perhaps individual, or it appears individual, and may conform; but we are hardly likely to find that it is one and not the other.

To proceed to a more intelligible exposition of the relation of the poet to the past: he can neither take the past as a lump, an indiscriminate bolus, nor can he form himself wholly on one or two private admirations, nor can he form himself wholly upon one preferred period. The first course is inadmissible, the second is an important experience of youth, and the third is a pleasant and highly desirable supplement. The poet must be very conscious of the main current, which does not at all flow invariably through the most distinguished reputations. He must be quite aware of the obvious fact that art never improves, but that the material of art is never quite the same. He must be aware that the mind of Europe – the mind of his own country – a mind which he learns in time to be much more important than his own private mind – is a mind which changes, and that this change is a development which abandons nothing *en route*, which does not superannuate either Shakespeare, or Homer, or the rock drawing of the Magdalenian draughtsmen. That this development, refinement perhaps, complication certainly, is not, from the point of view of the artist, any improvement. Perhaps not even an improvement from the point of view of the psychologist or not to the extent which we imagine; perhaps only in the end based upon a complication in economics and machinery. But the difference between the present and the past is that the conscious present is an awareness of the past in a way and to an extent which the past's awareness of itself cannot show.

Someone said: 'The dead writers are remote from us because we *know* so much more than they did'. Precisely, and they are that which we know.

I am alive to a usual objection to what is clearly part of my programme for the *métier* of poetry. The objection is that the doctrine requires a ridiculous amount of erudition (pedantry), a claim which can be rejected by appeal to the lives of poets in any pantheon. It will even be affirmed that much learning deadens or perverts poetic sensibility. While, however, we persist in believing that a poet ought to know as much as will not encroach upon his necessary receptivity and necessary laziness, it is not desirable to confine knowledge to whatever can be put into a useful shape for examinations, drawing-rooms, or the still more pretentious modes of publicity. Some can absorb knowledge, the more tardy must sweat for it. Shakespeare acquired more essential history from Plutarch than most men could from the whole British Museum. What is to be insisted upon is that the poet must develop or procure the consciousness of the past and that he should continue to develop this consciousness throughout his career.

What happens is a continual surrender of himself as he is at the moment to something which is more valuable. The progress of an artist is a continual self-sacrifice, a continual extinction of personality.

There remains to define this process of depersonalization and its relation to the sense of tradition. It is in this depersonalization that art may be said to approach the condition of science. I therefore invite you to consider, as a suggestive analogy, the action which takes place when a bit of finely filiated platinum is introduced into a chamber containing oxygen and sulphur dioxide.

II

Honest criticism and sensitive appreciation is directed not upon the poet but upon the poetry. If we attend to the confused cries of the newspaper critics and the susurrus of popular repetition that follows, we shall hear the names of poets in great numbers; if we seek not Blue-book knowledge but the enjoyment of poetry, and ask for a poem, we shall seldom find it. I have tried to point out the importance of the relation of the poem to other poems by other authors, and suggested the conception of poetry as a living whole of all the poetry that has ever been written. The other aspect of this Impersonal theory of poetry is the relation of the poem to its author. And I hinted, by an analogy, that the mind of the mature poet differs from that of the immature one not precisely in any valuation of 'personality', not being necessarily more interesting, or having 'more to say', but rather by being a more finely perfected medium in which special, or very varied, feelings are at liberty to enter into new combinations. The analogy was that of the catalyst. When the two gases previously mentioned are mixed in the presence of a filament of platinum, they form sulphurous acid. This combination takes place only if the platinum is present; nevertheless the newly formed acid contains no trace of platinum, and the platinum itself is apparently unaffected: has remained inert, neutral, and unchanged. The mind of the poet is the shred of platinum. It may partly or exclusively operate upon the experience of the man himself; but, the more perfect the artist, the more completely separate in him will be the man who suffers and the mind which creates; the more perfectly will the mind digest and transmute the passions which are its material.

The experience, you will notice, the elements which enter the presence of the transforming catalyst, are of two kinds: emotions and feelings. The effect of a work of art upon the person who enjoys it is an experience different in kind from any experience not of art. It may be formed out of one emotion, or may be a combination of several; and various feelings, inhering for the writer in particular words or phrases or images, may be added to compose the final result. Or great poetry may be made without the direct use of any emotion whatever: composed out of feelings solely. Canto XV of the *Inferno* (Brunetto Latini) is a working up of the emotion evident in the situation; but the effect, though single as that of any work of art, is obtained by considerable complexity of detail. The last quatrain gives an image, a feeling attaching to an image, which 'came', which did not develop simply out of what precedes, but which was probably in suspension in the poet's mind until the proper combination arrived for it to add itself to. The poet's mind is in fact a receptacle for seizing and storing up numberless feelings, phrases, images, which remain there until all the particles which can unite to form a new compound are present together.

If you compare several representative passages of the greatest poetry you see how great is the variety of types of combination, and also how completely any semi-ethical criterion of 'sublimity' misses the mark. For it is not the 'greatness', the intensity, of the emotions, the components, but the intensity of the artistic process, the pressure, so to speak, under which the fusion takes place, that counts. The episode of Paolo and Francesca employs a definite emotion, but the intensity of the poetry is something quite different from whatever intensity in the supposed experience it may give the impression of. It is no more intense, furthermore, than Canto XXVI, the voyage of Ulysses, which has not the direct dependence upon an emotion. Great variety is possible in the process of transmutation of emotion: the murder of Agamemnon, or the agony of Othello, gives an artistic effect apparently closer to a possible original than the scenes from Dante. In the *Agamemnon*, the artistic emotion approximates to the emotion of an actual spectator; in *Othello* to the emotion of the protagonist himself. But the difference between art and the event is always absolute; the combination which is the murder of Agamemnon is probably as complex as that which is the voyage of Ulysses. In either case there has been a fusion of elements. The ode of Keats contains a number of feelings which have nothing particular to do with the nightingale, but which the nightingale, partly perhaps because of its attractive name, and partly because of its reputation, served to bring together.

The point of view which I am struggling to attack is perhaps related to the metaphysical theory of the substantial unity of the soul: for my meaning is, that the poet has, not a 'personality' to express, but a particular medium, which is only a medium and not a personality, in which impressions and experiences combine in peculiar and unexpected ways. Impressions and experiences which are important for the man may take no place in the poetry, and those which become important in the poetry may play quite a negligible part in the man, the personality.

I will quote a passage which is unfamiliar enough to be regarded with fresh attention in the light – or darkness – of these observations:

> *And now methinks I could e'en chide myself*
> *For doating on her beauty, though her death*
> *Shall be revenged after no common action.*
> *Does the silkworm expend her yellow labours*
> *For thee? For thee does she undo herself?*
> *Are lordships sold to maintain ladyships*
> *For the poor benefit of a bewildering minute?*
> *Why does yon fellow falsify highways,*
> *And put his life between the judge's lips,*
> *To refine such a thing – keeps horse and men*
> *To beat their valours for her? . . .*

In this passage (as is evident if it is taken in its context) there is a combination of positive and negative emotions: an intensely strong attraction toward beauty and an equally intense fascination by the ugliness which is contrasted with it and which destroys it. This balance of contrasted emotion is in the dramatic situation to

42

which the speech is pertinent, but that situation alone is inadequate to it. This is, so to speak, the structural emotion, provided by the drama. But the whole effect, the dominant tone, is due to the fact that a number of floating feelings, having an affinity to this emotion by no means superficially evident, having combined with it to give us a new art emotion.

It is not in his personal emotions, the emotions provoked by particular events in his life, that the poet is in any way remarkable or interesting. His particular emotions may be simple, or crude, or flat. The emotion in his poetry will be a very complex thing, but not with the complexity of the emotions of people who have very complex or unusual emotions in life. One error, in fact, of eccentricity in poetry is to seek for new human emotions to express; and in this search for novelty in the wrong place it discovers the perverse. The business of the poet is not to find new emotions, but to use the ordinary ones and, in working them up into poetry, to express feelings which are not in actual emotions at all. And emotions which he has never experienced will serve his turn as well as those familiar to him. Consequently, we must believe that 'emotion recollected in tranquillity' is an inexact formula. For it is neither emotion, nor recollection, nor without distortion of meaning, tranquillity. It is a concentration, and a new thing resulting from the concentration, of a very great number of experiences which to the practical and active person would not seem to be experiences at all; it is a concentration which does not happen consciously or of deliberation. These experiences are not 'recollected', and they finally unite in an atmosphere which is 'tranquil' only in that it is a passive attending upon the event. Of course this is not quite the whole story. There is a great deal, in the writing of poetry, which must be conscious and deliberate. In fact, the bad poet is usually unconscious where he ought to be conscious, and conscious where he ought to be unconscious. Both errors tend to make him 'personal'. Poetry is not a turning loose of emotion, but an escape from emotion; it is not the expression of personality, but an escape from personality. But, of course, only those who have personality and emotions know what it means to want to escape from these things.

III

ὁ δὲ νοῦς ἴσως θειότερόν τι καὶ ἀπαθές ἐστιν.

This essay proposes to halt at the frontiers of metaphysics or mysticism, and confine itself to such practical conclusions as can be applied by the responsible person interested in poetry. To

43

divert interest from the poet to the poetry is a laudable aim: for it would conduce to a juster estimation of actual poetry, good and bad. There are many people who appreciate the expression of sincere emotion in verse, and there is a smaller number of people who can appreciate technical excellence. But very few know when there is an expression of *significant* emotion, emotion which has its life in the poem and not in the history of the poet. The emotion of art is impersonal. And the poet cannot reach this impersonality without surrendering himself wholly to the work to be done. And he is not likely to know what is to be done unless he lives in what is not merely the present, but the present moment of the past, unless he is conscious, not of what is dead, but of what is already living.

HAMLET

Few critics have ever admitted that *Hamlet* the play is the primary problem, and Hamlet the character only secondary. And Hamlet the character has had an especial temptation for that most dangerous type of critic: the critic with a mind which is naturally of the creative order, but which through some weakness in creative power exercises itself in criticism instead. These minds often find in Hamlet a vicarious existence for their own artistic realization. Such a mind had Goethe, who made of Hamlet a Werther; and such had Coleridge, who made of Hamlet a Coleridge; and probably neither of these men in writing about Hamlet remembered that his first business was to study a work of art. The kind of criticism that Goethe and Coleridge produced, in writing of Hamlet, is the most misleading kind possible. For they both possessed unquestionable critical insight, and both make their critical aberrations the more plausible by the substitution – of their own Hamlet for Shakespeare's – which their creative gift effects. We should be thankful that Walter Pater did not fix his attention on this play.

Two writers of our time, Mr. J. M. Robertson and Professor Stoll of the University of Minnesota, have issued small books which can be praised for moving in the other direction. Mr. Stoll performs a service in recalling to our attention the labours of the critics of the seventeenth and eighteenth centuries,[1] observing that

they knew less about psychology than more recent Hamlet critics, but they were nearer in spirit to Shakespeare's art; and as they insisted on the importance of the effect of the whole rather than on the importance of the leading character, they were nearer, in their old-fashioned way, to the secret of dramatic art in general.

Qua work of art, the work of art cannot be interpreted; there is nothing to interpret; we can only criticize it according to standards, in comparison to other works of art; and for 'interpretation'

[1] I have never, by the way, seen a cogent refutation of Thomas Rymer's objections to *Othello*.

the chief task is the presentation of relevant historical facts which the reader is not assumed to know. Mr. Robertson points out, very pertinently, how critics have failed in their 'interpretation' of *Hamlet* by ignoring what ought to be very obvious: that *Hamlet* is a stratification, that it represents the efforts of a series of men, each making what he could out of the work of his predecessors. The *Hamlet* of Shakespeare will appear to us very differently if, instead of treating the whole action of the play as due to Shakespeare's design, we perceive his *Hamlet* to be superposed upon much cruder material which persists even in the final form.

We know that there was an older play by Thomas Kyd, that extraordinary dramatic (if not poetic) genius who was in all probability the author of two plays so dissimilar as the *Spanish Tragedy* and *Arden of Feversham*; and what this play was like we can guess from three clues: from the *Spanish Tragedy* itself, from the tale of Belleforest upon which Kyd's *Hamlet* must have been based, and from a version acted in Germany in Shakespeare's lifetime which bears strong evidence of having been adapted from the earlier, not from the later, play. From these three sources it is clear that in the earlier play the motive was a revenge motive simply; that the action or delay is caused, as in the *Spanish Tragedy*, solely by the difficulty of assassinating a monarch surrounded by guards; and that the 'madness' of Hamlet was feigned in order to escape suspicion, and successfully. In the final play of Shakespeare, on the other hand, there is a motive which is more important than that of revenge, and which explicitly 'blunts' the latter; the delay in revenge is unexplained on grounds of necessity or expediency; and the effect of the 'madness' is not to lull but to arouse the king's suspicion. The alteration is not complete enough, however, to be convincing. Furthermore, there are verbal parallels so close to the *Spanish Tragedy* as to leave no doubt that in places Shakespeare was merely *revising* the text of Kyd. And finally there are unexplained scenes – the Polonius-Laertes and the Polonius-Reynaldo scenes – for which there is little excuse; these scenes are not in the verse style of Kyd, and not beyond doubt in the style of Shakespeare. These Mr. Robertson believes to be scenes in the original play of Kyd reworked by a third hand, perhaps Chapman, before Shakespeare touched the play. And he concludes, with very strong show of reason, that the original play of Kyd was, like certain other revenge plays, in two parts of five acts each. The upshot of Mr. Robertson's examination is, we believe, irrefragable: that Shakespeare's *Hamlet*, so far as it is Shakespeare's, is a play dealing with the effect of a mother's guilt upon her son, and that

46

Shakespeare was unable to impose this motive successfully upon the 'intractable' material of the old play.

Of the intractability there can be no doubt. So far from being Shakespeare's masterpiece, the play is most certainly an artistic failure. In several ways the play is puzzling, and disquieting as is none of the others. Of all the plays it is the longest and is possibly the one on which Shakespeare spent most pains; and yet he has left in it superfluous and inconsistent scenes which even hasty revision should have noticed. The versification is variable. Lines like

> *Look, the morn, in russet mantle clad,*
> *Walks o'er the dew of yon high eastern hill,*

are of the Shakespeare of *Romeo and Juliet*. The lines in Act V. Sc. ii,

> *Sir, in my heart there was a kind of fighting*
> *That would not let me sleep . . .*
> *Up from my cabin,*
> *My sea-gown scarf'd about me, in the dark*
> *Grop'd I to find out them: had my desire;*
> *Finger'd their packet;*

are of his quite mature. Both workmanship and thought are in an unstable position. We are surely justified in attributing the play, with that other profoundly interesting play of 'intractable' material and astonishing versification, *Measure for Measure*, to a period of crisis, after which follow the tragic successes which culminate in *Coriolanus*. *Coriolanus* may be not as 'interesting' as *Hamlet*, but it is, with *Antony and Cleopatra*, Shakespeare's most assured artistic success. And probably more people have thought *Hamlet* a work of art because they found it interesting, than have found it interesting because it is a work of art. It is the 'Mona Lisa' of literature.

The grounds of *Hamlet's* failure are not immediately obvious. Mr. Robertson is undoubtedly correct in concluding that the essential emotion of the play is the feeling of a son towards a guilty mother:

[Hamlet's] tone is that of one who has suffered tortures on the score of his mother's degradation. . . . The guilt of a mother is an almost intolerable motive for drama, but it had to be maintained and emphasized to supply a psychological solution, or rather a hint of one.

This, however, is by no means the whole story. It is not merely the 'guilt of a mother' that cannot be handled as Shakespeare handled the suspicion of Othello, the infatuation of Antony, or the pride of Coriolanus. The subject might conceivably have expanded into a tragedy like these, intelligible, self-complete, in the sunlight. *Hamlet*, like the sonnets, is full of some stuff that the writer could not drag to light, contemplate, or manipulate into art. And when we search for this feeling, we find it, as in the sonnets, very difficult to localize. You cannot point to it in the speeches; indeed, if you examine the two famous soliloquies you see the versification of Shakespeare, but a content which might be claimed by another, perhaps by the author of the *Revenge of Bussy d'Ambois*, Act V. Sc. i. We find Shakespeare's *Hamlet* not in the action, not in any quotations that we might select, so much as in an unmistakable tone which is unmistakably not in the earlier play.

The only way of expressing emotion in the form of art is by finding an 'objective correlative'; in other words, a set of objects, a situation, a chain of events which shall be the formula of that *particular* emotion; such that when the external facts, which must terminate in sensory experience, are given, the emotion is immediately evoked. If you examine any of Shakespeare's most successful tragedies, you will find this exact equivalence; you will find that the state of mind of Lady Macbeth walking in her sleep has been communicated to you by a skilful accumulation of imagined sensory impressions; the words of Macbeth on hearing of his wife's death strike us as if, given the sequence of events, these words were automatically released by the last event in the series. The artistic 'inevitability' lies in this complete adequacy of the external to the emotion; and this is precisely what is deficient in *Hamlet*. Hamlet (the man) is dominated by an emotion which is inexpressible, because it is in *excess* of the facts as they appear. And the supposed identity of Hamlet with his author is genuine to this point: that Hamlet's bafflement at the absence of objective equivalent to his feelings is a prolongation of the bafflement of his creator in the face of his artistic problem. Hamlet is up against the difficulty that his disgust is occasioned by his mother, but that his mother is not an adequate equivalent for it; his disgust envelops and exceeds her. It is thus a feeling which he cannot understand; he cannot objectify it, and it therefore remains to poison life and obstruct action. None of the possible actions can satisfy it; and nothing that Shakespeare can do with the plot can express Hamlet for him. And it must be noticed that the very nature of the *données* of the problem precludes objective equivalence. To have heightened the criminality of Gertrude would have been to provide the formula for a totally different emotion in Hamlet; it is just *because* her character is so negative and insignificant that

48

she arouses in Hamlet the feeling which she is incapable of representing.

The 'madness' of Hamlet lay to Shakespeare's hand; in the earlier play a simple ruse, and to the end, we may presume, understood as a ruse by the audience. For Shakespeare it is less than madness and more than feigned. The levity of Hamlet, his repetition of phrase, his puns, are not part of a deliberate plan of dissimulation, but a form of emotional relief. In the character Hamlet it is the buffoonery of an emotion which can find no outlet in action; in the dramatist it is the buffoonery of an emotion which he cannot express in art. The intense feeling, ecstatic or terrible, without an object or exceeding its object, is something which every person of sensibility has known; it is doubtless a subject of study for pathologists. It often occurs in adolescence: the ordinary person puts these feelings to sleep, or trims down his feelings to fit the business world; the artist keeps them alive by his ability to intensify the world to his emotions. The Hamlet of Laforgue is an adolescent; the Hamlet of Shakespeare is not, he has not that explanation and excuse. We must simply admit that here Shakespeare tackled a problem which proved too much for him. Why he attempted it at all is an insoluble puzzle; under compulsion of what experience he attempted to express the inexpressibly horrible, we cannot ever know. We need a great many facts in his biography; and we should like to know whether, and when, and after or at the same time as what personal experience, he read Montaigne, II. xii, *Apologie de Raimond Sebond*. We should have, finally, to know something which is by hypothesis unknowable, for we assume it to be an experience which, in the manner indicated, exceeded the facts. We should have to understand things which Shakespeare did not understand himself.

THE PERFECT CRITIC

I

*'Eriger en lois ses impressions personnelles,
c'est le grand effort d'un homme s'il est sincère.'*
LETTRES À 'AMAZONE.

Coleridge was perhaps the greatest of English critics, and in a sense the last. After Coleridge we have Matthew Arnold; but Arnold – I think it will be conceded – was rather a propagandist for criticism than a critic, a popularizer rather than a creator of ideas. So long as this land remains an island (and we are no nearer the Continent than were Arnold's contemporaries) the work of Arnold will be important; it is still a bridge across the Channel, and it will always have been good sense. Since Arnold's attempt to correct his countrymen, English criticism has followed two directions. When a distinguished critic observed recently, in a newspaper article, that 'poetry is the most highly organized form of intellectual activity,' we were conscious that we were reading neither Coleridge nor Arnold. Not only have the words 'organized' and 'activity', occurring together in this phrase, that familiar vague suggestion of the scientific vocabulary which is characteristic of modern writing, but one asked questions which Coleridge and Arnold would not have permitted one to ask. How is it, for instance, that poetry is more 'highly organized' than astronomy, physics, or pure mathematics, which we imagine to be, in relation to the scientist who practises them, 'intellectual activity' of a pretty highly organized type? 'Mere strings of words,' our critic continues with felicity and truth, 'flung like dabs of paint across a blank canvas, may awaken surprise . . . but have no significance whatever in the history of literature.' The phrases by which Arnold is best known may be inadequate, they may assemble more doubts than they dispel, but they usually have some meaning. And if a phrase like 'the most highly organized form of intellectual activity' is the highest organization of thought of which contemporary criticism, in a distinguished representative, is capable, then, we conclude, modern criticism is degenerate.

50

The verbal disease above noticed may be reserved for diagnosis by and by. It is not a disease from which Mr. Arthur Symons (for the quotation was, of course, not from Mr. Symons) notably suffers. Mr. Symons represents the other tendency; he is a representative of what is always called 'aesthetic criticism' or 'impressionistic criticism'. And it is this form of criticism which I propose to examine at once. Mr. Symons, the critical successor of Pater, and partly of Swinburne (I fancy that the phrase 'sick or sorry' is the common property of all three), is the 'impressionistic critic'. He, if anyone, would be said to expose a sensitive and cultivated mind – cultivated, that is, by the accumulation of a considerable variety of impressions from all the arts and several languages – before an 'object'; and his criticism, if anyone's, would be said to exhibit to us, like the plate, the faithful record of the impressions, more numerous or more refined than our own, upon a mind more sensitive than our own. A record, we observe, which is also an interpretation, a translation; for it must itself impose impressions upon us, and these impressions are as much created as transmitted by the criticism. I do not say at once that this is Mr. Symons; but it is the 'impressionistic' critic, and the impressionistic critic is supposed to be Mr. Symons.

At hand is a volume which we may test.[1] Ten of these thirteen essays deal with single plays of Shakespeare, and it is therefore fair to take one of these ten as a specimen of the book:

> *Antony and Cleopatra* is the most wonderful, I think, of all Shakespeare's plays . . .

and Mr. Symons reflects that Cleopatra is the most wonderful of all women:

> The queen who ends the dynasty of the Ptolemies has been the star of poets, a malign star shedding baleful light, from Horace and Propertius down to Victor Hugo; and it is not to poets only . . .

What, we ask, is this for? as a page on Cleopatra, and on her possible origin in the dark lady of the Sonnets, unfolds itself. And we find, gradually, that this is not an essay on a work of art or a work of intellect; but that Mr. Symons is living through the play as one might live it through in the theatre; recounting, commenting:

> In her last days Cleopatra touches a certain elevation . . . she would die a thousand times, rather than live to be a mockery and a scorn in

[1] *Studies in Elizabethan Drama.* By Arthur Symons.

men's mouths . . . she is a woman to the last . . . so she dies . . . the plays
ends with a touch of grave pity . . .

Presented in this rather unfair way, torn apart like the leaves
of an artichoke, the impressions of Mr. Symons come to resemble
a common type of popular literary lecture, in which the stories of
plays or novels are retold, the motives of the characters set forth,
and the work of art therefore made easier for the beginner. But
this is not Mr. Symons' reason for writing. The reason why we
find a similarity between his essay and this form of education is
that *Antony and Cleopatra* is a play with which we are pretty well
acquainted, and of which we have, therefore, our own impressions. We can please ourselves with our own impressions of the
characters and their emotions; and we do not find the impressions
of another person, however sensitive, very significant. But if we
can recall the time when we were ignorant of the French sym-
bolists, and met with *The Symbolist Movement in Literature*, we
remember that book as an introduction to wholly new feelings,
as a revelation. After we have read Verlaine and Laforgue and
Rimbaud and return to Mr. Symons' book, we may find that our
own impressions dissent from his. The book has not, perhaps, a
permanent value for the one reader, but it has led to results of
permanent importance for him.

The question is not whether Mr. Symons' impressions are
'true' or 'false'. So far as you can isolate the 'impression', the pure
feeling, it is, of course, neither true nor false. The point is that
you never rest at the pure feeling; you react in one of two ways,
or, as I believe Mr. Symons does, in a mixture of the two ways.
The moment you try to put the impressions into words, you
either begin to analyse and construct, to 'ériger en lois', or you
begin to create something else. It is significant that Swinburne,
by whose poetry Mr. Symons may at one time have been influenced, is one man in his poetry and a different man in his
criticism; to this extent and in this respect only, that he is
satisfying a different impulse; he is criticizing, expounding,
arranging. You may say this is not the criticism of a critic, that it
is emotional, not intellectual – though of this there are two
opinions, but it is in the direction of analysis and construction, a
beginning to 'ériger en lois', and not in the direction of creation.
So I infer that Swinburne found an adequate outlet for the
creative impulse in his poetry; and none of it was forced back and
out through his critical prose. The style of the latter is essentially
a prose style; and Mr. Symons' prose is much more like Swinburne's poetry than it is like his prose. I imagine – though here
one's thought is moving in almost complete darkness – that Mr.

Symons is far more disturbed, far more profoundly affected, by his reading than was Swinburne, who responded rather by a violent and immediate and comprehensive burst of admiration which may have left him internally unchanged. The disturbance in Mr. Symons is almost, but not quite, to the point of creating; the reading sometimes fecundates his emotions to produce something new which is not criticism, but is not the expulsion, the ejection, the birth of creativeness.

The type is not uncommon, although Mr. Symons is far superior to most of the type. Some writers are essentially of the type that reacts in excess of the stimulus, making something new out of the impressions, but suffer from a defect of vitality or an obscure obstruction which prevents nature from taking its course. Their sensibility alters the object, but never transforms it. Their reaction is that of the ordinary emotional person developed to an exceptional degree. For this ordinary emotional person, experiencing a work of art, has a mixed critical and creative reaction. It is made up of comment and opinion, and also new emotions which are vaguely applied to his own life. The sentimental person, in whom a work of art arouses all sorts of emotions which have nothing to do with that work of art whatever, but are accidents of personal association, is an incomplete artist. For in an artist these suggestions made by a work of art, which are purely personal, become fused with a multitude of other suggestions from multitudinous experience, and result in the production of a new object which is no longer purely personal, because it is a work of art itself.

It would be rash to speculate, and is perhaps impossible to determine, what is unfulfilled in Mr. Symons' charming verse that overflows into his critical prose. Certainly we may say that in Swinburne's verse the circuit of impression and expression is complete; and Swinburne was therefore able, in his criticism, to be more a critic than Mr. Symons. This gives us an intimation why the artist is – each within his own limitations – oftenest to be depended upon as a critic; his criticism will be criticism, and not the satisfaction of a suppressed creative wish – which, in most other persons, is apt to interfere fatally.

Before considering what the proper critical reaction of artistic sensibility is, how far criticism is 'feeling' and how far 'thought', and what sort of 'thought' is permitted, it may be instructive to prod a little into that other temperament, so different from Mr. Symons', which issues in generalities such as that quoted near the beginning of this article.

II

*'L'écrivain de style abstrait est presque toujours un
sentimental, du moins un sensitif. L'écrivain artiste n'est
presque jamais un sentimental, et très rarement un sensitif.'*
—LE PROBLÈME DU STYLE

The statement already quoted, that 'poetry is the most highly
organized form of intellectual activity,' may be taken as a specimen of the abstract style in criticism. The confused distinction
which exists in most heads between 'abstract' and 'concrete' is
due not so much to a manifest fact of the existence of two types
of mind, an abstract and a concrete, as to the existence of another
type of mind, the verbal, or philosophic. I, of course, do not
imply any general condemnation of philosophy; I am, for the
moment, using the word 'philosophic' to cover the unscientific
ingredients of philosophy; to cover, in fact, the greater part of the
philosophic output of the last hundred years. There are two ways
in which a word may be 'abstract'. It may have (the word 'activity',
for example) a meaning which cannot be grasped by appeal to
any of the senses; its apprehension may require a deliberate
suppression of analogies of visual or muscular experience, which
is none the less an effort of imagination. 'Activity' will mean for
the trained scientist, if he employ the term, either nothing at all
or something still more exact than anything it suggests to us. If we
are allowed to accept certain remarks of Pascal and Mr. Bertrand
Russell about mathematics, we believe that the mathematician
deals with objects – if he will permit us to call them objects –
which directly affect his sensibility. And during a good part of
history the philosopher endeavoured to deal with objects which
he believed to be of the same exactness as the mathematician's.
Finally Hegel arrived, and if not perhaps the first, he was certainly the most prodigious exponent of emotional systematization,
dealing with his emotions as if they were definite objects which
had aroused those emotions. His followers have as a rule taken for
granted that words have definite meanings, overlooking the
tendency of words to become indefinite emotions. (No one who
had not witnessed the event could imagine the conviction in the
tone of Professor Eucken as he pounded the table and exclaimed
Was ist Geist? Geist ist . . .) If verbalism were confined to professional philosophers, no harm would be done. But their corruption has extended very far. Compare a mediaeval theologian
or mystic, compare a seventeenth-century preacher, with any
'liberal' sermon since Schleiermacher, and you will observe that

words have changed their meanings. What they have lost is definite, and what they have gained is indefinite.

The vast accumulations of knowledge – or at least of information – deposited by the nineteenth century have been responsible for an equally vast ignorance. When there is so much to be known, when there are so many fields of knowledge in which the same words are used with different meanings, when every one knows a little about a great many things, it becomes increasingly difficult for anyone to know whether he knows what he is talking about or not. And when we do not know, or when we do not know enough, we tend always to substitute emotions for thoughts. The sentence so frequently quoted in this essay will serve for an example of this process as well as any, and may be profitably contrasted with the opening phrases of the *Posterior Analytics*. Not only all knowledge, but all feeling, is in perception. The inventor of poetry as the most highly organized form of intellectual activity was not engaged in perceiving when he composed this definition; he had nothing to be aware of except his own emotion about 'poetry'. He was, in fact, absorbed in a very different 'activity' not only from that of Mr. Symons, but from that of Aristotle.

Aristotle is a person who has suffered from the adherence of persons who must be regarded less as his disciples than as his sectaries. One must be firmly distrustful of accepting Aristotle in a canonical spirit; this is to lose the whole living force of him. He was primarily a man of not only remarkable but universal intelligence; and universal intelligence means that he could apply his intelligence to anything. The ordinary intelligence is good only for certain classes of objects; a brilliant man of science, if he is interested in poetry at all, may conceive grotesque judgments: like one poet because he reminds him of himself, or another because he expresses emotions which he admires; he may use art, in fact, as the outlet for the egotism which is suppressed in his own speciality. But Aristotle had none of these impure desires to satisfy; in whatever sphere of interest, he looked solely and steadfastly at the object; in his short and broken treatise he provides an eternal example – not of laws, or even of method, for there is no method except to be very intelligent, but of intelligence itself swiftly operating the analysis of sensation to the point of principle and definition.

It is far less Aristotle than Horace who has been the model for criticism up to the nineteenth century. A precept, such as Horace, or Boileau gives us, is merely an unfinished analysis. It appears as a law, a rule, because it does not appear in its most general form; it is empirical. When we understand necessity, as Spinoza knew, we are free because we assent. The dogmatic critic, who lays down a rule, who affirms a value, has left his labour incomplete. Such statements may often be justifiable as a saving of time; but in matters of great importance the critic must not coerce, and he must not make judgments of worse and better. He must simply elucidate: the reader will form the correct judgment for himself.

And again, the purely 'technical' critic – the critic, that is, who writes to expound some novelty or impart some lesson to practitioners of an art – can be called a critic only in a narrow sense. He may be analysing perceptions and the means for arousing perceptions, but his aim is limited and is not the disinterested exercise of intelligence. The narrowness of the aim makes easier the detection of the merit or feebleness of the work; even of these writers there are very few – so that their 'criticism' is of great importance within its limits. So much suffices for Campion. Dryden is far more disinterested; he displays much free intelligence; and yet even Dryden – or any *literary* critic of the seventeenth century – is not quite a free mind, compared, for instance, with such a mind as Rochefoucauld's. There is always a tendency to legislate rather than to inquire, to revise accepted laws, even to overturn, but to reconstruct out of the same material. And the free intelligence is that which is wholly devoted to inquiry.

Coleridge, again, whose natural abilities, and some of whose performances, are probably more remarkable than those of any other modern critic, cannot be estimated as an intelligence completely free. The nature of the restraint in his case is quite different from that which limited the seventeenth-century critics, and is much more personal. Coleridge's metaphysical interest was quite genuine, and was, like most metaphysical interest, an affair of his emotions. But a literary critic should have no emotions except those immediately provoked by a work of art – and these (as I have already hinted) are, when valid, perhaps not to be called emotions at all. Coleridge is apt to take leave of the data of criticism, and arouse the suspicion that he has been diverted into a metaphysical hare-and-hounds. His end does not always appear to be the return to the work of art with improved perception and intensified, because more conscious, enjoyment; his centre of interest changes, his feelings are impure. In the derogatory sense he is more 'philosophic' than Aristotle. For everything that Aristotle says illuminates the literature which is the occasion for saying it; but Coleridge only now and then. It is one more instance of the pernicious effect of emotion.

Aristotle had what is called the scientific mind – a mind which, as it is rarely found among scientists except in fragments, might better be called the intelligent mind. For there is no other

56

intelligence than this, and so far as artists and men of letters are intelligent (we may doubt whether the level of intelligence among men of letters is as high as among men of science) their intelligence is of this kind. Sainte-Beuve was a physiologist by training; but it is probable that his mind, like that of the ordinary scientific specialist, was limited in its interest, and that this was not, primarily, an interest in art. If he was a critic, there is no doubt that he was a very good one; but we may conclude that he earned some other name. Of all modern critics, perhaps Remy de Gourmont had most of the general intelligence of Aristotle. An amateur, though an excessively able amateur, in physiology, he combined to a remarkable degree sensitiveness, erudition, sense of fact and sense of history, and generalizing power.

We assume the gift of a superior sensibility. And for sensibility wide and profound reading does not mean merely a more extended pasture. There is not merely an increase of understanding, leaving the original acute impression unchanged. The new impressions modify the impressions received from the objects already known. An impression needs to be constantly refreshed by new impressions in order that it may persist at all; it needs to take its place in a system of impressions. And this system tends to become articulate in a generalized statement of literary beauty.

There are, for instance, many scattered lines and tercets in the *Divine Comedy* which are capable of transporting even a quite uninitiated reader, just sufficiently acquainted with the roots of the language to decipher the meaning, to an impression of overpowering beauty. This impression may be so deep that no subsequent study and understanding will intensify it. But at this point the impression is emotional; the reader in the ignorance which we postulate is unable to distinguish the poetry from an emotional state aroused in himself by the poetry, a state which may be merely an indulgence of his own emotions. The poetry may be an accidental stimulus. The end of the enjoyment of poetry is a pure contemplation from which all the accidents of personal emotion are removed; thus we aim to see the object as it really is and find a meaning for the words of Arnold. And without a labour which is largely a labour of the intelligence, we are unable to attain that stage of vision *amor intellectualis Dei*.

Such considerations, cast in this general form, may appear commonplaces. But I believe that it is always opportune to call attention to the torpid superstition that appreciation is one thing, and 'intellectual' criticism something else. Appreciation in popular psychology is one faculty, and criticism another, an arid cleverness building theoretical scaffolds upon one's own perceptions or those of others. On the contrary, the true generalization

57

is not something superposed upon an accumulation of perceptions; the perceptions do not, in a really appreciative mind, accumulate as a mass, but form themselves as a structure; and criticism is the statement in language of this structure; it is a development of sensibility. The bad criticism, on the other hand, is that which is nothing but an expression of emotion. And emotional people – such as stockbrokers, politicians, men of science – and a few people who pride themselves on being unemotional – detest or applaud great writers such as Spinoza or Stendhal because of their 'frigidity'.

The writer of the present essay once committed himself to the statement that 'The poetic critic is criticizing poetry in order to create poetry.' He is now inclined to believe that the 'historical' and the 'philosophical' critics had better be called historians and philosophers quite simply. As for the rest, there are merely various degrees of intelligence. It is fatuous to say that criticism is for the sake of 'creation' or creation for the sake of criticism. It is also fatuous to assume that there are ages of criticism and ages of creativeness, as if by plunging ourselves into intellectual darkness we were in better hopes of finding spiritual light. The two directions of sensibility are complementary; and as sensibility is rare, unpopular, and desirable, it is to be expected that the critic and the creative artist should frequently be the same person.

THE METAPHYSICAL POETS

By collecting these poems[1] from the work of a generation more often named than read, and more often read than profitably studied, Professor Grierson has rendered a service of some importance. Certainly the reader will meet with many poems already preserved in other anthologies, at the same time that he discovers poems such as those of Aurelian Townshend or Lord Herbert of Cherbury here included. But the function of such an anthology as this is neither that of Professor Saintsbury's admirable edition of Caroline poets nor that of the *Oxford Book of English Verse*. Mr. Grierson's book is in itself a piece of criticism, and a provocation of criticism; and we think that he was right in including so many poems of Donne, elsewhere (though not in many editions) accessible, as documents in the case of 'metaphysical poetry'. The phrase has long done duty as a term of abuse, or as the label of a quaint and pleasant taste. The question is to what extent the so-called metaphysicals formed a school (in our own time we should say a 'movement'), and how far this so-called school or movement is a digression from the main current.

Not only is it extremely difficult to define metaphysical poetry, but difficult to decide what poets practise it and in which of their verses. The poetry of Donne (to whom Marvell and Bishop King are sometimes nearer than any of the other authors) is late Elizabethan, its feeling often very close to that of Chapman. The 'courtly' poetry is derivative from Jonson, who borrowed liberally from the Latin; it expires in the next century with the sentiment and witticism of Prior. There is finally the devotional verse of Herbert, Vaughan, and Crashaw (echoed long after by Christina Rossetti and Francis Thompson); Crashaw, sometimes more profound and less sectarian than the others, has a quality which returns through the Elizabethan period to the early Italians. It is difficult to find any precise use of metaphor, simile, or other conceit, which is common to all the poets and at the same time

[1] *Metaphysical Lyrics and Poems of the Seventeenth Century:* Donne to Butler. Selected and edited, with an Essay, by Herbert J. C. Grierson (Oxford: Clarendon Press, London: Milford).

important enough as an element of style to isolate these poets as a group. Donne, and often Cowley, employ a device which is sometimes considered characteristically 'metaphysical'; the elaboration (contrasted with the condensation) of a figure of speech to the furthest stage to which ingenuity can carry it. Thus Cowley develops the commonplace comparison of the world to a chess-board through long stanzas (*To Destiny*), and Donne, with more grace, in *A Valediction*, the comparison of two lovers to a pair of compasses. But elsewhere we find, instead of the mere explication of the content of a comparison, a development by rapid association of thought which requires considerable agility on the part of the reader.

> *On a round ball*
> *A workeman that hath copies by, can lay*
> *An Europe, Afrique, and an Asia,*
> *And quickly make that, which was nothing, All,*
> > *So doth each teare,*
> > *Which thee doth weare,*
> *A globe, yea world by that impression grow,*
> *Till thy tears mixt with mine doe overflow*
> *This world, by waters sent from thee, my heaven dissolved so.*

Here we find at least two connections which are not implicit in the first figure, but are forced upon it by the poet: from the geographer's globe to the tear, and the tear to the deluge. On the other hand, some of Donne's most successful and characteristic effects are secured by brief words and sudden contrasts:

> *A bracelet of bright hair about the bone,*

where the most powerful effect is produced by the sudden contrast of associations of 'bright hair' and of 'bone'. This telescoping of images and multiplied associations is characteristic of the phrase of some of the dramatists of the period which Donne knew: not to mention Shakespeare, it is frequent in Middleton, Webster, and Tourneur, and is one of the sources of the vitality of their language.

Johnson, who employed the term 'metaphysical poets', apparently having Donne, Cleveland, and Cowley chiefly in mind, remarks of them that 'the most heterogeneous ideas are yoked by violence together'. The force of this impeachment lies in the failure of the conjunction, the fact that often the ideas are yoked but not united; and if we are to judge of styles of poetry by their abuse, enough examples may be found in Cleveland to justify
60

Johnson's condemnation. But a degree of heterogeneity of material compelled into unity by the operation of the poet's mind is omnipresent in poetry. We need not select for illustration such a line as:

Notre âme est un trois-mâts cherchant son Icarie;

we may find it in some of the best lines of Johnson himself (*The Vanity of Human Wishes*):

> *His fate was destined to a barren strand,*
> *A petty fortress, and a dubious hand;*
> *He left a name at which the world grew pale,*
> *To point a moral, or adorn a tale.*

where the effect is due to a contrast of ideas, different in degree but the same in principle, as that which Johnson mildly reprehended. And in one of the finest poems of the age (a poem which could not have been written in any other age), the *Exequy* of Bishop King, the extended comparison is used with perfect success: the idea and the simile become one, in the passage in which the Bishop illustrates his impatience to see his dead wife, under the figure of a journey:

> *Stay for me there; I will not faile*
> *To meet thee in that hollow Vale.*
> *And think not much of my delay;*
> *I am already on the way,*
> *And follow thee with all the speed*
> *Desire can make, or sorrows breed.*
> *Each minute is a short degree,*
> *And ev'ry houre a step towards thee.*
> *At night when I betake to rest,*
> *Next morn I rise nearer my West*
> *Of life, almost by eight houres sail,*
> *Than when sleep breath'd his drowsy gale. . . .*
> *But heark! My Pulse, like a soft Drum*
> *Beats my approach, tells* Thee *I come;*
> *And slow howere my marches be,*
> *I shall at last sit down by* Thee.

(In the last few lines there is that effect of terror which is several times attained by one of Bishop King's admirers, Edgar Poe.) Again, we may justly take these quatrains from Lord Herbert's

Ode, stanzas which would, we think, be immediately pronounced to be of the metaphysical school:

> *So when from hence we shall be gone,*
> *And be no more, nor you, nor I,*
> *As one another's mystery,*
> *Each shall be both, yet both but one.*
>
> *This said, in her up-lifted face,*
> *Her eyes, which did that beauty crown,*
> *Were like two starrs, that having faln down,*
> *Look up again to find their place:*
>
> *While such a moveless silent peace*
> *Did seize on their becalmed sense,*
> *One would have thought some influence*
> *Their ravished spirits did possess.*

There is nothing in these lines (with the possible exception of the stars, a simile not at once grasped, but lovely and justified) which fits Johnson's general observations on the metaphysical poets in his essay on Cowley. A good deal resides in the richness of association which is at the same time borrowed from and given to the word 'becalmed'; but the meaning is clear, the language simple and elegant. It is to be observed that the language of these poets is as a rule simple and pure; in the verse of George Herbert this simplicity is carried as far as it can go – a simplicity emulated without success by numerous modern poets. The *structure* of the sentences, on the other hand, is sometimes far from simple, but this is not a vice; it is a fidelity to thought and feeling. The effect, at its best, is far less artificial than that of an ode by Gray. And as this fidelity induces variety of thought and feeling, so it induces variety of music. We doubt whether, in the eighteenth century, could be found two poems in nominally the same metre, so dissimilar as Marvell's *Coy Mistress* and Crashaw's *Saint Teresa*; the one producing an effect of great speed by the use of short syllables, and the other an ecclesiastical solemnity by the use of long ones:

> *Love thou art absolute sole lord*
> *Of life and death.*

If so shrewd and sensitive (though so limited) a critic as Johnson failed to define metaphysical poetry by its faults, it is worth while to inquire whether we may not have more success by adopting the opposite method: by assuming that the poets of the seventeenth century (up to the Revolution) were the direct and normal development of the precedent age; and, without prejudicing their case by the adjective 'metaphysical', consider whether their virtue was not something permanently valuable, which subsequently disappeared, but ought not to have disappeared. Johnson has hit, perhaps by accident, on one of their peculiarities, when he observed that 'their attempts were always analytic'; he would not agree that, after the dissociation, they put the material together again in a new unity.

It is certain that the dramatic verse of the later Elizabethan and early Jacobean poets expresses a degree of development of sensibility which is not found in any of the prose, good as it often is. If we except Marlowe, a man of prodigious intelligence, these dramatists were directly or indirectly (it is at least a tenable theory) affected by Montaigne. Even if we except also Jonson and Chapman, these two were notably erudite, and were notably men who incorporated their erudition into their sensibility: their mode of feeling was directly and freshly altered by their reading and thought. In Chapman especially there is a direct sensuous apprehension of thought, or a recreation of thought into feeling, which is exactly what we find in Donne:

> *in this one thing, all the discipline*
> *Of manners and of manhood is contained;*
> *A man to join himself with th' Universe*
> *In his main sway, and make in all things fit*
> *One with that All, and go on, round as it;*
> *Not plucking from the whole his wretched part*
> *And into straits, or into nought revert,*
> *Wishing the complete Universe might be*
> *Subject to such a rag of it as he;*
> *But to consider great Necessity.*

We compare this with some modern passage:

> *No, when the fight begins within himself,*
> *A man's worth something. God stoops o'er his head,*
> *Satan looks up between his feet – both tug –*
> *He's left, himself, i' the middle; the soul wakes*
> *And grows. Prolong that battle through his life!*

It is perhaps somewhat less fair, though very tempting as both poets are concerned with the perpetuation of love by offspring), to compare with the stanzas already quoted from Lord Herbert's Ode the following from Tennyson:

63

One walked between his wife and child,
With measured footfall firm and mild,
And now and then he gravely smiled.
The prudent partner of his blood
Leaned on him, faithful, gentle, good
Wearing the rose of womanhood.
And in their double love secure,
The little maiden walked demure,
Pacing with downward eyelids pure.
These three made unity so sweet,
My frozen heart began to beat,
Remembering its ancient heat.

The difference is not a simple difference of degree between poets. It is something which had happened to the mind of England between the time of Donne or Lord Herbert of Cherbury and the time of Tennyson and Browning; it is the difference between the intellectual poet and the reflective poet. Tennyson and Browning are poets, and they think; but they do not feel their thought as immediately as the odour of a rose. A thought to Donne was an experience; it modified his sensibility. When a poet's mind is perfectly equipped for its work, it is constantly amalgamating disparate experience; the ordinary man's experience is chaotic, irregular, fragmentary. The latter falls in love, or reads Spinoza, and these two experiences have nothing to do with each other, or with the noise of the typewriter or the smell of cooking; in the mind of the poet these experiences are always forming new wholes.

We may express the difference by the following theory: The poets of the seventeenth century, the successors of the dramatists of the sixteenth, possessed a mechanism of sensibility which could devour any kind of experience. They are simple, artificial, difficult, or fantastic, as their predecessors were; no less nor more than Dante, Guido Cavalcanti, Guinicelli, or Cino. In the seventeenth century a dissociation of sensibility set in, from which we have never recovered; and this dissociation, as is natural, was aggravated by the influence of the two most powerful poets of the century, Milton and Dryden. Each of these men performed certain poetic functions so magnificently well that the magnitude of the effect concealed the absence of others. The language went on and in some respects improved; the best verse of Collins, Gray, Johnson, and even Goldsmith satisfies some of our fastidious demands better than that of Donne or Marvell or King. But while the language became more refined, the feeling became more crude. The feeling, the sensibility, expressed in the *Country*

64

Churchyard (to say nothing of Tennyson and Browning) is cruder than that in the *Coy Mistress*.

The second effect of the influence of Milton and Dryden followed from the first, and was therefore slow in manifestation. The sentimental age began early in the eighteenth century, and continued. The poets revolted against the ratiocinative, the descriptive; they thought and felt by fits, unbalanced; they reflected. In one or two passages of Shelley's *Triumph of Life*, in the second *Hyperion* there are traces of a struggle toward unification of sensibility. But Keats and Shelley died, and Tennyson and Browning ruminated.

After this brief exposition of a theory – too brief, perhaps, to carry conviction – we may ask, what would have been the fate of the 'metaphysical' had the current of poetry descended in a direct line from them, as it descended in a direct line to them? They would not, certainly, be classified as metaphysical. The possible interests of a poet are unlimited; the more intelligent he is the better; the more intelligent he is the more likely that he will have interests: our only condition is that he turn them into poetry, and not merely meditate on them poetically. A philosophical theory which has entered into poetry is established, for its truth or falsity in one sense ceases to matter, and its truth in another sense is proved. The poets in question have, like other poets, various faults. But they were, at best, engaged in the task of trying to find the verbal equivalent for states of mind and feeling. And this means both that they are more mature, and that they wear better, than later poets of certainly not less literary ability.

It is not a permanent necessity that poets should be interested in philosophy, or in any other subject. We can only say that it appears likely that poets in our civilization, as it exists at present, must be *difficult*. Our civilization comprehends great variety and complexity, and this variety and complexity, playing upon a refined sensibility, must produce various and complex results. The poet must become more and more comprehensive, more allusive, more indirect, in order to force, to dislocate if necessary, language into his meaning. (A brilliant and extreme statement of this view, with which it is not requisite to associate oneself, is that of M. Jean Epstein, *La Poésie d'aujourd-hui*.) Hence we get something which looks very much like the conceit – we get, in fact, a method curiously similar to that of the 'metaphysical poets', similar also in its use of obscure words and of simple phrasing.

> *O géraniums diaphanes, guerroyeurs sortilèges,*
> *Sacrilèges monomanes!*
> *Emballages, dévergondages, douches! O pressoirs*

65

Des vendanges des grands soirs!
Layettes aux abois,
Thyrses au fond des bois!
Transfusions, représailles,
Relevailles, compresses et l'éternal potion,
Angélus! n'en pouvoir plus
De débâcles nuptiales! de débâcles nuptiales!

The same poet could write also simply:

Elle est bien loin, elle pleure,
Le grand vent se lamente aussi . . .

Jules Laforgue, and Tristan Corbière in many of his poems, are nearer to the 'school of Donne' than any modern English poet. But poets more classical than they have the same essential quality of transmuting ideas into sensations, of transforming an observation into a state of mind.

Pour l'enfant, amoureux de cartes et d'estampes,
L'univers est égal à son vaste appétit.
Ah, que le monde est grand à la clarté des lampes!
Aux yeux du souvenir que le monde est petit!

In French literature the great master of the seventeenth century – Racine – and the great master of the nineteenth – Baudelaire – are in some ways more like each other than they are like anyone else. The greatest two masters of diction are also the greatest two psychologists, the most curious explorers of the soul. It is interesting to speculate whether it is not a misfortune that two of the greatest masters of diction in our language, Milton and Dryden, triumph with a dazzling disregard of the soul. If we continued to produce Miltons and Drydens it might not so much matter, but as things are it is a pity that English poetry has remained so incomplete. Those who object to the 'artificiality' of Milton or Dryden sometimes tell us to 'look into our hearts and write'. But that is not looking deep enough; Racine or Donne looked into a good deal more than the heart. One must look into the cerebral cortex, the nervous system, and the digestive tracts.

May we not conclude, then, that Donne, Crashaw, Vaughan, Herbert and Lord Herbert, Marvell, King, Cowley at his best, are in the direct current of English poetry, and that their faults should be reprimanded by this standard rather than coddled by antiquarian affection? They have been enough praised in terms which are implicit limitations because they are 'metaphysical' or

66

'witty', 'quaint' or 'obscure', though at their best they have not these attributes more than other serious poets. On the other hand, we must not reject the criticism of Johnson (a dangerous person to disagree with) without having mastered it, without having assimilated the Johnsonian canons of taste. In reading the celebrated passage in his essay on Cowley we must remember that by wit he clearly means something more serious than we usually mean today; in his criticism of their versification we must remember in what a narrow discipline he was trained, but also how well trained; we must remember that Johnson tortures chiefly the chief offenders, Cowley and Cleveland. It would be a fruitful work, and one requiring a substantial book, to break up the classification of Johnson (for there has been none since) and exhibit these poets in all their difference of kind and of degree, from the massive music of Donne to the faint, pleasing tinkle of Aurelian Townshend – whose *Dialogue between a Pilgrim and Time* is one of the few regrettable omissions from the excellent anthology of Professor Grierson.

THE FUNCTION OF CRITICISM

I

Writing several years ago on the subject of the relation of the new to the old in art, I formulated a view to which I still adhere, in sentences which I take the liberty of quoting, because the present paper is an application of the principle they express:

'The existing monuments form an ideal order among themselves, which is modified by the introduction of the new (the really new) work of art among them. The existing order is complete before the new work arrives; for order to persist after the supervention of novelty, the *whole* existing order must be, if ever so slightly, altered; and so the relations, proportions, values of each work of art toward the whole are readjusted; and this is conformity between the old and the new. Whoever has approved this idea of order, of the form of European, of English literature, will not find it preposterous that the past should be altered by the present as much as the present is directed by the past.'

I was dealing then with the artist, and the sense of tradition which, it seemed to me, the artist should have; but it was generally a problem of order; and the function of criticism seems to be essentially a problem of order too. I thought of literature then, as I think of it now, of the literature of the world, of the literature of Europe, of the literature of a single country, not as a collection of the writings of individuals, but as 'organic wholes', as systems in relation to which, and only in relation to which, individual works of literary art, and the works of individual artists, have their significance. There is accordingly something outside of the artist to which he owes allegiance, a devotion to which he must surrender and sacrifice himself in order to earn and to obtain his unique position. A common inheritance and a common cause unite artists consciously or unconsciously: it must be admitted that the union is mostly unconscious. Between the true artists of any time there is, I believe, an unconscious community. And, as our instincts of tidiness imperatively command us not to leave to the haphazard of unconsciousness what we can ..ttempt to do consciously, we are forced to conclude that what happens

68

unconsciously we could bring about, and form into a purpose, if we made a conscious attempt. The second-rate artist, of course, cannot afford to surrender himself to any common action; for his chief task is the assertion of all the trifling differences which are his distinction: only the man who has so much to give that he can forget himself in his work can afford to collaborate, to exchange, to contribute.

If such views are held about art, it follows that *a fortiori* whoever holds them must hold similar views about criticism. When I say criticism, I mean of course in this place the commentation and exposition of works of art by means of written words; for of the general use of the word 'criticism' to mean such writings, as Matthew Arnold uses it in his essay, I shall presently make several qualifications. No exponent of criticism (in this limited sense) has, I presume, ever made the preposterous assumption that criticism is an autotelic activity. I do not deny that art may be affirmed to serve ends beyond itself; but art is not required to be aware of these ends, and indeed performs its function, whatever that may be, according to various theories of value, much better by indifference to them. Criticism, on the other hand, must always profess an end in view, which, roughly speaking, appears to be the elucidation of works of art and the correction of taste. The critic's task, therefore, appears to be quite clearly cut out for him; and it ought to be comparatively easy to decide whether he performs it satisfactorily, and in general, what kinds of criticism are useful and what are otiose. But on giving the matter a little attention, we perceive that criticism, far from being a simple and orderly field of beneficent activity, from which impostors can be readily ejected, is no better than a Sunday park of contending and contentious orators, who have not even arrived at the articulation of their differences. Here, one would suppose, was a place for quiet cooperative labour. The critic, one would suppose, if he is to justify his existence, should endeavour to discipline his personal prejudices and cranks – tares to which we are all subject – and compose his differences with as many of his fellows as possible, in the common pursuit of true judgment. When we find that quite the contrary prevails, we begin to suspect that the critic owes his livelihood to the violence and extremity of his opposition to other critics, or else to some trifling oddities of his own with which he contrives to season the opinions which men already hold, and which out of vanity or sloth they prefer to maintain. We are tempted to expel the lot.

Immediately after such an eviction, or as soon as relief has abated our rage, we are compelled to admit that there remain certain books, certain essays, certain sentences, certain men, who have been 'useful' to us. And our next step is to attempt to classify these, and find out whether we establish any principles for deciding what kinds of book should be preserved, and what aims and methods of criticism should be followed.

II

The view of the relation of the work of art to art, of the work of literature to literature, of 'criticism' to criticism, which I have outlined above, seemed to me natural and self-evident. I owe to Mr. Middleton Murry my perception of the contentious character of the problem; or rather, my perception that there is a definite and final choice involved. To Mr. Murry I feel an increasing debt of gratitude. Most of our critics are occupied in labour of obnubilation; in reconciling, in hushing up, in patting down, in squeezing in, in glozing over, in concocting pleasant sedatives, in pretending that the only difference between themselves and others is that they are nice men and the others of very doubtful repute. Mr. Murry is not one of these. He is aware that there are definite positions to be taken, and that now and then one must actually reject something and select something else. He is not the anonymous writer who in a literary paper several years ago asserted that Romanticism and Classicism are much the same thing, and that the true Classical Age in France was the Age which produced the Gothic cathedrals and – Jeanne d'Arc. With Mr. Murry's formulation of Classicism and Romanticism I cannot agree; the difference seems to me rather the difference between the complete and the fragmentary, the adult and the immature, the orderly and the chaotic. But what Mr. Murry does show is that there are at least two attitudes toward literature and toward everything, and that you cannot hold both. And the attitude which he professes appears to imply that the other has no standing in England whatever. For it is made a national, a racial issue.

Mr. Murry makes his issue perfectly clear. 'Catholicism', he says, 'stands for the principle of unquestioned spiritual authority outside the individual; that is also the principle of Classicism in literature.' Within the orbit within which Mr. Murry's discussion moves, this seems to me an unimpeachable definition, though it is of course not all that there is to be said about either Catholicism or Classicism. Those of us who find ourselves supporting what Mr. Murry calls Classicism believe that men cannot get on without giving allegiance to something outside themselves. I am aware that 'outside' and 'inside' are terms which provide unlimited opportunity for quibbling, and that no psychologist would tolerate a discussion which shuffled such base coinage; but I will presume that Mr. Murry and myself can agree that for our purpose these counters are adequate, and concur in disregarding the admonitions of our psychological friends. If you find that you have to imagine it as outside, then it is outside. If, then, a man's interest is political, he must, I presume, profess an allegiance to principles, or to a form of government, or to a monarch; and if he is interested in religion, and has one, to a Church; and if he happens to be interested in literature, he must acknowledge, it seems to me, just that sort of allegiance which I endeavoured to put forth in the preceding section. There is, nevertheless, an alternative, which Mr. Murry has expressed. 'The English writer, the English divine, the English statesman, inherit no rules from their forebears; they inherit only this: a sense that in the last resort they must depend upon the inner voice.' This statement does, I admit, appear to cover certain cases; it throws a flood of light upon Mr Lloyd George. But why 'in the last resort'? Do they, then, avoid the dictates of the inner voice up to the last extremity? My belief is that those who possess this inner voice are ready enough to hearken to it, and will hear no other. The inner voice, in fact, sounds remarkably like an old principle which has been formulated by an elder critic in the now familiar phrase of 'doing as one likes'. The possessors of the inner voice ride ten in a compartment to a football match at Swansea, listening to the inner voice, which breathes the eternal message of vanity, fear, and lust.

Mr. Murry will say, with some show of justice, that this is a wilful misrepresentation. He says: 'If they (the English writer, divine, statesman) dig *deep enough* in their pursuit of self-knowledge – a piece of mining done not with the intellect alone, but with the whole man – they will come upon a self that is universal' – an exercise far beyond the strength of our football enthusiasts. It is an exercise, however, which I believe was of enough interest to Catholicism for several handbooks to be written on its practice. But the Catholic practitioners were, I believe, with the possible exception of certain heretics, not palpitating Narcissi; the Catholic did not believe that God and himself were identical. 'The man who truly interrogates himself will ultimately hear the voice of God', Mr. Murry says. In theory, this leads to a form of pantheism which I maintain is not European – just as Mr. Murry maintains that 'Classicism' is not English. For its practical results, one may refer to the verses of *Hudibras*.

I did not realize that Mr. Murry was the spokesman for a considerable sect, until I read in the editorial columns of a dignified daily that 'magnificent as the representatives of the classical genius have been in England, they are not the sole expressions of the English character, which remains at bottom obstinately "humorous" and nonconformist'. This writer is moderate in using the qualification *sole*, and brutally frank in attributing this 'humorousness' to 'the unreclaimed Teutonic element in us'. But it strikes me that Mr. Murry, and this other voice, are either too obstinate or too tolerant. The question is, the first question, *not* what comes natural or what comes *easy* to us, but what is right? Either one attitude is better than the other, or else it is indifferent. But how can such a choice be indifferent? Surely the reference to racial origins, or the mere statement that the French are thus, and the English otherwise, is not expected to settle the question: which, of two antithetical views, is *right*? And I cannot understand why the opposition between Classicism and Romanticism should be profound enough in Latin countries (Mr. Murry says it is) and yet of no significance among ourselves. For if the French are *naturally* classical, why should there be any 'opposition' in France, any more than there is here? And if Classicism is not natural to them, but something acquired, why not acquire it here? Were the French in the year 1600 classical, and the English in the same year romantic? A more important difference, to my mind, is that the French in the year 1600 *had already a more mature prose.*

III

This discussion may seem to have led us a long way from the subject of this paper. But it was worth my while to follow Mr. Murry's comparison of Outside Authority with the Inner Voice. For to those who obey the inner voice (perhaps 'obey' is not the word) nothing that I can say about criticism will have the slightest value. For they will not be interested in the attempt to find any common principles for the pursuit of criticism. Why have principles, when one has the inner voice? If I like a thing, that is all I want; and if enough of us, shouting all together, like it, that should be all that *you* (who don't like it) ought to want. The law of art, said Mr. Clutton Brock, is all case law. And we can not only like whatever we like to like but we can like it for any reason we choose. We are not, in fact, concerned with literary *perfection* at all – the search for perfection is a sign of pettiness, for it shows that the writer has admitted the existence of an unquestioned spiritual authority outside himself, to which he has attempted to *conform*. We are not in fact interested in art. We will not worship Baal. 'The principle of classical leadership is that obeisance is made to

72

the office or to the tradition, never to the man.' And we want, not principles, but men.

Thus speaks the Inner Voice. It is a voice to which, for convenience, we may give a name: and the name I suggest is Whiggery.

IV

Leaving, then, those whose calling and election are sure and returning to those who shamefully depend upon tradition and the accumulated wisdom of time, and restricting the discussion to those who sympathize with each other in this frailty, we may comment for a moment upon the use of the terms 'critical' and 'creative' by one whose place, on the whole, is with the weaker brethren. Matthew Arnold distinguishes far too bluntly, it seems to me, between the two activities: he overlooks the capital importance of criticism in the work of creation itself. Probably, indeed, the larger part of the labour of an author in composing his work is critical labour; the labour of sifting, combining, constructing, expunging, correcting, testing: this frightful toil is as much critical as creative. I maintain even that the criticism employed by a trained and skilled writer on his own work is the most vital, the highest kind of criticism; and (as I think I have said before) that some creative writers are superior to others solely because their critical faculty is superior. There is a tendency, and I think it is a whiggery tendency, to decry this critical toil of the artist; to propound the thesis that the great artist is an unconscious artist, unconsciously inscribing on his banner the words Muddle Through. Those of us who are Inner Deaf Mutes are, however, sometimes compensated by a humble conscience, which, though without oracular expertness, counsels us to do the best we can, reminds us that our compositions ought to be as free from defects as possible (to atone for their lack of inspiration), and, in short, makes us waste a good deal of time. We are aware, too, that the critical discrimination which comes so hardly to us has in more fortunate men flashed in the very heat of creation; and we do not assume that because works have been composed without apparent critical labour, no critical labour has been done. We do not know what previous labours have prepared, or what goes on, in the way of criticism, all the time in the minds of the creators.

But this affirmation recoils upon us. If so large a part of creation is really criticism, is not a large part of what is called 'critical writing' really creative? If so, is there not creative criticism in the ordinary sense? The answer seems to be, that there is no equation. I have assumed as axiomatic that a creation, a work of art, is

73

autotelic; and that criticism, by definition, is *about* something other than itself. Hence you cannot fuse creation with criticism as you can fuse criticism with creation. The critical activity finds its highest, its true fulfilment in a kind of union with creation in the labour of the artist.

But no writer is completely self-sufficient, and many creative writers have a critical activity which is not all discharged into their work. Some seem to require to keep their critical powers in condition for the real work by exercising them miscellaneously; others, on completing a work, need to continue the critical activity by commenting on it. There is no general rule. And as men can learn from each other, so some of these treatises have been useful to other writers. And some of them have been useful to those who were not writers.

At one time I was inclined to take the extreme position that the *only* critics worth reading were the critics who practised, and practised well, the art of which they wrote. But I had to stretch this frame to make some important inclusions; and I have since been in search of a formula which should cover everything I wished to include, even if it included more than I wanted. And the most important qualification which I have been able to find, which accounts for the peculiar importance of the criticism of practitioners, is that a critic must have a very highly developed sense of fact. This is by no means a trifling or frequent gift. And it is not one which easily wins popular commendations. The sense of fact is something very slow to develop, and its complete development means perhaps the very pinnacle of civilization. For there are so many spheres of fact to be mastered, and our outermost sphere of fact, of knowledge, of control, will be ringed with narcotic fancies in the sphere beyond. To the member of the Browning Study Circle, the discussion of poets about poetry may seem arid, technical, and limited. It is merely that the practitioners have clarified and reduced to a state of fact all the feelings that the member can only enjoy in the most nebulous form; the dry technique implies, for those who have mastered it, all that the member thrills to; only that has been made into something precise, tractable, under control. That, at all events, is one reason for the value of the practitioner's criticism – he is dealing with his facts, and he can help us to do the same.

And at every level of criticism I find the same necessity regnant. There is a large part of critical writing which consists in 'interpreting' an author, a work. This is not on the level of the Study Circle either; it occasionally happens that one person obtains an understanding of another, or a creative writer, which he can partially communicate, and which we feel to be true and illumi-

74

nating. It is difficult to confirm the 'interpretation' by external evidence. To anyone who is skilled in fact on this level there will be evidence enough. But who is to prove his own skill? And for every success in this type of writing there are thousands of impostures. Instead of insight, you get a fiction. Your test is to apply it again and again to the original, with your view of the original to guide you. But there is no one to guarantee your competence, and once again we find ourselves in a dilemma.

We must ourselves decide what is useful to us and what is not; and it is quite likely that we are not competent to decide. But it is fairly certain that 'interpretation' (I am not touching upon the acrostic element in literature) is only legitimate when it is not interpretation at all, but merely putting the reader in possession of facts which he would otherwise have missed. I have had some experience of Extension lecturing, and I have found only two ways of leading any pupils to like anything with the right liking: to present them with a selection of the simpler kind of facts about a work – its conditions, its setting, its genesis – or else to spring the work on them in such a way that they were not prepared to be prejudiced against it. There were many facts to help them with Elizabethan drama: the poems of T. E. Hulme only needed to be read aloud to have immediate effect.

Comparison and analysis, I have said before, and Remy de Gourmont has said before me (a real master of fact – sometimes, I am afraid, when he moved outside of literature, a master illusionist of fact), are the chief tools of the critic. It is obvious indeed that they *are* tools, to be handled with care, and not employed in an inquiry into the number of times giraffes are mentioned in the English novel. They are not used with conspicuous success by many contemporary writers. You must know what to compare and what to analyse. The late Professor Ker had skill in the use of these tools. Comparison and analysis need only the cadavers on the table; but interpretation is always producing parts of the body from its pockets, and fixing them in place. And any book, any essay, any note in *Notes and Queries*, which produces a fact even of the lowest order about a work of art is a better piece of work than nine-tenths of the most pretentious critical journalism, in journals or in books. We assume, of course, that we are masters and not servants of facts, and that we know that the discovery of Shakespeare's laundry bills would not be of much use to us; but we must always reserve final judgment as to the futility of the research which has discovered them, in the possibility that some genius will appear who will know of a use to which to put them. Scholarship, even in its humblest forms, has its rights; we assume that we know how to use it, and how to

75

neglect it. Of course the multiplication of critical books and essays may create, and I have seen it create, a vicious taste for reading about works of art instead of reading the works themselves, it may supply opinion instead of educating taste. But *fact* cannot corrupt taste; it can at worst gratify one taste – a taste for history, let us say, or antiquities, or biography – under the illusion that it is assisting another. The real corrupters are those who supply opinion or fancy; and Goethe and Coleridge are not guiltless – for what is Coleridge's *Hamlet*: is it an honest inquiry as far as the data permit, or is it an attempt to present Coleridge in an attractive costume?

We have not succeeded in finding such a test as anyone can apply; we have been forced to allow ingress to innumerable dull and tedious books; but we have, I think, found a test which, for those who are able to apply it, will dispose of the really vicious ones. And with this test we may return to the preliminary statement of the polity of literature and of criticism. For the kinds of critical work which we have admitted, there is the possibility of cooperative activity, with the further possibility of arriving at something outside of ourselves, which may provisionally be called truth. But if anyone complains that I have not defined truth, or fact, or reality, I can only say apologetically that it was no part of my purpose to do so, but only to find a scheme into which, whatever they are, they will fit, if they exist.

from PREFACE TO ANABASIS

I am by no means convinced that a poem like *Anabasis* requires a preface at all. It is better to read such a poem six times, and dispense with a preface. But when a poem is presented in the form of a translation, people who have never heard of it are naturally inclined to demand some testimonial. So I give mine hereunder. . . .

For myself, once having had my attention drawn to the poem by a friend whose taste I trusted, there was no need for a preface. I did not need to be told, after one reading, that the word *anabasis* has no particular reference to Xenophon or the journey of the Ten Thousand, no particular reference to Asia *Minor*; and that no map of its migrations could be drawn up. Mr. Perse is using the word *anabasis* in the same literal sense in which Xenophon himself used it. The poem is a series of images of migration, of conquest of vast spaces in Asiatic wastes, of destruction and foundation of cities and civilizations of any races or epochs of the ancient East.

I may, I trust, borrow from Mr. Fabre two notions which may be of use to the English reader. The first is that any obscurity of the poem, on first readings, is due to the suppression of 'links in the chain', of explanatory and connecting matter, and not to incoherence, or to the love of cryptogram. The justification of such abbreviation of method is that the sequence of images coincides and concentrates into one intense impression of barbaric civilization. The reader has to allow the images to fall into his memory successively without questioning the reasonableness of each at the moment; so that, at the end, a total effect is produced.

Such selection of a sequence of images and ideas has nothing chaotic about it. There is a logic of the imagination as well as a logic of concepts. People who do not appreciate poetry always find it difficult to distinguish between order and chaos in the

77

arrangement of images; and even those who are capable of appreciating poetry cannot depend upon first impressions. I was not convinced of Mr. Perse's imaginative order until I had read the poem five or six times. And if, as I suggest, such an arrangement of imagery requires just as much 'fundamental brainwork' as the arrangement of an argument, it is to be expected that the reader of a poem should take at least as much trouble as a barrister reading an important decision on a complicated case. . . .

from THE USE OF POETRY AND THE USE OF CRITICISM

[*i* THE NECESSITY OF CRITICISM

. . . The important moment for the appearance of criticism seems to be the time when poetry ceases to be the expression of the mind of a whole people. The drama of Dryden, which furnishes the chief occasion for his critical writing, is formed by Dryden's perception that the possibilities of writing in the mode of Shakespeare were exhausted; the form persists in the tragedies of such a writer as Shirley (who is much more up to date in his comedies), after the mind and sensibility of England has altered. But Dryden was not writing plays for the whole people; he was writing in a form which had not grown out of popular tradition or popular requirements, a form the acceptance of which had therefore to come by diffusion through a small society. Something similar had been attempted by the Senecan dramatists. But the part of society to which Dryden's work, and that of the Restoration comedians, could immediately appeal constituted something like an intellectual aristocracy; when the poet finds himself in an age in which there is no intellectual aristocracy, when power is in the hands of a class so democratized that whilst still a class it represents itself to be the whole nation; when the only alternatives seem to be to talk to a coterie or to soliloquize, the difficulties of the poet and the necessity of criticism become greater. . . .

[*ii* CRITICISM AND THE MEANING OF POETRY

. . . The critical mind operating *in* poetry, the critical effort which goes to the writing of it, may always be in advance of the critical mind operating *upon* poetry, whether it be one's own or some one else's. I only affirm that there is a significant relation between the best poetry and the best criticism of the same period. The age of criticism is also the age of critical poetry. And when I speak of modern poetry as being extremely critical, I mean that the contemporary poet, who is not merely a composer of graceful verses,

79

– is forced to ask himself such questions as 'what is poetry for?'; not merely 'what am I to say?' but rather 'how and to whom am I to say it?' We have to communicate – if it is communication, for the word may beg the question – an experience which is not an experience in the ordinary sense, for it may only exist, formed out of many personal experiences ordered in some way which may be very different from the way of valuation of practical life, in the expression of it. *If* poetry is a form of 'communication', yet that which is to be communicated is the poem itself, and only incidentally the experience and the thought which have gone into it. The poem's existence is somewhere between the writer and the reader; it has a reality which is not simply the reality of what the writer is trying to 'express', or of his experience of writing it, or of the experience of the reader or of the writer as reader. Consequently the problem of what a poem 'means' is a good deal more difficult than it at first appears. If a poem of mine entitled *Ash-Wednesday* ever goes into a second edition, I have thought of prefixing to it the lines of Byron from *Don Juan*:

> *Some have accused me of a strange design*
> *Against the creed and morals of this land,*
> *And trace it in this poem, every line.*
> *I don't pretend that I quite understand*
> *My own meaning when I would be very fine;*
> *But the fact is that I have nothing planned*
> *Except perhaps to be a moment merry . . .*

There is some sound critical admonition in these lines. But a poem is not just either what the poet 'planned' or what the reader conceives, nor is its 'use' restricted wholly to what the author intended or to what it actually does for readers. Though the amount and the quality of the pleasure which any work of art has given since it came into existence is not irrelevant, still we never judge it by that; and we do not ask, after being greatly moved by the sight of a piece of architecture or the audition of a piece of music, 'what has been my benefit or profit from seeing this temple or hearing this music?' In one sense the question implied by the phrase 'the use of poetry' is nonsense. But there is another meaning to the question. Apart from the variety of ways in which poets have used their art, with greater or less success, with designs of instruction or persuasion, there is no doubt that a poet wishes to give pleasure, to entertain or divert people; and he should normally be glad to be able to feel that the entertainment or diversion is enjoyed by as large and various a number of people as possible. When a poet deliberately restricts his public by his choice of style of writing or of subject-matter, this is a special situation demanding explanation and extenuation, but I doubt whether this ever happens. It is one thing to write in a style which is already popular, and another to hope that one's writing may eventually become popular. From one point of view, the poet aspires to the condition of the music-hall comedian. Being incapable of altering his wares to suit a prevailing taste, if there be any, he naturally desires a state of society in which they may become popular, and in which his own talents will be put to the best use. He is accordingly vitally interested in the *use* of poetry....

[*iii* SHELLEY

Shelley both had views about poetry and made use of poetry for expressing views. With Shelley we are struck from the beginning by the number of things poetry is expected to do; from a poet who tells us, in a note on vegetarianism, that 'the orang-outang perfectly resembles man both in the order and the number of his teeth', we shall not know what not to expect. The notes to *Queen Mab* express, it is true, only the views of an intelligent and enthusiastic schoolboy, but a schoolboy who knows how to write; and throughout his work, which is of no small bulk for a short life, he does not, I think, let us forget that he took his ideas seriously. The ideas of Shelley seem to me always to be ideas of adolescence – as there is every reason why they should be. And an enthusiasm for Shelley seems to me also to be an affair of adolescence: for most of us, Shelley has marked an intense period before maturity, but for how many does Shelley remain the companion of age? I confess that I never open the volume of his poems simply because I want to read poetry, but only with some special reason for reference. I find his ideas repellent; and the difficulty of separating Shelley from his ideas and beliefs is still greater than with Wordsworth. And the biographical interest which Shelley has always excited makes it difficult to read the poetry without remembering the man: and the man was humourless, pedantic, self-centred, and sometimes almost a blackguard. Except for an occasional flash of shrewd sense, when he is speaking of someone else and not concerned with his own affairs or with fine writing, his letters are insufferably dull. He makes an astonishing contrast with the attractive Keats. On the other hand, I admit that Wordsworth does not present a very pleasing personality either; yet I not only enjoy his poetry as I cannot enjoy Shelley's, but I enjoy it more than when I first read it. I can only fumble (abating my prejudices as best I can) for reasons why

Shelley's abuse of poetry does me more violence than Words-worth's.

Shelley seems to have had to a high degree the unusual faculty of passionate apprehension of abstract ideas. Whether he was not sometimes confused about his own feelings, as we may be tempted to believe when confounded by the philosophy of *Epipsychidion*, is another matter. I do not mean that Shelley had a metaphysical or philosophical mind; his mind was in some ways a very confused one: he was able to be at once and with the same enthusiasm an eighteenth-century rationalist and a cloudy Platon-ist. But abstractions could excite in him strong emotion. His views remained pretty fixed, though his poetic gift matured. It is open to us to guess whether his mind would have matured too; certainly, in his last, and to my mind greatest though unfinished poem, *The Triumph of Life*, there is evidence not only of better writing than in any previous long poem, but of greater wisdom:

> Then what I thought was an old root that grew
> To strange distortion out of the hillside,
> Was indeed one of those (sic) deluded crew
> And that the grass, which methought hung so wide
> And white, was but his thin discoloured hair
> And that the holes he vainly sought to hide
> Were or had been eyes . . .

There is a precision of image and an economy here that is new to Shelley. But so far as we can judge, he never quite escaped from the tutelage of Godwin, even when he saw through the humbug as a man; and the weight of Mrs. Shelley must have been pretty heavy too. And, taking his work as it is, and without vain con-jectures about the future, we may ask: is it possible to ignore the 'ideas' in Shelley's poems, so as to be able to enjoy the poetry?

Mr. I. A. Richards deserves the credit of having done the pioneer work in the problem of Belief in the enjoyment of poetry; and any methodical pursuit of the problem I must leave to him and to those who are qualified after him. But Shelley raises the question in another form than that in which it presented itself to me in a note on the subject which I appended to an essay on Dante. There, I was concerned with two hypothetical readers, one of whom accepts the philosophy of the poet, and the other of whom rejects it; and so long as the poets in question were such as Dante and Lucretius, this seemed to cover the matter. I am not a Buddhist, but some of the early Buddhist scriptures affect me as parts of the Old Testament do; I can still enjoy Fitz-gerald's *Omar*, though I do not hold that rather smart and shallow

82

view of life. But some of Shelley's views I positively dislike, and that hampers my enjoyment of the poems in which they occur; and others seem to me so puerile that I cannot enjoy the poems in which they occur. And I do not find it possible to skip these passages and satisfy myself with the poetry in which no proposition pushes itself forward to claim assent. What complicates the problem still further is that in poetry so fluent as Shelley's there is a good deal which is just bad jingling. The following, for instance:

> *On a battle-trumpet's blast*
> *I fled hither, fast, fast, fast,*
> *Mid the darkness upward cast.*
> *From the dust of creeds outworn,*
> *From the tyrant's banner torn,*
> *Gathering round me, onward borne,*
> *There was mingled many a cry —*
> *Freedom! Hope! Death! Victory!*

Walter Scott seldom fell as low as this, though Byron more often. But in such lines, harsh and untunable, one is all the more affronted by the ideas, the ideas which Shelley bolted whole and never assimilated, visible in the catchwords of creeds outworn, tyrants and priests, which Shelley employed with such reiteration. And the bad parts of a poem can contaminate the whole, so that when Shelley rises to the heights, at the end of the poem:

> *To suffer woes which Hope thinks infinite;*
> *To forgive wrongs darker than death or night;*
> *To defy Power, which seems omnipotent;*
> *To love, and bear; to hope till Hope creates*
> *From its own wreck the thing it contemplates . . .*

lines to the content of which belief is neither given nor denied, we are unable to enjoy them fully. One does not expect a poem to be equally sustained throughout; and in some of the most successful long poems there is a relation of the more tense to the more relaxed passages, which is itself part of the pattern of beauty. But good lines amongst bad can never give more than a regretful pleasure. In reading *Epipsychidion* I am thoroughly gravelled by lines like:

> *True love in this differs from gold and clay,*
> *That to divide is not to take away . . .*
> *I never was attached to that great sect*
> *Whose doctrine is, that each one should select*

83

> *Out of the crowd, a mistress or a friend*
> *And all the rest, though fair and wise, commend*
> *To cold oblivion. . .*

so that when I come, a few lines later, upon a lovely image like:

> *A vision like incarnate April, warning*
> *With smiles and tears, Frost the anatomy*
> *Into his summer grave,*

I am as much shocked at finding it in such indifferent company as pleased by finding it at all. And we must admit that Shelley's finest long poems, as well as some of his worst, are those in which he took his ideas very seriously.[1] It was these ideas that blew the 'fading coal' to life; no more than with Wordsworth, can we ignore them without getting something no more Shelley's poetry than a wax effigy would be Shelley.

Shelley said that he disliked didactic poetry; but his own poetry is chiefly didactic, though (in fairness) not exactly in the sense in which he was using that word. Shelley's professed view of poetry is not dissimilar to that of Wordsworth. The language in which he clothes it in the 'Defence of Poetry' is very magniloquent, and with the exception of the magnificent image which Joyce quotes somewhere in *Ulysses* ('the mind in creation is as a fading coal, which some invisible influence, like an inconstant wind, awakens to transitory brightness') it seems to me an inferior piece of writing to Wordsworth's great preface. He says other fine things too; but the following is more significant of the way in which he relates poetry to the social activity of the age:

'The most unfailing herald, companion and follower of the awakening of a great people to work a beneficial change in opinion or institution, is poetry. At such periods there is an accumulation of the power of communicating and receiving intense and impassioned conceptions respecting man and nature. The persons in whom this power resides may often, so far as regards many portions of their nature, have little apparent correspondence with that spirit of good of which they are the ministers. But even whilst they deny and abjure, they are yet compelled to serve, the power which is seated on the throne of their own soul.'

I know not whether Shelley had in mind, in his reservations about 'the persons in whom this power resides', the defects of Byron or those of Wordsworth; he is hardly likely to have been

[1] He did not, for instance, appear to take his ideas very seriously in *The Witch of Atlas*, which, with all its charm, I think we may dismiss as a trifle.

84

contemplating his own. But this is a statement, and is either true or false. If he is suggesting that great poetry always tends to accompany a popular 'change in opinion or institution', that we know to be false. Whether at such periods the power of 'communicating and receiving intense and impassioned conceptions respecting man and nature' accumulates is doubtful; one would expect people to be too busy in other ways. Shelley does not appear, in this passage, to imply that poetry itself helps to operate these changes, and accumulate this power, nor does he assert that poetry is a usual by-product of change of these kinds; but he does affirm some relation between the two; and in consequence, a particular relation between his own poetry and the events of his own time; from which it would follow that the two throw light upon each other. This is perhaps the first appearance of the kinetic or revolutionary theory of poetry; for Wordsworth did not generalize to this point.

We may now return to the question how far it is possible to enjoy Shelley's poetry without approving the use to which he put it; that is, without sharing his views and sympathies. Dante, of course, was about as thoroughgoing a didacticist as one could find; and I have maintained elsewhere, and still maintain, that it is not essential to share Dante's beliefs in order to enjoy his poetry.[1] If in this instance I may appear to be extending the tolerance of a biassed mind, the example of Lucretius will do as well: one may share the essential beliefs of Dante and yet enjoy Lucretius to the full. Why then should this general indemnity not extend to Wordsworth and to Shelley? Here Mr. Richards comes very patly to our help:[2]

'Coleridge, when he remarked that a "willing suspension of disbelief" accompanied much poetry, was noting an important fact, but not quite in the happiest terms, for we are neither aware of a disbelief nor voluntarily suspending it in these cases. It is better to say that the question of belief or disbelief, in the intellectual sense, never arises when we are reading well. If unfortunately it does arise, either through the poet's fault or our own, we have for the moment ceased to be reading and have become astronomers, or theologians, or moralists, persons engaged in quite a different type of activity.'

We may be permitted to infer, in so far as the distaste of a

---

[1] Mr. A. E. Housman has affirmed (*The Name and Nature of Poetry*, p. 34) that 'good religious poetry, whether in Keble or Dante or Job, is likely to be most justly appreciated and most discriminatingly relished by the undevout'. There is a hard atom of truth in this, but if taken literally it would end in nonsense.

[2] *Practical Criticism*, p. 277.

person like myself for Shelley's poetry is not attributable to irrelevant prejudices or to a simple blind spot, but is due to a peculiarity in the poetry and not in the reader, that it is not the presentation of beliefs which I do not hold, or – to put the case as extremely as possible – of beliefs that excite my abhorrence, that makes the difficulty. Still less is it that Shelley is deliberately making use of his poetic gifts to propagate a doctrine; for Dante and Lucretius did the same thing. I suggest that the position is somewhat as follows. When the doctrine, theory, belief, or 'view of life' presented in a poem is one which the mind of the reader can accept as coherent, mature, and founded on the facts of experience, it interposes no obstacle to the reader's enjoyment, whether it be one that he accept or deny, approve or deprecate. When it is one which the reader rejects as childish or feeble, it may, for a reader of well-developed mind, set up an almost complete check. I observe in passing that we may distinguish, but without precision, between poets who employ their verbal, rhythmic and imaginative gift in the service of ideas which they hold passionately, and poets who employ the ideas which they hold with more or less settled conviction as material for a poem; poets may vary indefinitely between these two hypothetical extremes, and at what point we place any particular poet must remain incapable of exact calculation. And I am inclined to think that the reason why I was intoxicated by Shelley's poetry at the age of fifteen, and now find it almost unreadable, is not so much that at that age I accepted his ideas, and have since come to reject them, as that at that age 'the question of belief or disbelief', as Mr. Richards puts it, did not arise. It is not so much that thirty years ago I was able to read Shelley under an illusion which experience has dissipated, as that because the question of belief or disbelief did not arise I was in a much better position to enjoy the poetry. I can only regret that Shelley did not live to put his poetic gifts, which were certainly of the first order, at the service of more tenable beliefs – which need not have been, for my purposes, beliefs more acceptable to me. . . .

[*iv* THE EXHAUSTIVE CRITIC

From time to time, every hundred years or so, it is desirable that some critic shall appear to review the past of our literature, and set the poets and the poems in a new order. This task is not one of revolution but of readjustment. What we observe is partly the same scene, but in a different and more distant perspective; there are new and strange objects in the foreground, to be drawn accurately in proportion to the more familiar ones which now approach the horizon, where all but the most eminent become invisible to the naked eye. The exhaustive critic, armed with a powerful glass, will be able to sweep the distance and gain an acquaintance with minute objects in the landscape with which to compare minute objects close at hand; he will be able to gauge nicely the position and proportion of the objects surrounding us, in the whole of the vast panorama. This metaphorical fancy only represents the ideal; but Dryden, Johnson and Arnold have each performed the task as well as human frailty will allow. The majority of critics can be expected only to parrot the opinions of the last master of criticism; among more independent minds a period of destruction, of preposterous over-estimation, and of successive fashions takes place, until a new authority comes to introduce some order. And it is not merely the passage of time and accumulation of new artistic experience, nor the ineradicable tendency of the great majority of men to repeat the opinions of those few who have taken the trouble to think, nor the tendency of a nimble but myopic minority to progenerate heterodoxies, that makes new assessments necessary. It is that no generation is interested in Art in quite the same way as any other; each generation, like each individual, brings to the contemplation of art its own categories of appreciation, makes its own demands upon art, and has its own uses for art. 'Pure' artistic appreciation is to my thinking only an ideal, when not merely a figment, and must be, so long as the appreciation of art is an affair of limited and transient human beings existing in space and time. Both artist and audience are limited. There is for each time, for each artist, a kind of alloy required to make the metal workable into art; and each generation prefers its own alloy to any other. Hence each new master of criticism performs a useful service merely by the fact that his errors are of a different kind from the last; and the longer the sequence of critics we have, the greater amount of correction is possible. . . .

[v ORIGIN AND USES OF POETRY

I speak of Mr. Richards's views with some diffidence. Some of the problems he discusses are themselves very difficult, and only those are qualified to criticize who have applied themselves to the same specialized studies and have acquired proficiency in this kind of thinking. But here I limit myself to passages in which he does not seem to be speaking as a specialist, and in which I have no advantage of special knowledge either. There are two reasons why the writer of poetry must not be thought to have any great advantage. One is that a discussion of poetry such as this takes us far outside the limits within which a poet may speak with authority; the other is that the poet does many things upon instinct, for which he can give no better account than anybody else. A poet can try, of course, to give an honest report of the way in which he himself writes: the result may, if he is a good observer, be illuminating. And in one sense, but a very limited one, he knows better what his poems 'mean' than can anyone else; he may know the history of their composition, the material which has gone in and come out in an unrecognizable form, and he knows what he was trying to do and what he was meaning to mean. But what a poem means is as much what it means to others as what it means to the author; and indeed, in the course of time a poet may become merely a reader in respect to his own works, forgetting his original meaning – or without forgetting, merely changing. So that, when Mr. Richards asserts that *The Waste Land* effects 'a complete severance between poetry and *all* beliefs' I am no better qualified to say No! than is any other reader. I will admit that I think that either Mr. Richards is wrong, or I do not understand his meaning. The statement might mean that it was the first poetry to do what all poetry in the past would have been the better for doing: I can hardly think that he intended to pay me such an unmerited compliment. It might also mean that the present situation is radically different from any in which poetry has been produced in the past: namely, that now there is nothing in which to believe, that Belief itself is dead; and that therefore my poem is the first to respond properly to the modern situation and not call upon Make-Believe. And it is in this connection, apparently, that Mr. Richards observes that 'poetry is capable of saving us'.

A discussion of Mr. Richards's theories of knowledge, value and meaning would be by no means irrelevant to this assertion, but it would take us far afield, and I am not the person to undertake it. We cannot of course refute the statement 'poetry is capable of saving us' without knowing which one of the multiple definitions of salvation Mr. Richards has in mind.[1] (A good many people behave as if they thought so too: otherwise their interest in poetry is difficult to explain.) I am sure, from the differences of environment, of period, and of mental furniture, that salvation by poetry is not quite the same thing for Mr. Richards as it was for Arnold; but so far as I am concerned these are merely different shades of blue. In *Practical Criticism*[2] Mr. Richards provides a recipe which I think throws some light upon his theological ideas. He says:

[1] See his *Mencius on the Mind*. There is of course a locution in which we say of someone 'he is not one of *us*'; it is possible that the 'us' of Mr. Richards's statement represents an equally limited and select number.

[2] Second Impression, p. 290.

'Something like a technique or ritual for heightening sincerity might well be worked out. When our response to a poem after our best efforts remains uncertain, when we are unsure whether the feelings it excites come from a deep source in our experience, whether our liking or disliking is genuine, is *ours*, or an accident of fashion, a response to surface details or to essentials, we may perhaps help ourselves by considering it in a frame of feelings whose sincerity is beyond our questioning. Sit by the fire (with eyes shut and fingers pressed firmly upon the eyeballs) and consider with as full "realisation" as possible –' . . .

That there is an analogy between mystical experience and some of the ways in which poetry is written I do not deny; and I think that the Abbé Brémond has observed very well the differences as well as the likenesses; though, as I have said, whether the analogy is of significance for the student of religion, or only to the psychologist, I do not know. I know, for instance, that some forms of ill-health, debility or anaemia, may (if other circumstances are favourable) produce an efflux of poetry in a way approaching the condition of automatic writing – though, in contrast to the claims sometimes made for the latter, the material has obviously been incubating within the poet, and cannot be suspected of being a present from a friendly or impertinent demon. What one writes in this way may succeed in standing the examination of a more normal state of mind; it gives me the impression, as I have just said, of having undergone a long incubation, though we do not know until the shell breaks what kind of egg we have been sitting on. To me it seems that at these moments, which are characterized by the sudden lifting of the burden of anxiety and fear which presses upon our daily life so steadily that we are unaware of it, what happens is something *negative*: that is to say, not 'inspiration' as we commonly think of it, but the breaking down of strong habitual barriers – which tend to re-form very quickly.[1]

[1] I should like to quote a confirmation of my own experience from Mr. A. E. Housman's *Name and Nature of Poetry*: 'In short I think that the production of poetry, in its first stage, is less an active than a passive and involuntary process; and if I were obliged, not to define poetry, but to name the class of things to which it belongs, I should call it a secretion; whether a natural secretion, like turpentine in the fir, or a morbid secretion, like the pearl in the oyster. I think that my own case, though I may not deal with the matter so cleverly as the oyster does, is the latter; because I have seldom written poetry unless I was rather out of health, and the experience, though pleasurable, was generally agitating and exhausting.' I take added satisfaction in the fact that I only read Mr. Housman's essay some time after my own lines were written.

Some obstruction is momentarily whisked away. The accompanying feeling is less like what we know as positive pleasure, than a sudden relief from an intolerable burden. I agree with Brémond, and perhaps go even further, in finding that this disturbance of our quotidian character which results in an incantation, an outburst of words which we hardly recognize as our own (because of the effortlessness), is a very different thing from mystical illumination. The latter is a vision which may be accompanied by the realization that you will never be able to communicate it to anyone else, or even by the realization that when it is past you will not be able to recall it to yourself; the former is not a vision but a motion terminating in an arrangement of words on paper. . . .

The way in which poetry is written is not, so far as our knowledge of these obscure matters as yet extends, any clue to its value. . . . The faith in mystical inspiration is responsible for the exaggerated repute of *Kubla Khan*. The imagery of that fragment, certainly, whatever its origins in Coleridge's reading, sank to the depths of Coleridge's feeling, was saturated, transformed there – 'those are pearls that were his eyes' – and brought up into daylight again. But it is not *used*: the poem has not been written. A single verse is not poetry unless it is a one-verse poem; and even the finest line draws its life from its context. Organization is necessary as well as 'inspiration'. The re-creation of word and image which happens fitfully in the poetry of such a poet as Coleridge happens almost incessantly with Shakespeare. Again and again, in his use of a word, he will give a new meaning or extract a latent one; again and again the right imagery saturated while it lay in the depths of Shakespeare's memory, will rise like Anadyomene from the sea. In Shakespeare's poetry this reborn image or word will have its rational use and justification; in much good poetry the organization will not reach to so rational a level. I will take an example which I have used elsewhere: I am glad of the opportunity to use it again, as on the previous occasion I had an inaccurate text. It is from Chapman's *Bussy D'Ambois*:

> *Fly where the evening from the Iberian vales*
> *Takes on her swarthy shoulders Hecate*
> *Crowned with a grove of oaks: fly where men feel*
> *The burning axletree, and those that suffer*
> *Beneath the chariot of the snowy Bear. . . .*

Chapman borrowed this, as Dr. Boas points out, from Seneca's *Hercules Œteus*:

> *dic sub Aurora positis Sabaeis*
> *dic sub occasu positis Hiberis*

quique sub plaustro patiuntur ursae
quique ferventi quatiuntur axe

and probably also from the same author's *Hercules Furens*:

sub ortu solis, an sub cardine
glacialis ursae?

There is first the probability that this imagery had some personal saturation value, so to speak, for Seneca; another for Chapman, and another for myself, who have borrowed it twice from Chapman. I suggest that what gives it such intensity as it has in each case is its saturation – I will not say with 'associations', for I do not want to revert to Hartley – but with feelings too obscure for the authors even to know quite what they were. And of course only a part of an author's imagery comes from his reading. It comes from the whole of his sensitive life since early childhood. Why, for all of us, out of all that we have heard, seen, felt, in a lifetime, do certain images recur, charged with emotion, rather than others? The song of one bird, the leap of one fish, at a particular place and time, the scent of one flower, an old woman on a German mountain path, six ruffians seen through an open window playing cards at night at a small French railway junction where there was a water-mill: such memories may have symbolic value, but of what we cannot tell, for they come to represent the depths of feeling into which we cannot peer. We might just as well ask why, when we try to recall visually some period in the past, we find in our memory just the few meagre arbitrarily chosen set of snapshots that we do find there, the faded poor souvenirs of passionate moments.[1]

Thus far is as far as my experience will take me in this direction. My purpose has not been to examine thoroughly any one type of theory of poetry, still less to confute it; but rather to indicate the kinds of defect and excess that we must expect to find in each, and to suggest that the current tendency is to expect too much, rather than too little, of poetry. No one of us, when he thinks about poetry, is without his own bias; and Abbé Brémond's preoccupation with mysticism and Mr. Richards's lack of interest

---

[1] In chapter xxii of *Principles of Literary Criticism* Mr. Richards discusses these matters in his own way. As evidence that there are other approaches as well, see a very interesting article *Le symbolisme et l'âme primitive* by E. Cailliet and J. A. Bédé in the *Revue de litterature comparée* for April–June 1932. The authors, who have done field-work in Madagascar, apply the theories of Lévy-Bruhl: the pre-logical mentality persists in civilized man, but becomes available only to or through the poet.

in theology are equally significant. One voice was raised, in our time, to express a view of a different kind; that of a man who wrote several remarkable poems himself, and who also had an aptitude for theology. It is that of T. E. Hulme:

'There is a general tendency to think that verse means little else than the expression of unsatisfied emotion. People say: "But how can you have verse without sentiment?" You see what it is; the prospect alarms them. A classical revival to them would mean the prospect of an arid desert and the death of poetry as they understand it, and could only come to fill the gulf caused by that death. Exactly why this dry classical spirit should have a positive and legitimate necessity to express itself in poetry is utterly inconceivable to them. . . . The great aim is accurate, precise and definite description. The first thing is to realize how extraordinarily difficult this is. . . . Language has its own special nature, its own conventions and communal ideas. It is only by a concentrated effort of the mind that you can hold it fixed to your own purpose.'

This is, we must remark at once, not a general theory of poetry, but an assertion of the claims of a particular kind of poetry for the writer's own time. It may serve to remind us how various are the kinds of poetry, and how variously poetry may appeal to different minds and generations equally qualified to appreciate it.

The extreme of theorizing about the nature of poetry, the essence of poetry if there is any, belongs to the study of aesthetics and is no concern of the poet or of a critic with my limited qualifications. Whether the self-consciousness involved in aesthetics and in psychology does not risk violating the frontier of consciousness, is a question which I need not raise here; it is perhaps only my private eccentricity to believe that such researches are perilous if not guided by sound theology. The poet is much more vitally concerned with the social 'uses' of poetry, and with his own place in society; and this problem is now perhaps more importunately pressed upon his conscious attention than at any previous time. The uses of poetry certainly vary as society alters, as the public to be addressed changes. In this context something should be said about the vexed question of obscurity and unintelligibility. The difficulty of poetry (and modern poetry is supposed to be difficult) may be due to one of several reasons. First, there may be personal causes which make it impossible for a poet to express himself in any but an obscure way; while this may be regrettable, we should be glad, I think, that the man has been able to express himself at all. Or difficulty may be due just to novelty: we know the ridicule accorded in turn to Wordsworth, Shelley and Keats, Tennyson and Browning – but

must remark that Browning was the first to be *called* difficult;
hostile critics of the earlier poets found them difficult, but called
them silly. Or difficulty may be caused by the reader's having
been told, or having suggested to himself, that the poem is going
to prove difficult. The ordinary reader, when warned against the
obscurity of a poem, is apt to be thrown into a state of consterna-
tion very unfavourable to poetic receptivity. Instead of beginning,
as he should, in a state of sensitivity, he obfuscates his senses by
the desire to be clever and to look very hard for something, he
doesn't know what – or else by the desire not to be taken in. There
is such a thing as stage fright, but what such readers have is pit or
gallery fright. The more seasoned reader, he who has reached, in
these matters, a state of greater *purity*, does not bother about
understanding; not, at least, at first. I know that some of the
poetry to which I am most devoted is poetry which I did not
understand at first reading; some is poetry which I am not sure I
understand yet: for instance, Shakespeare's. And finally, there is
the difficulty caused by the author's having left out something
which the reader is used to finding; so that the reader, bewildered,
gropes about for what is absent, and puzzles his head for a kind of
'meaning' which is not there, and is not meant to be there.

The chief use of the 'meaning' of a poem, in the ordinary sense,
may be (for here again I am speaking of some kinds of poetry and
not all) to satisfy one habit of the reader, to keep his mind diverted
and quiet, while the poem does its work upon him: much as the
imaginary burglar is always provided with a bit of nice meat for
the house-dog. This is a normal situation of which I approve. But
the minds of all poets do not work that way; some of them, assuming that there are other minds like their own, become impatient of
this 'meaning' which seems superfluous, and perceive possibilities
of intensity through its elimination. I am not asserting that this
situation is ideal; only that we must write our poetry as we can,
and take it as we find it. It may be that for some periods of society
a more relaxed form of writing is right, and for others a more
concentrated. I believe that there must be many people who feel,
as I do, that the effect of some of the greater nineteenth-century
poets is diminished by their bulk. Who now, for the pure pleasure
of it, reads Wordsworth, Shelley and Keats even, certainly
Browning and Swinburne and most of the French poets of the
century – entire? I by no means believe that the 'long poem' is a
thing of the past; but at least there must be more in it for the
length than our grandparents seemed to demand; and for us, anything that can be said as well in prose can be said better in prose.
And a great deal, in the way of meaning, belongs to prose rather
than to poetry. The doctrine of 'art for art's sake', a mistaken

one, and more advertised than practised, contained this true impulse behind it, that it is a recognition of the error of the poet's trying to do other people's work. But poetry has as much to learn from prose as from other poetry; and I think that an interaction between prose and verse, like the interaction between language and language, is a condition of vitality in literature.

To return to the question of obscurity: when all exceptions have been made, and after admitting the possible existence of minor 'difficult' poets whose public must always be small, I believe that the poet naturally prefers to write for as large and miscellaneous an audience as possible, and that it is the half-educated and ill-educated, rather than the uneducated, who stand in his way: I myself should like an audience which could neither read nor write.[1] The most useful poetry, socially, would be one which could cut across all the present stratifications of public taste – stratifications which are perhaps a sign of social disintegration. The ideal medium for poetry, to my mind, and the most direct means of social 'usefulness' for poetry, is the theatre. In a play of Shakespeare you get several levels of significance. For the simplest auditors there is the plot, for the more thoughtful the character and conflict of character, for the more literary the words and phrasing, for the more musically sensitive the rhythm, and for auditors of greater sensitiveness and understanding a meaning which reveals itself gradually. And I do not believe that the classification of audience is so clear-cut as this; but rather that the sensitiveness of every auditor is acted upon by all these elements at once, though in different degrees of consciousness. At none of these levels is the auditor bothered by the presence of that which he does not understand, or by the presence of that in which he is not interested. I may make my meaning a little clearer by a simple instance. I once designed, and drafted a couple of scenes, of a verse play. My intention was to have one character whose sensibility and intelligence should be on the plane of the most sensitive and intelligent members of the audience; his speeches should be addressed to them as much as to the other personages in the play – or rather, should be addressed to the latter, who were to be material, literal-minded and visionless, with the consciousness of being overheard by the former. There was to be an understanding between this protagonist and a small number of the audience, while the rest of the audience would share the responses of the other characters in the play. Perhaps this is all too deliberate, but one must experiment as one can.

[1] On the subject of education, there are some helpful remarks in Lawrence's *Fantasia of the Unconscious*.

Every poet would like, I fancy, to be able to think that he had some direct social utility. By this, as I hope I have already made clear, I do not mean that he should meddle with the tasks of the theologian, the preacher, the economist, the sociologist or anybody else; that he should do anything but write poetry, poetry not defined in terms of something else. He would like to be something of a popular entertainer, and be able to think his own thoughts behind a tragic or a comic mask. He would like to convey the pleasures of poetry, not only to a larger audience, but to larger groups of people collectively; and the theatre is the best place in which to do it. There might, one fancies, be some fulfilment in exciting this communal pleasure, to give an immediate compensation for the pains of turning blood into ink. As things are, and as fundamentally they must always be, poetry is not a career, but a mug's game. No honest poet can ever feel quite sure of the permanent value of what he has written: he may have wasted his time and messed up his life for nothing. All the better, then, if he could have at least the satisfaction of having a part to play in society as worthy as that of the music-hall comedian. Furthermore, the theatre, by the technical exactions which it makes and limitations which it imposes upon the author, by the obligation to keep for a definite length of time the sustained interest of a large and unprepared and not wholly perceptive group of people, by its problems which have constantly to be solved, has enough to keep the poet's *conscious* mind fully occupied, as the painter's by the manipulation of his tools. If, beyond keeping the interest of a crowd of people for that length of time, the author can make a play which is real poetry, so much the better.

I have not attempted any definition of poetry, because I can think of none which does not assume that the reader already knows what it is, or which does not falsify by leaving out much more than it can include. Poetry begins, I dare say, with a savage beating a drum in a jungle, and it retains that essential of percussion and rhythm; hyperbolically one might say that the poet is *older* than other human beings – but I do not want to be tempted to ending on this sort of flourish. I have insisted rather on the variety of poetry, variety so great that all the kinds seem to have nothing in common except the rhythm of verse instead of the rhythm of prose: and that does not tell you much about all poetry. Poetry is of course not to be defined by its uses. If it commemorates a public occasion, or celebrates a festival, or decorates a religious rite, or amuses a crowd, so much the better. It may effect revolutions in sensibility such as are periodically needed; may help to break up the conventional modes of perception and valuation which are perpetually forming, and make people see the world afresh, or some new part of it. It may make us from time to time a little more aware of the deeper, unnamed feelings which form the substratum of our being, to which we rarely penetrate; for our lives are mostly a constant evasion of ourselves, and an evasion of the visible and sensible world. But to say all this is only to say what you know already, if you have felt poetry and thought about your feelings. And I fear that I have already, throughout these lectures, trespassed beyond the bounds which a little self-knowledge tells me are my proper frontier. If, as James Thomson observed, 'lips only sing when they cannot kiss', it may also be that poets only talk when they cannot sing. I am content to leave my theorizing about poetry at this point. The sad ghost of Coleridge beckons to me from the shadows.

RELIGION AND LITERATURE

What I have to say is largely in support of the following propositions: Literary criticism should be completed by criticism from a definite ethical and theological standpoint. In so far as in any age there is common agreement on ethical and theological matters, so far can literary criticism be substantive. In ages like our own, in which there is no such common agreement, it is the more necessary for Christian readers to scrutinize their reading, especially of works of imagination, with explicit ethical and theological standards. The 'greatness' of literature cannot be determined solely by literary standards; though we must remember that whether it is literature or not can be determined only by literary standards.[1]

We have tacitly assumed, for some centuries past, that there is *no* relation between literature and theology. This is not to deny that literature – I mean, again, primarily works of imagination – has been, is, and probably always will be judged by some moral standards. But moral judgments of literary works are made only according to the moral code accepted by each generation, whether it lives according to that code or not. In an age which accepts some precise Christian theology, the common code may be fairly orthodox: though even in such periods the common code may exalt such concepts as 'honour,' 'glory' or 'revenge' to a position quite intolerable to Christianity. The dramatic ethics of the Elizabethan Age offers an interesting study. But when the common code is detached from its theological background, and is consequently more and more merely a matter of habit, it is exposed both to prejudice and to change. At such times morals are open to being altered *by* literature; so that we find in practice that what is 'objectionable' in literature is merely what the present generation is not used to. It is a commonplace that what shocks one generation is accepted quite calmly by the next. This adaptability to change of moral standards is sometimes greeted with

[1] As an example of literary criticism given greater significance by theological interests, I would call attention to Theodor Haecker: *Virgil* (Sheed and Ward).

satisfaction as an evidence of human perfectibility: whereas it is only evidence of what unsubstantial foundations people's moral judgments have.

I am not concerned here with religious literature but with the application of our religion to the criticism of any literature. It may be as well, however, to distinguish first what I consider to be the three senses in which we can speak of 'religious literature'. The first is that of which we say that it is 'religious literature' in the same way that we speak of 'historical literature' or of 'scientific literature'. I mean that we can treat the Authorized translation of the Bible, or the works of Jeremy Taylor, as literature, in the same way that we treat the historical writing of Clarendon or of Gibbon – our two great English historians – as literature; or Bradley's *Logic*, or Buffon's *Natural History*. All of these writers were men who, incidentally to their religious, or historical, or philosophic purpose, had a gift of language which makes them delightful to read to all those who can enjoy language well written even if they are unconcerned with the objects which the writers had in view. And I would add that though a scientific, or historical, or theological, or philosophic work which is also 'literature', may become superannuated as anything but literature, yet it is not likely to be 'literature' unless it had its scientific or other value for its own time. While I acknowledge the legitimacy of this enjoyment, I am more acutely aware of its abuse. The persons who enjoy these writings *solely* because of their literary merit are essentially parasites; and we know that parasites, when they become too numerous, are pests. I could fulminate against the men of letters who have gone into ecstasies over 'the Bible as literature', the Bible as 'the noblest monument of English prose'. Those who talk of the Bible as a 'monument of English prose' are merely admiring it as a monument over the grave of Christianity. I must try to avoid the by-paths of my discourse: it is enough to suggest that just as the work of Clarendon, or Gibbon, or Buffon or Bradley would be of inferior literary value if it were insignificant as history, science and philosophy respectively, so the Bible has had a *literary* influence upon English literature *not* because it has been considered as literature, but because it has been considered as the report of the Word of God. And the fact that men of letters now discuss it as 'literature' probably indicates the *end* of its 'literary' influence.

The second kind of relation of religion to literature is that which is found in what is called 'religious' or 'devotional' poetry. Now what is the usual attitude of the lover of poetry – and I mean the person who is a genuine and first-hand enjoyer and appreciator of poetry, not the person who follows the admirations of others –

towards this department of poetry? I believe, all that may be implied in his calling it a *department*. He believes, not always explicitly, that when you qualify poetry as 'religious' you are indicating very clear limitations. For the great majority of people who love poetry, '*religious* poetry' is a variety of *minor* poetry: the religious poet is not a poet who is treating the whole subject matter of poetry in a religious spirit, but a poet who is dealing with a confined part of this subject matter: who is leaving out what men consider their major passions, and thereby confessing his ignorance of them. I think that this is the real attitude of most poetry lovers towards such poets as Vaughan, or Southwell, or Crashaw, or George Herbert, or Gerard Hopkins.

But what is more, I am ready to admit that up to a point these critics are right. For there is a kind of poetry, such as most of the work of the authors I have mentioned, which is the product of a special religious awareness, which may exist without the general awareness which we expect of the major poet. In some poets, or in some of their works, this general awareness may have existed; but the preliminary steps which represent it may have been suppressed, and only the end-product presented. Between these, and those in which the religious or devotional genius represents the *special* and limited awareness, it may be very difficult to discriminate. I do not pretend to offer Vaughan, or Southwell, or George Herbert, or Hopkins as major poets:[1] I feel sure that the first three, at least, are poets of this limited awareness. They are not great religious poets in the sense in which Dante, or Cornielle, or Racine, even in those of their plays which do not touch upon Christian themes, are great Christian religious poets. Or even in the sense in which Villon and Baudelaire, with all their imperfections and delinquencies, are Christian poets. Since the time of Chaucer, Christian poetry (in the sense in which I shall mean it) has been limited in England almost exclusively to minor poetry.

I repeat that when I am considering Religion and Literature, I speak of these things only to make clear that I am not concerned primarily with Religious Literature. I am concerned with what should be the relation between Religion and all Literature. Therefore the third type of 'religious literature' may be more quickly passed over. I mean the literary works of men who are sincerely desirous of forwarding the cause of religion: that which

[1] I note that in an address delivered in Swansea some years later (subsequently published in *The Welsh Review* under the title of 'What Is Minor Poetry?') I stated with some emphasis my opinion that Herbert is a major, not a minor poet. I agree with my later opinion.

[1949]

may come under the heading of Propaganda. I am thinking, of course, of such delightful fiction as Mr. Chesterton's *Man Who Was Thursday*, or his *Father Brown*. No one admires and enjoys these things more than I do; I would only remark that when the same effect is aimed at by zealous persons of less talent than Mr. Chesterton the effect is negative. But my point is that such writings do not enter into any serious consideration of the relation of Religion and Literature: because they are conscious operations in a world in which it is assumed that Religion and Literature are not related. It is a conscious and limited relating. What I want is a literature which should be *un*consciously, rather than deliberately and defiantly, Christian: because the work of Mr. Chesterton has its point from appearing in a world which is definitely not Christian.

I am convinced that we fail to realize how completely, and yet how irrationally, we separate our literary from our religious judgments. If there could be a complete separation, perhaps it might not matter: but the separation is not, and never can be, complete. If we exemplify literature by the novel – for the novel is the form in which literature affects the greatest number – we may remark this gradual secularization of literature during at least the last three hundred years. Bunyan, and to some extent Defoe, had moral purposes: the former is beyond suspicion, the latter may be suspect. But since Defoe the secularization of the novel has been continuous. There have been three chief phases. In the first, the novel took the Faith, in its contemporary version, for granted, and omitted it from its picture of life. Fielding, Dickens and Thackeray belong to this phase. In the second, it doubted, worried about, or contested the Faith. To this phase belong George Eliot, George Meredith and Thomas Hardy. To the third phase, in which we are living, belong nearly all contemporary novelists except Mr. James Joyce. It is the phase of those who have never heard the Christian Faith spoken of as anything but an anachronism.

Now, do people in general hold a definite opinion, that is to say religious or anti-religious; and do they read novels, or poetry for that matter, with a separate compartment of their minds? The common ground between religion and fiction is behaviour. Our religion imposes our ethics, our judgment and criticism of ourselves, and our behaviour toward our fellow men. The fiction that we read affects our behaviour towards our fellow men, affects our patterns of ourselves. When we read of human beings behaving in certain ways, with the approval of the author, who gives his benediction to this behaviour by his attitude towards the result of the behaviour arranged by himself, we can be influenced towards behaving in the same way.[1] When the contemporary novelist is an individual thinking for himself in isolation, he may have something important to offer to those who are able to receive it. He who is alone may speak to the individual. But the majority of novelists are persons drifting in the stream, only a little faster. They have some sensitiveness, but little intellect.

We are expected to be broadminded about literature, to put aside prejudice or conviction, and to look at fiction as fiction and at drama as drama. With what is inaccurately called 'censorship' in this country - with what is much more difficult to cope with than an official censorship, because it represents the opinions of individuals in an irresponsible democracy – I have very little sympathy; partly because it so often suppresses the wrong books, and partly because it is little more effective than Prohibition of Liquor; partly because it is one manifestation of the desire that state control should take the place of decent domestic influence; and wholly because it acts only from custom and habit, not from decided theological and moral principles. Incidentally, it gives people a false sense of security in leading them to believe that books which are *not* suppressed are harmless. Whether there *is* such a thing as a harmless book I am not sure: but there very likely are books so utterly unreadable as to be incapable of injuring anybody. But it is certain that a book is not harmless merely because no one is consciously offended by it. And if we, as readers, keep our religious and moral convictions in one compartment, and take our reading merely for entertainment, or on a higher plane, for aesthetic pleasure, I would point out that the author, whatever his conscious intentions in writing, in practice recognizes no such distinctions. The author of a work of imagination is trying to affect us wholly, as human beings, whether he knows it or not; and we are affected by it, as human beings, whether we intend to be or not. I suppose that everything we eat has some other effect upon us than merely the pleasure of taste and mastication; it affects us during the process of assimilation and digestion; and I believe that exactly the same is true of anything we read.

The fact that what we read does not concern merely something called our *literary taste*, but that it affects directly, though only amongst many other influences, the whole of what we are, is best elicited, I think, by a conscientious examination of the history of our individual literary education. Consider the adolescent reading of any person with some literary sensibility. Everyone, I

[1] Here and later I am indebted to Montgomery Belgion, *The Human Parrot* (chapter on The Irresponsible Propagandist).

believe, who is at all sensible to the seductions of poetry, can remember some moment in youth when he or she was completely carried away by the work of one poet. Very likely he was carried away by several poets, one after the other. The reason for this passing infatuation is not merely that our sensibility to poetry is keener in adolescence than in maturity. What happens is a kind of inundation, of invasion of the undeveloped personality by the stronger personality of the poet. The same thing may happen at a later age to persons who have not done much reading. One author takes complete possession of us for a time; then another; and finally they begin to affect each other in our mind. We weigh one against another; we see that each has qualities absent from others, and qualities incompatible with the qualities of others: we begin to be, in fact, critical; and it is our growing critical power which protects us from excessive possession by any one literary personality. The good critic – and we should all try to be critics, and not leave criticism to the fellows who write reviews in the papers – is the man who, to a keen and abiding sensibility, joins wide and increasingly discriminating reading. Wide reading is not valuable as a kind of hoarding, an accumulation of knowledge, or what sometimes is meant by the term 'a well-stocked mind'. It is valuable because in the process of being affected by one powerful personality after another, we cease to be dominated by any one, or by any small number. The very different views of life, cohabiting in our minds, affect each other, and our own personality asserts itself and gives each a place in some arrangement peculiar to ourself.

It is simply not true that works of fiction, prose or verse, that is to say works depicting the actions, thoughts and words and passions of imaginary human beings, *directly* extend our knowledge of life. Direct knowledge of life is knowledge directly in relation to ourselves, it is our knowledge of *how* people behave in general, of *what* they are like in general, in so far as that part of life in which we ourselves have participated gives us material for generalization. Knowledge of life obtained through fiction is only possible by another stage of self-consciousness. That is to say, it can only be a knowledge of other people's knowledge of life, not of life itself. So far as we are taken up with the happenings in any novel in the same way in which we are taken up with what happens under our eyes, we are acquiring at least as much falsehood as truth. But when we are developed enough to say: 'This is the view of life of a person who was a good observer within his limits, Dickens, or Thackeray, or George Eliot, or Balzac; but he looked at it in a different way from me, because he was a different man; he even selected rather different things to look at, or the same things in a different order of importance, because he was a different man; so what I am looking at is the world as seen by a particular mind' – then we are in a position to gain something from reading fiction. We are learning *something* about life from these authors direct, just as we learn something from the reading of history direct; but these authors are only really helping us when we can see, and allow for, their differences from ourselves.

Now what we get, as we gradually grow up and read more and more, and read a greater diversity of authors, is a variety of views of life. But what people commonly assume, I suspect, is that we gain this experience of other men's views of life only by 'improving reading'. This, it is supposed, is a reward we get by applying ourselves to Shakespeare, and Dante, and Goethe, and Emerson, and Carlyle, and dozens of other respectable writers. The rest of our reading for amusement is merely killing time. But I incline to come to the alarming conclusion that it is just the literature that we read for 'amusement', or 'purely for pleasure' that may have the greatest and least suspected influence upon us. It is the literature which we read with the least effort that can have the easiest and most insidious influence upon us. Hence it is that the influence of popular novelists, and of popular plays of contemporary life, requires to be scrutinized most closely. And it is chiefly *contemporary* literature that the majority of people ever read in this attitude of 'purely for pleasure', of pure passivity.

The relation to my subject of what I have been saying should now be a little more apparent. Though we may read literature merely for pleasure, of 'entertainment' or of 'aesthetic enjoyment', this reading never affects simply a sort of special sense: it affects us as entire human beings; it affects our moral and religious existence. And I say that while individual modern writers of eminence can be improving, contemporary literature as a whole tends to be degrading. And that even the effect of the better writers, in an age like ours, may be degrading to some readers; for we must remember that what a writer does to people is not necessarily what he intends to do. It may be only what people are capable of having done to them. People exercise an unconscious selection in being influenced. A writer like D. H. Lawrence may be in his effect either beneficial or pernicious. I am not sure that I have not had some pernicious influence myself.

At this point I anticipate a rejoinder from the liberal-minded, from all those who are convinced that if everybody says what he thinks, and does what he likes, things will somehow, by some automatic compensation and adjustment, come right in the end. 'Let everything be tried', they say, 'and if it is a mistake, then we shall learn by experience.' This argument might have some value, if we were always the same generation upon earth; or if, as we know to be not the case, people ever learned much from the experience of their elders. These liberals are convinced that only by what is called unrestrained individualism will truth ever emerge. Ideas, views of life, they think, issue distinct from independent heads, and in consequence of their knocking violently against each other, the fittest survive, and truth rises triumphant. Anyone who dissents from this view must be either a mediaevalist, wishful only to set back the clock, or else a fascist, and probably both.

If the mass of contemporary authors were really individualists, every one of them inspired Blakes, each with his separate vision, and if the mass of the contemporary public were really a mass of *individuals* there might be something to be said for this attitude. But this is not, and never has been, and never will be. It is not only that the reading individual today (or at any day) is not enough an individual to be able to absorb all the 'views of life' of all the authors pressed upon us by the publishers' advertisements and the reviewers, and to be able to arrive at wisdom by considering one against another. It is that the contemporary authors are not individuals enough either. It is not that the world of separate individuals of the liberal democrat is undesirable; it is simply that this world does not exist. For the reader of contemporary literature is not, like the reader of the established great literature of all time, exposing himself to the influence of divers and contradictory personalities; he is exposing himself to a mass movement of writers who, each of them, think that they have something individually to offer, but are really all working together in the same direction. And there never was a time, I believe, when the reading public was so large, or so helplessly exposed to the influences of its own time. There never was a time, I believe, when those who read at all, read so many more books by living authors than books by dead authors; there never was a time so completely parochial, so shut off from the past. There may be too many publishers; there are certainly too many books published; and the journals ever incite the reader to 'keep up' with what is being published. Individualistic democracy has come to high tide: and it is more difficult today to be an individual than it ever was before.

Within itself, modern literature has perfectly valid distinctions of good and bad, better and worse: and I do not wish to suggest that I confound Mr. Bernard Shaw with Mr. Noel Coward, Mrs. Woolf with Miss Mannin. On the other hand, I should like it to be clear that I am not defending a 'high'-brow against a 'low'-brow literature. What I do wish to affirm is that the whole of modern literature is corrupted by what I call Secularism, that it is simply unaware of, simply cannot understand the meaning of, the primacy of the supernatural over the natural life: of something which I assume to be our primary concern.

I do not want to give the impression that I have delivered a mere fretful jeremiad against contemporary literature. Assuming a common attitude between my readers, or some of my readers, and myself, the question is not so much, what is to be done about it? as, how should we behave towards it?

I have suggested that the liberal attitude towards literature will not work. Even if the writers who make their attempt to impose their 'view of life' upon us were really distinct individuals, even if we as readers were distinct individuals, what would be the result? It would be, surely, that each reader would be impressed, in his reading, merely by what he was previously prepared to be impressed by; he would follow the 'line of least resistance', and there would be no assurance that he would be made a better man. For literary judgment we need to be acutely aware of two things at once: of 'what we like', and of 'what we *ought* to like'. Few people are honest enough to know either. The first means knowing what we really feel: very few know that. The second involves understanding our shortcomings; for we do not really know what we ought to like unless we also know why we ought to like it, which involves knowing why we don't yet like it. It is not enough to understand what we ought to be, unless we know what we are; and we do not understand what we are, unless we know what we ought to be. The two forms of self-consciousness, knowing what we are and what we ought to be, must go together.

It is our business, as readers of literature, to know what we like. It is our business, as Christians, *as well as* readers of literature, to know what we ought to like. It is our business as honest men not to assume that whatever we like is what we ought to like; and it is our business as honest Christians not to assume that we do like what we ought to like. And the last thing I would wish for would be the existence of two literatures, one for Christian consumption and the other for the pagan world. What I believe to be incumbent upon all Christians is the duty of maintaining consciously certain standards and criteria of criticism over and above those applied by the rest of the world; and that by these criteria and standards everything that we read must be tested. We must remember that the greater part of our current reading matter is written for us by people who have no real belief in a supernatural order, though some of it may be written by people with individual notions of a supernatural order which are not ours. And the greater part of our reading matter is coming to be written by people who not only

105

have no such belief, but are even ignorant of the fact that there are still people in the world so 'backward' or so 'eccentric' as to continue to believe. So long as we are conscious of the gulf fixed between ourselves and the greater part of contemporary literature, we are more or less protected from being harmed by it, and are in a position to extract from it what good it has to offer us.

There are a very large number of people in the world today who believe that all ills are fundamentally economic. Some believe that various specific economic changes alone would be enough to set the world right; others demand more or less drastic changes in the social as well, changes chiefly of two opposed types. These changes demanded, and in some places carried out, are alike in one respect, that they hold the assumptions of what I call Secularism: they concern themselves only with changes of a temporal, material, and external nature; they concern themselves with morals only of a collective nature. In an exposition of one such new faith I read the following words:

'In our morality the one single test of any moral question is whether it impedes or destroys in any way the power of the individual to serve the State. [The individual] must answer the questions: "Does this action injure the nation? Does it injure other members of the nation? Does it injure my ability to serve the nation?" And if the answer is clear on all those questions, the individual has absolute liberty to do as he will.'

Now I do not deny that this is a kind of morality, and that it is capable of great good within limits; but I think that we should all repudiate a morality which had no higher ideal to set before us than that. It represents, of course, one of the violent reactions we are witnessing, against the view that the community is solely for the benefit of the individual; but it is equally a gospel of this world, and of this world alone. My complaint against modern literature is of the same kind. It is not that modern literature is in the ordinary sense 'immoral' or even 'amoral'; and in any case to prefer that charge would not be enough. It is simply that it repudiates, or is wholly ignorant of, our most fundamental and important beliefs; and that in consequence its tendency is to encourage its readers to get what they can out of life while it lasts, to miss no 'experience' that presents itself, and to sacrifice themselves, if they make any sacrifice at all, only for the sake of tangible benefits to others in this world either now or in the future. We shall certainly continue to read the best of its kind, of what our time provides; but we must tirelessly criticize it according to our own principles, and not merely according to the principles admitted by the writers and by the critics who discuss it in the public press.

from THE MUSIC OF POETRY[1]

The poet, when he talks or writes about poetry, has peculiar qualifications and peculiar limitations: if we allow for the latter we can better appreciate the former – a caution which I recommend to poets themselves as well as to the readers of what they say about poetry. I can never re-read any of my own prose writings without acute embarrassment: I shirk the task, and consequently may not take account of all the assertions to which I have at one time or another committed myself; I may often repeat what I have said before, and I may often contradict myself. But I believe that the critical writings of poets, of which in the past there have been some very distinguished examples, owe a great deal of their interest to the fact that the poet, at the back of his mind, if not as his ostensible purpose, is always trying to defend the kind of poetry he is writing, or to formulate the kind that he wants to write. Especially when he is young, and actively engaged in battling for the kind of poetry which he practises, he sees the poetry of the past in relation to his own: and his gratitude to those dead poets from whom he has learned, as well as his indifference to those whose aims have been alien to his own, may be exaggerated. He is not so much a judge as an advocate. His knowledge even is likely to be partial: for his studies will have led him to concentrate on certain authors to the neglect of others. When he theorizes about poetic creation, he is likely to be generalizing one type of experience; when he ventures into aesthetics, he is likely to be less, rather than more competent than the philosopher; and he may do best merely to report, for the information of the philosopher, the data of his own introspection. What he writes about poetry, in short, must be assessed in relation to the poetry he writes. We must return to the scholar for ascertainment of facts, and to the more detached critic for impartial judgment. The critic, certainly, should be something of a scholar, and the scholar something of a critic. Ker, whose attention was devoted mainly to

[1] The third W. P. Ker Memorial Lecture, delivered at Glasgow University in 1942, and published by Glasgow University Press in the same year.

the literature of the past, and to problems of historical relationship, must be put in the category of scholars; but he had in a high degree the sense of value, the good taste, the understanding of critical canons and the ability to apply them, without which the scholar's contribution can be only indirect.

There is another, more particular respect in which the scholar's and the practitioner's acquaintance with versification differ. Here, perhaps, I should be prudent to speak only of myself. I have never been able to retain the names of feet and metres, or to pay the proper respect to the accepted rules of scansion. At school, I enjoyed very much reciting Homer or Virgil – in my own fashion. Perhaps I had some instinctive suspicion that nobody really knew how Greek ought to be pronounced, or what interweaving of Greek and native rhythms the Roman ear might appreciate in Virgil; perhaps I had only an instinct of protective laziness. But certainly, when it came to applying rules of scansion to English verse, with its very different stresses and variable syllabic values, I wanted to know why one line was good and another bad; and this, scansion could not tell me. The only way to learn to manipulate any kind of English verse seemed to be by assimilation and imitation, by becoming so engrossed in the work of a particular poet that one could produce a recognizable derivative. This is not to say that I consider the analytical study of metric, of the abstract forms which sound so extraordinarily different when handled by different poets, to be an utter waste of time. It is only that a study of anatomy will not teach you how to make a hen lay eggs. I do not recommend any other way of beginning the study of Greek and Latin verse than with the aid of those rules of scansion which were established by grammarians after most of the poetry had been written; but if we could revive those languages sufficiently to be able to speak and hear them as the authors did, we could regard the rules with indifference. We have to learn a dead language by an artificial method, and we have to approach its versification by an artificial method, and our methods of teaching have to be applied to pupils most of whom have only a moderate gift for language. Even in approaching the poetry of our own language, we may find the classification of metres, of lines with different numbers of syllables and stresses in different places, useful at a preliminary stage, as a simplified map of a complicated territory: but it is only the study, not of poetry but of poems, that can train our ear. It is not from rules, or by cold-blooded imitation of style, that we learn to write: we learn by imitation indeed, but by a deeper imitation than is achieved by analysis of style. When we imitated Shelley, it was not so much from a desire to write as he did, as from an invasion of the adolescent self by Shelley, which

108

made Shelley's way, for the time, the only way in which to write.

The practice of English versification has, no doubt, been affected by awareness of the rules of prosody: it is a matter for the historical scholar to determine the influence of Latin upon the innovators Wyatt and Surrey. The great grammarian Otto Jespersen has maintained that the structure of English grammar has been misunderstood in our attempts to make it conform to the categories of Latin – as in the supposed 'subjunctive'. In the history of versification, the question whether poets have misunderstood the rhythms of the language in imitating foreign models does not arise: we must accept the practices of great poets of the past, because they are practices upon which our ear has been trained and must be trained. I believe that a number of foreign influences have gone to enrich the range and variety of English verse. Some classical scholars hold the view – this is a matter beyond my competence – that the native measure of Latin poetry was accentual rather than syllabic, that it was overlaid by the influence of a very different language – Greek – and that it reverted in something approximating to its early form, in poems such as the *Pervigilium Veneris* and the early Christian hymns. If so, I cannot help suspecting that to the cultivated audience of the age of Virgil, part of the pleasure in the poetry arose from the presence in it of two metrical schemes in a kind of counterpoint: even though the audience may not necessarily have been able to analyse the experience. Similarly, it may be possible that the beauty of some English poetry is due to the presence of more than one metrical structure in it. Deliberate attempts to devise English metres on Latin models are usually very frigid. Among the most successful are a few exercises by Campion, in his brief but too little read treatise on metrics; among the most eminent failures, in my opinion, are the experiments of Robert Bridges – I would give all his ingenious inventions for his earlier and more traditional lyrics. But when a poet has so thoroughly absorbed Latin poetry that its movement informs his verse without deliberate artifice – as with Milton and in some of Tennyson's poems – the result can be among the great triumphs of English versification.

What I think we have, in English poetry, is a kind of amalgam of systems of divers sources (though I do not like to use the word 'system', for it has a suggestion of conscious invention rather than growth): an amalgam like the amalgam of races, and indeed partly due to racial origins. The rhythms of Anglo-Saxon, Celtic, Norman French, of Middle English and Scots, have all made their mark upon English poetry, together with the rhythms of Latin, and, at various periods, of French, Italian and Spanish. As with

human beings in a composite race, different strains may be dominant in different individuals, even in members of the same family,
so one or another element in the poetic compound may be more
congenial to one or another poet or to one or another period. The
kind of poetry we get is determined, from time to time, by the
influence of one or another contemporary literature in a foreign
language; or by circumstances which make one period of our own
past more sympathetic than another; or by the prevailing emphasis
in education. But there is one law of nature more powerful than
any of these varying currents, or influences from abroad or from
the past: the law that poetry must not stray too far from the
ordinary everyday language which we use and hear. Whether
poetry is accentual or syllabic, rhymed or rhymeless, formal or
free, it cannot afford to lose its contact with the changing language
of common intercourse.

It may appear strange, that when I profess to be talking about
the 'music' of poetry, I put such emphasis upon conversation. But
I would remind you, first, that the music of poetry is not something which exists apart from the meaning. Otherwise, we could
have poetry of great musical beauty which made no sense, and I
have never come across such poetry. The apparent exceptions
only show a difference of degree: there are poems in which we are
moved by the music and take the sense for granted, just as there
are poems in which we attend to the sense and are moved by the
music without noticing it. Take an apparently extreme example –
the nonsense verse of Edward Lear. His non-sense is not vacuity
of sense: it is a parody of sense, and that is the sense of it. *The
Jumblies* is a poem of adventure, and of nostalgia for the romance
of foreign voyage and exploration; *The Yongy-Bongy Bo* and *The
Dong with a Luminous Nose* are poems of unrequited passion –
'blues' in fact. We enjoy the music, which is of a high order, and
we enjoy the feeling of irresponsibility towards the sense. Or take
a poem of another type, the *Blue Closet* of William Morris. It is a
delightful poem, though I cannot explain what it means and I
doubt whether the author could have explained it. It has an effect
somewhat like that of a rune or charm, but runes and charms are
very practical formulae designed to produce definite results, such
as getting a cow out of a bog. But its obvious intention (and I
think the author succeeds) is to produce the effect of a dream. It
is not necessary, in order to enjoy the poem, to know what the
dream means; but human beings have an unshakeable belief that
dreams mean something: they used to believe – and many still
believe – that dreams disclose the secrets of the future; the orthodox modern faith is that they reveal the secrets – or at least the
more horrid secrets – of the past. It is a commonplace to observe

that the meaning of a poem may wholly escape paraphrase. It is not quite so commonplace to observe that the meaning of a poem may be something larger than its author's conscious purpose, and something remote from its origins. One of the more obscure of modern poets was the French writer Stéphane Mallarmé, of whom the French sometimes say that his language is so peculiar that it can be understood only by foreigners. The late Roger Fry, and his friend Charles Mauron, published an English translation with notes to unriddle the meanings: when I learn that a difficult sonnet was inspired by seeing a painting on the ceiling reflected on the polished top of a table, or by seeing the light reflected from the foam on a glass of beer, I can only say that this may be a correct embryology, but it is not the meaning. If we are moved by a poem, it has meant something, perhaps something important, to us; if we are not moved, then it is, as poetry, meaningless. We can be deeply stirred by hearing the recitation of a poem in a language of which we understand no word; but if we are then told that the poem is gibberish and has no meaning, we shall consider that we have been deluded – this was no poem, it was merely an imitation of instrumental music. If, as we are aware, only a part of the meaning can be conveyed by paraphrase, that is because the poet is occupied with frontiers of consciousness beyond which words fail, though meanings still exist. A poem may appear to mean very different things to different readers, and all of these meanings may be different from what the author thought he meant. For instance, the author may have been writing some peculiar personal experience, which he saw quite unrelated to anything outside; yet for the reader the poem may become the expression of a general situation, as well as of some private experience of his own. The reader's interpretation may differ from the author's and be equally valid – it may even be better. There may be much more in a poem than the author was aware of. The different interpretations may all be partial formulations of one thing; the ambiguities may be due to the fact that the poem means more, not less, than ordinary speech can communicate.

So, while poetry attempts to convey something beyond what can be conveyed in prose rhythms, it remains, all the same, one person talking to another; and this is just as true if you sing it, for singing is another way of talking. The immediacy of poetry to conversation is not a matter on which we can lay down exact laws. Every revolution in poetry is apt to be, and sometimes to announce itself to be a return to common speech. That is the revolution which Wordsworth announced in his prefaces, and he was right: but the same revolution had been carried out a century before by Oldham, Waller, Denham and Dryden; and the same revolution was due again something over a century later. The followers of a revolution develop the new poetic idiom in one direction or another; they polish or perfect it; meanwhile the spoken language goes on changing, and the poetic idiom goes out of date. Perhaps we do not realize how natural the speech of Dryden must have sounded to the most sensitive of his contemporaries. No poetry, of course, is ever exactly the same speech that the poet talks and hears: but it has to be in such a relation to the speech of his time that the listener or reader can say 'that is how I should talk if I could talk poetry'. This is the reason why the best contemporary poetry can give us a feeling of excitement and a sense of fulfilment different from any sentiment aroused by even very much greater poetry of a past age.

The music of poetry, then, must be a music latent in the common speech of its time. And that means also that it must be latent in the common speech of the poet's *place*. It would not be to my present purpose to inveigh against the ubiquity of standardized, or 'B.B.C.' English. If we all came to talk alike there would no longer be any point in our not writing alike: but until that time comes – and I hope it may be long postponed – it is the poet's business to use the speech which he finds about him, that with which he is most familiar. I shall always remember the impression of W. B. Yeats reading poetry aloud. To hear him read his own works was to be made to recognize how much the Irish way of speech is needed to bring out the beauties of Irish poetry: to hear Yeats reading William Blake was an experience of a different kind, more astonishing than satisfying. Of course, we do not want the poet merely to reproduce exactly the conversational idiom of himself, his family, his friends and his particular district: but what he finds there is the material out of which he must make his poetry. He must, like the sculptor, be faithful to the material in which he works; it is out of sounds that he has heard that he must make his melody and harmony.

It would be a mistake, however, to assume that all poetry ought to be melodious, or that melody is more than one of the components of the music of words. Some poetry is meant to be sung; most poetry, in modern times, is meant to be spoken – and there are many other things to be spoken of besides the murmur of innumerable bees or the moan of doves in immemorial elms. Dissonance, even cacophony, has its place: just as, in a poem of any length, there must be transitions between passages of greater and less intensity, to give a rhythm of fluctuating emotion essential to the musical structure of the whole; and the passages of less intensity will be, in relation to the level on which the total poem operates, prosaic – so that, in the sense implied by that context, it may be said that no poet can write a poem of amplitude unless he is a master of the prosaic.[1]

What matters, in short, is the whole poem: and if the whole poem need not be, and often should not be, wholly melodious, it follows that a poem is not made only out of 'beautiful words'. I doubt whether, from the point of view of *sound* alone, any word is more or less beautiful than another – within its own language, for the question whether some languages are not more beautiful than others is quite another question. The ugly words are the words not fitted for the company in which they find themselves; there are words which are ugly because of rawness or because of antiquation; there are words which are ugly because of foreignness or ill-breeding (e.g. *television*): but I do not believe that any word well-established in its own language is either beautiful or ugly. The music of a word is, so to speak, at a point of intersection: it arises from its relation first to the words immediately preceding and following it, and indefinitely to the rest of its context; and from another relation, that of its immediate meaning in that context to all the other meanings which it has had in other contexts, to its greater or less wealth of association. Not all words, obviously, are equally rich and well-connected: it is part of the business of the poet to dispose the richer among the poorer, at the right points, and we cannot afford to load a poem too heavily with the former – for it is only at certain moments that a word can be made to insinuate the whole history of a language and a civilization. This is an 'allusiveness' which is not the fashion or eccentricity of a peculiar type of poetry; but an allusiveness which is in the nature of words, and which is equally the concern of every kind of poet. My purpose here is to insist that a 'musical poem' is a poem which has a musical pattern of sound and a musical pattern of the secondary meanings of the words which compose it, and that these two patterns are indissoluble and one. And if you object that it is only the pure sound, apart from the sense, to which the adjective 'musical' can be rightly applied, I can only reaffirm my previous assertion that the sound of a poem is as much an abstraction from the poem as is the sense. . . .

I think that a poet may gain much from the study of music: how much technical knowledge of musical form is desirable I do not know, for I have not that technical knowledge myself. But I believe that the properties in which music concerns the poet most nearly, are the sense of rhythm and the sense of structure. I think that it might be possible for a poet to work too closely to musical

---

[1] This is the complementary doctrine to that of the 'touchstone' line or passage of Matthew Arnold: this test of the greatness of a poet is the way he writes his less intense, but structurally vital, matter.

analogies: the result might be an effect of artificiality; but I know that a poem, or a passage of a poem, may tend to realize itself first as a particular rhythm before it reaches expression in words, and that this rhythm may bring to birth the idea and the image; and I do not believe that this is an experience peculiar to myself. The use of recurrent themes is as natural to poetry as to music. There are possibilities for verse which bear some analogy to the development of a theme by different groups of instruments; there are possibilities of transitions in a poem comparable to the different movements of a symphony or a quartet; there are possibilities of contrapuntal arrangement of subject-matter. It is in the concert room, rather than in the opera house, that the germ of a poem may be quickened. . . .

WHAT IS A CLASSIC?[1]

The subject which I have taken is simply the question: 'What is a classic?' It is not a new question. There is, for instance, a famous essay by Ste. Beuve with this title. The pertinence of asking this question, with Virgil particularly in mind, is obvious: whatever the definition we arrive at, it cannot be one which excludes Virgil – we may say confidently that it must be one which will expressly reckon with him. But before I go farther, I should like to dispose of certain prejudices and anticipate certain misunderstandings. I do not aim to supersede, or to outlaw, any use of the word 'classic' which precedent has made permissible. The word has, and will continue to have, several meanings in several contexts: I am concerned with one meaning in one context. In defining the term in this way, I do not bind myself, for the future, not to use the term in any of the other ways in which it has been used. If, for instance, I am discovered on some future occasion, in writing, in public speech, or in conversation, to be using the word 'classic' merely to mean a 'standard author' in any language – using it merely as an indication of the greatness, or of the permanence and importance of a writer in his own field, as when we speak of *The Fifth Form at St. Dominic's* as a classic of schoolboy fiction, or *Handley Cross* as a classic of the hunting field – no one should expect one to apologize. And there is a very interesting book called *A Guide to the Classics*, which tells you how to pick the Derby winner. On other occasions, I permit myself to mean by 'the classics', either Latin and Greek literature *in toto*, or the greatest authors of those languages, as the context indicates. And, finally, I think that the account of the classic which I propose to give here should remove it from the area of the antithesis between 'classic' and 'romantic' – a pair of terms belonging to literary politics, and therefore arousing winds of passion which I ask Aeolus, on this occasion, to contain in the bag.

This leads me to my next point. By the terms of the classic-romantic controversy, to call any work of art 'classical', implies

[1] The Presidential Address to the Virgil Society in 1944. Published by Faber & Faber 1945.

either the highest praise or the most contemptuous abuse, according to the party to which one belongs. It implies certain particular merits or faults: either the perfection of form, or the absolute zero of frigidity. But I want to define one kind of art, and am not concerned that it is absolutely and in every respect *better* or *worse* than another kind. I shall enumerate certain qualities which I should expect the classic to display. But I do not say that, if a literature is to be a great literature, it must have any one author, or any one period, in which all these qualities are manifested. If, as I think, they are all to be found in Virgil, that is not to assert that he is the greatest poet who ever wrote – such an assertion about any poet seems to me meaningless – and it is certainly not to assert that Latin literature is greater than any other literature. We need not consider it as a defect of any literature, if no one author, or no one period, is completely classical; or if, as is true of English literature, the period which most nearly fills the classical definition is not the greatest. I think that those literatures, of which English is one of the most eminent, in which the classical qualities are scattered between various authors and several periods, may well be the richer. Every language has its own resources, and its own limitations. The conditions of a language, and the conditions of the history of the people who speak it, may put out of question the expectation of a classical period, or a classical author. That is not in itself any more a matter for regret than it is for gratulation. It did happen that the history of Rome was such, the character of the Latin language was such, that at a certain moment a uniquely classical poet was possible: though we must remember that it needed that particular poet, and a lifetime of labour on the part of that poet, to make the classic out of his material. And, of course, Virgil couldn't know that *that* was what he was doing. He was, if any poet ever was, acutely aware of what he was trying to do; the one thing he couldn't aim at, or know that he was doing, was to compose a classic: for it is only by hindsight, and in historical perspective, that a classic can be known as such.

If there is one word on which we can fix, which will suggest the maximum of what I mean by the term 'a classic', it is the word *maturity*. I shall distinguish between the universal classic, like Virgil, and the classic which is only such in relation to the other literature in its own language, or according to the view of life of a particular period. A classic can only occur when a civilization is mature; when a language and a literature are mature; and it must be the work of a mature mind. It is the importance of that civilization and of that language, as well as the comprehensiveness of the mind of the individual poet, which gives the universality. To define *maturity* without assuming that the hearer already knows what it means, is almost impossible: let us say then, that if we are properly mature, as well as educated persons, we can recognize maturity in a civilization and in a literature, as we do in the other human beings whom we encounter. To make the meaning of maturity really apprehensible – indeed, even to make it acceptable – to the immature, is perhaps impossible. But if we are mature we either recognize maturity immediately, or come to know it on more intimate acquaintance. No reader of Shakespeare, for instance, can fail to recognize, increasingly as he himself grows up, the gradual ripening of Shakespeare's mind: even a less developed reader can perceive the rapid development of Elizabethan literature and drama as a whole, from early Tudor crudity to the plays of Shakespeare, and perceive a decline in the work of Shakespeare's successors. We can also observe, upon a little conversance, that the plays of Christopher Marlowe exhibit a greater maturity of mind and of style, than the plays which Shakespeare wrote at the same age: it is interesting to speculate whether, if Marlowe had lived as long as Shakespeare, his development would have continued at the same pace. I doubt it: for we observe some minds maturing earlier than others, and we observe that those which mature very early do not always develop very far. I raise this point as a reminder, first that the value of maturity depends upon the value of that which matures, and second, that we should know when we are concerned with the maturity of individual writers, and when with the relative maturity of literary periods. A writer who individually has a more mature mind, may belong to a less mature period than another, so that in that respect his work will be less mature. The maturity of a literature is the reflection of that of the society in which it is produced: an individual author – notably Shakespeare and Virgil – can do much to develop his language: but he cannot bring that language to maturity unless the work of his predecessors has prepared it for his final touch. A mature literature, therefore, has a history behind it: a history, that is not merely a chronicle, an accumulation of manuscripts and writings of this kind and that, but an ordered though unconscious progress of a language to realize its own potentialities within its own limitations.

It is to be observed, that a society, and a literature, like an individual human being, do not necessarily mature equally and concurrently in every respect. The precocious child is often, in some obvious ways, childish for his age in comparison with ordinary children. Is there any one period of English literature to which we can point as being fully mature, comprehensively and in equilibrium? I do not think so: and, as I shall repeat later, I hope it is not so. We cannot say that any individual poet in English has in the course of his life become a more mature man than Shakespeare: we cannot even say that any poet has done so much, to make the English language capable of expressing the most subtle thought or the most refined shades of feeling. Yet we cannot but feel that a play like Congreve's *Way of the World* is in some way more mature than any play of Shakespeare's: but only in this respect, that it reflects a more mature society – that is, it reflects a greater maturity of *manners*. The society for which Congreve wrote was, from our point of view, coarse and brutal enough: yet it is nearer to ours than the society of the Tudors: perhaps for that reason we judge it the more severely. Nevertheless, it was a society more polished and less provincial: its mind was shallower, its sensibility more restricted; it has lost some promise of maturity but realized another. So to maturity of *mind* we must add maturity of *manners*.

The progress towards maturity of language is, I think, more easily recognized and more readily acknowledged in the development of prose, than in that of poetry. In considering prose we are less distracted by individual differences in greatness, and more inclined to demand approximation towards a common standard, a common vocabulary and a common sentence structure: it is often, in fact, the prose which departs the farthest from these common standards, which is individual to the extreme, that we are apt to denominate 'poetic prose'. At a time when England had already accomplished miracles in poetry, her prose was relatively immature, developed sufficiently for certain purposes but not for others: at that same time, when the French language had given little promise of poetry as great as that in English, French prose was much more mature than English prose. You have only to compare any Tudor writer with Montaigne – and Montaigne himself, as a stylist, is only a precursor, his style not ripe enough to fulfil the French requirements for the classic. Our prose was ready for some tasks before it could cope with others: a Malory could come long before a Hooker, a Hooker before a Hobbes, and a Hobbes before an Addison. Whatever difficulties we have in applying this standard to poetry, it is possible to see that the development of a classic prose is the development towards a *common style*. By this I do not mean that the best writers are indistinguishable from each other. The essential and characteristic differences remain: it is not that the differences are less, but that they are more subtle and refined. To a sensitive palate the difference between the prose of Addison and that of Swift will be as marked as the difference between two vintage wines to a connoisseur. What we find, in a period of classic prose, is not a mere common convention of writing, like the common style of newspaper leader writers, but a community of taste. The age which precedes a classic age, may exhibit both eccentricity and monotony: monotony because the resources of the language have not yet been explored, and eccentricity because there is yet no generally accepted standard – if, indeed, that can be called eccentric where there is no centre. Its writing may be at the same time pedantic and licentious. The age following a classic age, may also exhibit eccentricity and monotony: monotony because the resources of the language have, for the time at least, been exhausted, and eccentricity because originality comes to be more valued than correctness. But the age in which we find a common style, will be an age when society has achieved a moment of order and stability, of equilibrium and harmony; as the age which manifests the greatest extremes of individual style will be an age of immaturity or an age of senility.

Maturity of language may naturally be expected to accompany maturity of mind and manners. We may expect the language to approach maturity at the moment when men have a critical sense of the past, a confidence in the present, and no conscious doubt of the future. In literature, this means that the poet is aware of his predecessors, and that we are aware of the predecessors behind his work, as we may be aware of ancestral traits in a person who is at the same time individual and unique. The predecessors should be themselves great and honoured: but their accomplishment must be such as to suggest still undeveloped resources of the language, and not such as to oppress the younger writers with the fear that everything that can be done has been done, in their language. The poet, certainly, in a mature age, may still obtain stimulus from the hope of doing something that his predecessors have not done; he may even be in revolt against them, as a promising adolescent may revolt against the beliefs, the habits and the manners of his parents; but, in retrospect, we can see that he is also the continuer of their traditions, that he preserves essential family characteristics, and that his difference of behaviour is a difference in the circumstances of another age. And, on the other hand, just as we sometimes observe men whose lives are overshadowed by the fame of a father or grandfather, men of whom any achievement of which they are capable appears comparatively insignificant, so a late age of poetry may be consciously impotent to compete with its distinguished ancestry. We meet poets of this kind at the end of any age, poets with a sense of the past only, or alternatively, poets whose hope of the future is founded upon the attempt to renounce the past. The persistence of literary creativeness in any people, accordingly, consists in the maintenance of an unconscious balance between tradition in the larger sense – the collective personality, so to speak, realized in the literature of the past – and the originality of the living generation.

We cannot call the literature of the Elizabethan period, great as it is, wholly mature: we cannot call it classical. No close parallel can be drawn between the development of Greek and Latin literature, for Latin had Greek behind it; still less can we draw a parallel between these and any modern literature, for modern literatures have both Latin and Greek behind them. In the Renaissance there is an early semblance of maturity, which is borrowed from antiquity. We are aware of approaching nearer to maturity with Milton. Milton was in a better position to have a critical sense of the past – of a past in English literature – than his great predecessors. To read Milton is to be confirmed in respect for the genius of Spenser, and in gratitude to Spenser for having contributed towards making the verse of Milton possible. Yet the style of Milton is not a classic style: it is a style of a language still in formation, the style of a writer whose *masters* were not English, but Latin and to a less degree Greek. This, I think, is only saying what Johnson and in turn Landor said, when they complained of Milton's style not being quite English. Let us qualify this judgment by saying immediately that Milton did much to develop the language. One of the signs of approach towards a classic style is a development towards greater complexity of sentence and period structure. Such development is apparent in the single work of Shakespeare, when we trace his style from the early to the late plays: we can even say that in his late plays he goes as far in the direction of complexity as is possible within the limits of dramatic verse, which are narrower than those of other kinds. But complexity for its own sake is not a proper goal: its purpose must be, first, the precise expression of finer shades of feeling and thought; second, the introduction of greater refinement and variety of music. When an author appears, in his love of the elaborate structure, to have lost the ability to say anything simply; when his addiction to pattern becomes such that he says things elaborately which should properly be said simply, and thus limits his range of expression, the process of complexity ceases to be quite healthy, and the writer is losing touch with the spoken language. Nevertheless, as verse develops, in the hands of one poet after another, it tends from monotony to variety, from simplicity to complexity; as it declines, it tends towards monotony again, though it may perpetuate the formal structure to which genius gave life and meaning. You will judge for yourselves how far this generalization is applicable to the predecessors and followers of Virgil: we can all see this secondary monotony in the eighteenth-century imitators of Milton – who himself is never monotonous. There comes a time when a new simplicity, even a relative crudity, may be the only alternative.

You will have anticipated the conclusion towards which I have been drawing: that those qualities of the classic which I have so far mentioned – maturity of mind, maturity of manners, maturity of language and perfection of the common style – are most nearly to be illustrated, in English literature, in the eighteenth century; and, in poetry, most in the poetry of Pope. If that were all I had to say on the matter, it would certainly not be new, and it would not be worth saying. That would be merely proposing a choice between two errors at which men have arrived before: one, that the eighteenth century is the finest period of English literature; and the other, that the classical idea should be wholly discredited. My own opinion is, that we have no classic age, and no classic poet, in English; that when we see why this is so, we have not the slightest reason for regret; but that, nevertheless, we must maintain the classic ideal before our eyes. Because we must maintain it, and because the English genius of language has had other things to do than to realize it, we cannot afford either to reject or to overrate the age of Pope; we cannot see English literature as a whole, or aim rightly in the future, without a critical appreciation of the degree to which the classical qualities are exemplified in the work of Pope: which means that unless we are able to enjoy the work of Pope, we cannot arrive at a full understanding of English poetry.

It is fairly obvious that the realization of classical qualities by Pope was obtained at a high price – to the exclusion of some greater potentialities of English verse. Now, to some extent, the sacrifice of some potentialities in order to realize others, is a condition of artistic creation, as it is a condition of life in general. In life the man who refuses to sacrifice anything, to gain anything else, ends in mediocrity or failure; though, on the other hand, there is the specialist who has sacrificed too much for too little, or who has been born too completely the specialist to have had anything to sacrifice. But in the English eighteenth century, we have reason for feeling that too much was excluded. There was the mature mind: but it was a narrow one. English society and English letters were not provincial, in the sense that they were not isolated from, and not lingering behind, the best European society and letters. Yet the age itself was, in a manner of speaking, a provincial age. When one thinks of a Shakespeare, a Jeremy Taylor, a Milton, in England – of a Racine, a Molière, a Pascal, in France – in the seventeenth century, one is inclined to say that the eighteenth century had perfected its formal garden, only by restricting the area under cultivation. We feel that if the classic is really a worthy ideal, it must be capable of exhibiting an amplitude, a catholicity, to which the eighteenth century cannot lay claim; qualities which are present in some great authors, like Chaucer, who cannot be regarded in my sense as classics of English literature; and which are fully present in the mediaeval mind of Dante. For in the Divine Comedy, if anywhere, we find the classic in a modern European language. In the eighteenth century, we are oppressed by the limited range of sensibility, and especially in the scale of religious feeling. It is not that, in England at least, the poetry is not Christian. It is not even that the poets were not devout Christians; for a pattern of orthodoxy of principle, and sincere piety of feeling, you may look long before you find a poet more genuine than Samuel Johnson. Yet there are evidences of a deeper religious sensibility in the poetry of Shakespeare, whose belief and practice can be only a matter of conjecture. And this restriction of religious sensibility itself produces a kind of provinciality (though we must add that in this sense the nineteenth century was more provincial still): the provinciality which indicates the disintegration of Christendom, the decay of a common belief and a common culture. It would seem then, that our eighteenth century, in spite of its classical achievement – an achievement, I believe, which still has great importance as an example for the future – was lacking some condition which makes the creation of a true classic possible. What this condition is, we must return to Virgil to discover.

I should like first to rehearse the characteristics which I have already attributed to the classic, with special application to Virgil, to his language, his civilization, and the particular moment in the history of that language and civilization at which he arrived. Maturity of mind: this needs history, and the consciousness of history. Consciousness of history cannot be fully awake, except where there is other history than the history of the poet's own people: we need this in order to see our own place in history. There must be the knowledge of the history of at least one other highly civilized people, and of a people whose civilization is sufficiently cognate to have influenced and entered into our own. This is a consciousness which the Romans had, and which the Greeks, however much more highly we may estimate their achievement – and indeed, we may respect it all the more on this account – could not possess. It was a consciousness, certainly, which Virgil himself did much to develop. From the beginning, Virgil, like his contemporaries and immediate predecessors, was constantly adapting and using the discoveries, traditions and inventions of Greek poetry: to make use of a foreign literature in this way marks a further stage of civilization beyond making use only of the earlier stages of one's own – though I think we can say that no poet has ever shown a finer sense of proportion than Virgil, in the uses he made of Greek and of earlier Latin poetry. It is this development of one literature, or one civilization, in relation to another, which gives a peculiar significance to the subject of Virgil's epic. In Homer, the conflict between the Greeks and the Trojans is hardly larger in scope than a feud between one Greek city-state and a coalition of other city-states: behind the story of Aeneas is the consciousness of a more radical distinction, a distinction, which is at the same time a statement of *relatedness*, between two great cultures, and, finally, of their reconciliation under an all-embracing destiny.

Virgil's maturity of mind, and the maturity of his age, are exhibited in this awareness of history. With maturity of mind I have associated maturity of manners and absence of provinciality. I suppose that, to a modern European suddenly precipitated into the past, the social behaviour of the Romans and the Athenians would seem indifferently coarse, barbarous and offensive. But if the poet can portray something superior to contemporary practice, it is not in the way of anticipating some later, and quite different code of behaviour, but by an insight into what the conduct of his own people at his own time might be, at its best. House parties of the wealthy, in Edwardian England, were not exactly what we read of in the pages of Henry James: but Mr. James's society was an idealization, of a kind, of *that* society, and not an anticipation of any other. I think that we are conscious, in Virgil more than in any other Latin poet – for Catullus and Propertius seem ruffians, and Horace somewhat plebeian, by comparison – of a refinement of manners springing from a delicate sensibility, and particularly in that test of manners, private and public conduct between the sexes. It is not for me, in a gathering of people, all of whom may be better scholars than I, to review the story of Aeneas and Dido. But I have always thought the meeting of Aeneas with the shade of Dido, in Book VI, not only one of the most poignant, but one of the most civilized passages in poetry. It is complex in meaning and economical in expression, for it not only tells us about the attitude of Dido – still more important is what it tells us about the attitude of Aeneas. Dido's behaviour appears almost as a projection of Aeneas' own conscience: this, we feel, is the way in which Aeneas' conscience would *expect* Dido to behave to him. The point, it seems to me, is not that Dido is unforgiving – though it is important that, instead of railing at him, she merely snubs him – perhaps the most telling snub in all poetry: what matters most is, that Aeneas does not forgive himself – and this, significantly, in spite of the fact of which he is well aware, that all that he has done has

been in compliance with destiny, or in consequence of the machi-
nations of gods who are themselves, we feel, only instruments of a
greater inscrutable power. Here, what I chose as an instance of
civilized manners, proceeds to testify to civilized consciousness
and conscience: but all of the levels at which we may consider a
particular episode, belong to one whole. It will be observed,
finally, that the behaviour of Virgil's characters (I might except
Turnus, the man without a destiny) never appears to be according
to some purely local or tribal code of manners: it is in its time,
both Roman and European. Virgil certainly, on the plane of
manners, is not provincial.

To attempt to demonstrate the maturity of language and style
of Virgil is, for the present occasion, a superflous task: many of
you could perform it better than I, and I think that we should all
be in accord. But it is worth repeating that Virgil's style would not
have been possible without a literature behind him, and without
his having a very intimate knowledge of this literature: so that he
was, in a sense, re-writing Latin poetry – as when he borrows a
phrase or a device from a predecessor and improves upon it. He
was a learned author, all of whose learning was relevant to his
task; and he had, for his use, just enough literature behind him
and not too much. As for maturity of style, I do not think that any
poet has ever developed a greater command of the complex structure, both of sense and sound, without losing the resource of
direct, brief and startling simplicity when the occasion required it.
On this I need not dilate: but I think it is worth while to say a
word more about the *common style*, because this is something
which we cannot perfectly illustrate from English poetry, and to
which we are apt to pay less than enough deference. In modern
European literature, the closest approximations to the ideal of a
common style, are probably to be found in Dante and Racine; the
nearest we have to it in English poetry is Pope, and Pope's is a
common style which, in comparison, is of a very narrow range. A
common style is one which makes us exclaim, not 'this is a man of
genius using the language' but 'this realizes the genius of the
language'. We do not say this when we read Pope, because we are
too conscious of all the resources of the English speech upon which
Pope does not draw; we can at most say 'this realizes the genius of
the English language of a particular epoch'. We do not say this
when we read Shakespeare or Milton, because we are always conscious of the greatness of the man, and of the miracles that *he* is
performing with the language; we come nearer perhaps with
Chaucer – but that Chaucer is using a different, from our point of
view a cruder speech. And Shakespeare and Milton, as later history shows, left open many possibilities of other uses of English in

poetry: whereas, after Virgil, it is truer to say that no great development was possible, until the Latin language became something different.

At this point I should like to return to a question which I have already suggested: the question whether the achievement of a classic, in the sense in which I have been using the term throughout, is, for the people and the language of its origin, altogether an unmixed blessing – even though it is unquestionably a ground for pride. To have this question raised in one's mind, it is almost enough simply to have contemplated Latin poetry after Virgil, to have considered the extent to which later poets lived and worked under the shadow of his greatness: so that we praise or dispraise them, according to standards which he set – admiring them, sometimes, for discovering some variation which was new, or even for merely rearranging patterns of words so as to give a pleasing faint reminder of the remote original. But English poetry, and French poetry also, may be considered fortunate in this: that the greatest poets have exhausted only particular areas. We cannot say that, since the age of Shakespeare, and respectively since the time of Racine, there has been any really first-rate poetic drama in England or in France; since Milton, we have had no great epic poem, though there have been great long poems. It is true that every supreme poet, classic or not, tends to exhaust the ground he cultivates, so that it must, after yielding a diminishing crop, finally be left in fallow for some generations.

Here it may be objected that the effect on a literature which I am imputing to the classic, results not from the classic character of that work, but simply from its greatness: for I have denied to Shakespeare and to Milton the title of classics, in the sense in which I am employing the term throughout, and yet have admitted that no supremely great poetry of the same kind has been written since. That every great work of poetry tends to make impossible the production of equally great works of the same kind is indisputable. The reason may be stated partly in terms of conscious purpose: no first-rate poet would attempt to do again, what has already been done as well as it can be done in his language. It is only after the language – its cadence, still more than vocabulary and syntax – has, with time and social change, sufficiently altered, that another dramatic poet as great as Shakespeare, or another epic poet as great as Milton, can become possible. Not only every great poet, but every genuine, though lesser poet, fulfils once for all some possibility of the language, and so leaves one possibility less for his successors. The vein that he has exhausted may be a very small one; or may represent some major form of poetry, the epic or dramatic. But what the great poet has exhausted is merely one form, and not the whole language. When the great poet is also a great classic poet, he exhausts, not a form only, but the language of his time; and the language of his time, as used by him, will be the language in its perfection. So that it is not the poet alone of whom we have to take account, but the language in which he writes: it is not merely that a classic poet exhausts the language, but that an exhaustible language is the kind which may produce a classic poet.

We may be inclined to ask, then, whether we are not fortunate in possessing a language which, instead of having produced a classic, can boast a rich variety in the past, and the possibility of further novelty in the future? Now while we are *inside* a literature, while we speak the same language, and have fundamentally the same culture as that which produced the literature of the past, we want to maintain two things: a pride in what our literature has already accomplished, and a belief in what it may still accomplish in the future. If we cease to believe in the future, the past would cease to be fully *our* past: it would become the past of a dead civilization. And this consideration must operate with particular cogency upon the minds of those who are engaged in the attempt to add to the store of English literature. There is no classic in English: therefore, any living poet can say, there is still hope that I – and those after me, for no one can face with equanimity, once he understands what is implied, the thought of being the *last* poet – may be able to write something which will be worth preserving. But from the aspect of eternity, such interest in the future has no meaning: when two languages are both dead languages, we cannot say that one is greater, because of the number and variety of its poets, or the other because its genius is more completely expressed in the work of one poet. What I wish to affirm, at one and the same time, is this: that, because English is a living language and the language in which we live, we may be glad that it has never completely realized itself in the work of one classic poet; but that, on the other hand, the classic criterion is of vital importance to us. We need it in order to judge our individual poets, though we refuse to judge our literature as a whole in comparison with one which has produced a classic. Whether a literature does culminate in a classic, is a matter of fortune. It is largely, I suspect, a question of the degree of fusion of the elements within that language; so that the Latin languages can approximate more closely to the classic, not simply because they are Latin, but because they are more homogeneous than English, and therefore tend more naturally towards the *common style*: whereas English, being the most various of great languages in its constituents, tends to variety rather than perfection, needs a longer time to realize its potency, and still contains, perhaps, more unexplored possibilities. It has, perhaps, the greatest capacity for changing and yet remaining itself.

I am now approaching the distinction between the relative and the absolute classic, the distinction between the literature which can be called classic in relation to its own language, and that which is classic in relation to a number of other languages. But first I wish to record one more characteristic of the classic, beyond those I have enumerated, which will help to establish this distinction, and to mark the difference between such a classic as Pope and such a classic as Virgil. It is convenient to recapitulate certain assertions which I made earlier.

I suggested, at the beginning, that a frequent, if not universal feature of the maturing of individuals may be a process of selection (not altogether conscious), of the development of some potentialities to the exclusion of others; and that a similarity may be found in the development of language and literature. If this is so, we should expect to find that in a minor classic literature, such as our own of the late seventeenth and the eighteenth century, the elements excluded, to arrive at maturity, will be more numerous or more serious; and that satisfaction in the result, will always be qualified by our awareness of the possibilities of the language, revealed in the work of earlier authors, which have been ignored. The classic age of English literature is not representative of the total genius of the race: as I have intimated, we cannot say that that genius is wholly realized in any one period – with the result that we can still, by referring to one or another period of the past, envisage possibilities for the future. The English language is one which offers wide scope for legitimate divergencies of style; it seems to be such that no one age, and certainly no one writer, can establish a norm. The French language has seemed to be much more closely tethered to a normal style; yet, even in French, though the language appeared to have established itself, once for all, in the seventeenth century, there is an *esprit gaulois*, an element of richness present in Rabelais and in Villon, the awareness of which may qualify our judgment of the *wholeness* of Racine or Molière, for we may feel that it is not only unrepresented but unreconciled. We may come to the conclusion, then, that the perfect classic must be one in which the whole genius of a people will be latent, if not all revealed; and that it can only appear in a language such that its whole genius can be present at once. We must accordingly add, to our list of characteristics of the classic, that of *comprehensiveness*. The classic must, within its formal limitations, express the maximum possible of the whole range of feeling which represents the character of the people who speak that language. It will represent this at its best, and it will also have the widest appeal: among the people to which it belongs, it will find its response among all classes and conditions of men.

When a work of literature has, beyond this comprehensiveness in relation to its own language, an equal significance in relation to a number of foreign literatures, we may say that it has also *universality*. We may for instance speak justly enough of the poetry of Goethe as constituting a classic, because of the place which it occupies in its own language and literature. Yet, because of its partiality, of the impermanence of some of its content, and the germanism of the sensibility; because Goethe appears, to a foreign eye, limited by his age, by his language, and by his culture, so that he is unrepresentative of the whole European tradition, and, like our own nineteenth-century authors, a little provincial, we cannot call him a *universal* classic. He is a universal author, in the sense that he is an author with whose works every European ought to be acquainted: but that is a different thing. Nor, on one count or another, can we expect to find the proximate approach to the classic in *any* modern language. It is necessary to go to the two dead languages: it is important that they are dead, because through their death we have come into our inheritance – the fact that they are dead would in itself give them no value, apart from the fact that all the peoples of Europe are their beneficiaries. And of all the great poets of Greece and Rome, I think that it is to Virgil that we owe the most for our standard of the classic: which, I will repeat, is not the same thing as pretending that he is the greatest, or the one to whom we are in every way the most indebted – it is of a particular debt that I speak. His comprehensiveness, his peculiar kind of comprehensiveness, is due to the unique position in our history of the Roman Empire and the Latin language; a position which may be said to conform to its *destiny*. This sense of destiny comes to consciousness in the *Aeneid*. Aeneas is himself, from first to last, a 'man in fate', a man who is neither an adventurer nor a schemer, neither a vagabond nor a careerist, a man fulfilling his destiny, not under compulsion or arbitrary decree, and certainly from no stimulus to glory, but by surrendering his will to a higher power behind the gods who would thwart or direct him. He would have preferred to stop in Troy, but he becomes an exile, and something greater and more significant than any exile; he is exiled for a purpose greater than he can know, but which he recognizes; and he is not, in a human sense, a happy or successful man. But he is the symbol of Rome; and, as Aeneas is to Rome, so is ancient Rome to Europe. Thus Virgil acquires the centrality of the unique classic; he is at the centre of European civilization, in a position which no other poet

128

can share or usurp. The Roman Empire and the Latin language were not any empire and any language, but an empire and a language with a unique destiny in relation to ourselves; and the poet in whom that Empire and that language came to consciousness and expression is a poet of unique destiny.

If Virgil is thus the consciousness of Rome and the supreme voice of her language, he must have a significance for us which cannot be expressed wholly in terms of literary appreciation and criticism. Yet, adhering to the problems of literature, or to the terms of literature in dealing with life, we may be allowed to imply more than we state. The value of Virgil to us, in literary terms, is in providing us with a criterion. We may, as I have said, have reasons to rejoice that this criterion is provided by a poet writing in a different language from our own: but that is not a reason for rejecting the criterion. To preserve the classical standard, and to measure every individual work of literature by it, is to see that, while our literature as a whole may contain everything, every single work in it may be defective in something. This may be a necessary defect, a defect without which some quality present would be lacking: but we must see it as a defect, at the same time that we see it as a necessity. In the absence of this standard of which I speak, a standard we cannot keep clearly before us if we rely on our own literature alone, we tend, first to admire works of genius for the wrong reasons – as we extol Blake for his *philosophy*, and Hopkins for his *style*: and from this we proceed to greater error, to giving the second-rate equal rank with the first-rate. In short, without the constant application of the classical measure, which we owe to Virgil more than to any other one poet, we tend to become provincial.

By 'provincial' I mean here something more than I find in the dictionary definitions. I mean more, for instance, than 'wanting the culture or polish of the capital', though, certainly, Virgil was of the Capital, to a degree which makes any later poet of equal stature look a little provincial; and I mean more that 'narrow in thought, in culture, in creed' – a slippery definition this, for, from a modern liberal point of view, Dante was 'narrow in thought, in culture, in creed', yet it may be the Broad Churchman, rather than the Narrow Churchman, who is the more provincial. I mean also a distortion of values, the exclusion of some, the exaggeration of others, which springs, not from lack of wide geographical perambulation, but from applying standards acquired within a limited area, to the whole of human experience; which confounds the contingent with the essential, the ephemeral with the permanent. In our age, when men seem more than ever prone to confuse wisdom with knowledge, and knowledge with information, and to try to solve problems of life in terms of engineering, there is coming into existence a new kind of provincialism which perhaps deserves a new name. It is a provincialism, not of space, but of time; one for which history is merely the chronicle of human devices which have served their turn and been scrapped, one for which the world is the property solely of the living, a property in which the dead hold no shares. The menace of this kind of provincialism is, that we can all, all the peoples on the globe, be provincials together; and those who are not content to be provincials, can only become hermits. If this kind of provincialism led to greater tolerance, in the sense of forbearance, there might be more to be said for it; but it seems more likely to lead to our becoming indifferent, in matters where we ought to maintain a distinctive dogma or standard, and to our becoming intolerant, in matters which might be left to local or personal preference. We may have as many varieties of religion as we like, provided we all send our children to the same schools. But my concern here is only with the corrective to provincialism in literature. We need to remind ourselves that, as Europe is a whole (and still, in its progressive mutilation and disfigurement, the organism out of which any greater world harmony must develop), so European literature is a whole, the several members of which cannot flourish, if the same blood-stream does not circulate throughout the whole body. The blood-stream of European literature is Latin and Greek — not as two systems of circulation, but one, for it is through Rome that our parentage in Greece must be traced. What common measure of excellence have we in literature, among our several languages, which is not the classical measure? What mutual intelligibility can we hope to preserve, except in our common heritage of thought and feeling in those two languages, for the understanding of which, no European people is in any position of advantage over any other? No modern language could aspire to the universality of Latin, even though it came to be spoken by millions more than ever spoke Latin, and even though it came to be the universal means of communication between peoples of all tongues and cultures. No modern language can hope to produce a classic, in the sense in which I have called Virgil a classic. Our classic, the classic of all Europe, is Virgil.

In our several literatures, we have much wealth of which to boast, to which Latin has nothing to compare; but each literature has its greatness, not in isolation, but because of its place in a larger pattern, a pattern set in Rome. I have spoken of the new seriousness — *gravity* I might say — the new insight into history, illustrated by the dedication of Aeneas to Rome, to a future far beyond his living achievement. *His* reward was hardly more than a narrow

130

beachhead and a political marriage in a weary middle age: his youth interred, its shadow moving with the shades the other side of Cumae. And so, I said, one envisages the destiny of ancient Rome. So we may think of Roman literature: at first sight, a literature of limited scope, with a poor muster of great names, yet universal as no other literature can be; a literature unconsciously sacrificing, in compliance to its destiny in Europe, the opulence and variety of later tongues, to produce, for us, the classic. It is sufficient that this standard should have been established once for all; the task does not have to be done again. But the maintenance of the standard is the price of our freedom, the defence of freedom against chaos. We may remind ourselves of this obligation, by our annual observance of piety towards the great ghost who guided Dante's pilgrimage: who, as it was his function to lead Dante towards a vision he could never himself enjoy, led Europe towards the Christian culture which he could never know; and who, speaking his final words in the new Italian speech, said in farewell

> *il temporal foco e l'eterno*
> *veduto hai, figlio, e sei venuto in parte*
> *dov' io per me più oltre non discerno.*

Son, the temporal fire and the eternal, hast thou seen, and art come to a place where I, of myself, discern no further.

POETRY AND DRAMA[1]

I

Reviewing my critical output for the last thirty-odd years, I am surprised to find how constantly I have returned to the drama, whether by examining the work of the contemporaries of Shakespeare, or by reflecting on the possibilities of the future. It may even be that people are weary of hearing me on this subject. But, while I find that I have been composing variations on this theme all my life, my views have been continually modified and renewed by increasing experience; so that I am impelled to take stock of the situation afresh at every stage of my own experimentation.

As I have gradually learned more about the problems of poetic drama, and the conditions which it must fulfil if it is to justify itself, I have made a little clearer to myself, not only my own reasons for wanting to write in this form, but the more general reasons for wanting to see it restored to its place. And I think that if I say something about these problems and conditions, it should make clearer to other people whether and if so why poetic drama has anything potentially to offer the playgoer, that prose drama cannot. For I start with the assumption that if poetry is merely a decoration, an added embellishment, if it merely gives people of literary tastes the pleasure of listening to poetry at the same time that they are witnessing a play, then it is superfluous. It must justify itself dramatically, and not merely be fine poetry shaped into a dramatic form. From this it follows that no play should be written in verse for which prose is *dramatically* adequate. And from this it follows, again, that the audience, its attention held by the dramatic action, its emotions stirred by the situation between the characters, should be too intent upon the play to be wholly conscious of the medium.

Whether we use prose or verse on the stage, they are both but means to an end. The difference, from one point of view, is not so great as we might think. In those prose plays which survive, which

[1] The first Theodore Spencer Memorial Lecture delivered at Harvard University and published by Faber & Faber and by the Harvard University Press in 1951.

132

are read and produced on the stage by later generations, the prose in which the characters speak is as remote, for the best part, from the vocabulary, syntax, and rhythm of our ordinary speech – with its fumbling for words, its constant recourse to approximation, its disorder, and its unfinished sentences – as verse is. Like verse, it has been written, and rewritten. Our two greatest prose stylists in the drama – apart from Shakespeare and the other Elizabethans who mixed prose and verse in the same play – are, I believe, Congreve and Bernard Shaw. A speech by a character of Congreve or of Shaw has – however clearly the characters may be differentiated – that unmistakable personal rhythm which is the mark of a prose style, and of which only the most accomplished conversationalists – who are for that matter usually monologuists – show any trace in their talk. We have all heard (too often!) of Molière's character who expressed surprise when told that he spoke prose. But it was M. Jourdain who was right, and not his mentor or his creator: he did not speak prose – he only talked. For I mean to draw a triple distinction: between prose, and verse, and our ordinary speech which is mostly below the level of either verse or prose. So if you look at it in this way, it will appear that prose, on the stage, is as artificial as verse: or alternatively, that verse can be as natural as prose.

But while the sensitive member of the audience will appreciate, when he hears fine prose spoken in a play, that this is something better than ordinary conversation, he does not regard it as a wholly different language from that which he himself speaks, for that would interpose a barrer between himself and the imaginary characters on the stage. Too many people, on the other hand, approach a play which they know to be in verse, with the consciousness of the difference. It is unfortunate when they are repelled by verse, but can also be deplorable when they are attracted by it – if that means that they are prepared to enjoy the play and the language of the play as two separate things. The chief effect of style and rhythm in dramatic speech, whether in prose or verse, should be unconscious.

From this it follows that a mixture of prose and verse in the same play is generally to be avoided: each transition makes the auditor aware, with a jolt, of the medium. It is, we may say, justifiable when the author wishes to produce this jolt: when, that is, he wishes to transport the audience violently from one plane of reality to another. I suspect that this kind of transition was easily acceptable to an Elizabethan audience, to whose ears both prose and verse came naturally; who liked high-falutin and low comedy in the same play; and to whom it seemed perhaps proper that the more humble and rustic characters should speak in a homely language, and that those of more exalted rank should rant in verse. But even in the plays of Shakespeare some of the prose passages seem to be designed for an effect of contrast which, when achieved, is something that can never become old-fashioned. The knocking at the gate in *Macbeth* is an example that comes to everyone's mind; but it has long seemed to me that the alternation of scenes in prose with scenes in verse in *Henry IV* points an ironic contrast between the world of high politics and the world of common life. The audience probably thought they were getting their accustomed chronicle play garnished with amusing scenes of low life; yet the prose scenes of both Part I and Part II provide a sardonic comment upon the bustling ambitions of the chiefs of the parties in the insurrection of the Percys.

Today, however, because of the handicap under which verse drama suffers, I believe that in verse drama prose should be used very sparingly indeed; that we should aim at a form of verse in which everything can be said that has to be said; and that when we find some situation which is intractable in verse, it is merely because our form of verse is inelastic. And if there prove to be scenes which we cannot put in verse, we must either develop our verse, or avoid having to introduce such scenes. For we have to accustom our audiences to verse to the point at which they will cease to be conscious of it; and to introduce prose dialogue would only be to distract their attention from the play itself to the medium of its expression. But if our verse is to have so wide a range that it can say anything that has to be said, it follows that it will not be 'poetry' all the time. It will only be 'poetry' when the dramatic situation has reached such a point of intensity that poetry becomes the natural utterance, because then it is the only language in which the emotions can be expressed at all.

It is indeed necessary for any long poem, if it is to escape monotony, to be able to say homely things without bathos, as well as to take the highest flights without sounding exaggerated. And it is still more important in a play, especially if it is concerned with contemporary life. The reason for writing even the more pedestrian parts of a verse play in verse instead of prose is, however, not only to avoid calling the audience's attention to the fact that it is at other moments listening to poetry. It is also that the verse rhythm should have its effect upon the hearers, without their being conscious of it. A brief analysis of one scene of Shakespeare's may illustrate this point. The opening scene of *Hamlet* – as well constructed an opening scene as that of any play ever written – has the advantage of being one that everybody knows.

What we do not notice, when we witness this scene in the theatre, is the great variation of style. Nothing is superfluous, and there is no line of poetry which is not justified by its dramatic value. The first twenty-two lines are built of the simplest words in the most homely idiom. Shakespeare had worked for a long time in the theatre, and written a good many plays, before reaching the point at which he could write those twenty-two lines. There is nothing quite so simplified and sure in his previous work. He first developed conversational, colloquial verse in the monologue of the character part – Faulconbridge in *King John*, and later the Nurse in *Romeo and Juliet*. It was a much further step to carry it unobtrusively into the dialogue of brief replies. No poet has begun to master dramatic verse until he can write lines which, like these in *Hamlet*, are *transparent*. You are consciously attending, not to the poetry, but to the meaning of the poetry. If you were hearing *Hamlet* for the first time, without knowing anything about the play, I do not think that it would occur to you to ask whether the speakers were speaking in verse or prose. The verse is having a different effect upon us from prose; but at the moment, what we are aware of is the frosty night, the officers keeping watch on the battlements, and the foreboding of a tragic action. I do not say that there is no place for the situation in which part of one's pleasure will be the enjoyment of hearing beautiful poetry – providing that the author gives it, in that place, dramatic inevitability. And of course, when we have both seen a play several times and read it between performances, we begin to analyse the means by which the author has produced his effects. But in the immediate impact of this scene we are unconscious of the medium of its expression.

From the short, brusque ejaculations at the beginning, suitable to the situation and to the character of the guards – but not expressing more character than is required for their function in the play – the verse glides into a slower movement with the appearance of the courtiers Horatio and Marcellus.

> *Horatio says 'tis but our fantasy*, . . .

and the movement changes again on the appearance of Royalty, the ghost of the King, into the solemn and sonorous

> *What art thou, that usurp'st this time of night*, . . .

(and note, by the way, this anticipation of the plot conveyed by the use of the verb *usurp*); and majesty is suggested in a reference reminding us whose ghost this is:

> *So frown'd he once, when, in an angry parle,*
> *He smote the sledded Polacks on the ice.*

There is an abrupt change to staccato in Horatio's words to the Ghost on its second appearance; this rhythm changes again with the words

> *We do it wrong, being so majestical,*
> *To offer it the show of violence;*
> *For it is, as the air, invulnerable,*
> *And our vain blows malicious mockery.*

The scene reaches a resolution with the words of Marcellus:

> *It faded on the crowing of the cock.*
> *Some say that ever 'gainst that season comes*
> *Wherein our Saviour's birth is celebrated,*
> *The bird of dawning singeth all night long; . . .*

and Horatio's answer:

> *So have I heard and do in part believe it.*
> *But, look, the morn, in russet mantle clad,*
> *Walks o'er the dew of yon high eastern hill.*
> *Break we our watch up.*

This is great poetry, and it is dramatic; but besides being poetic and dramatic, it is something more. There emerges, when we analyse it, a kind of musical design also which reinforces and is one with the dramatic movement. It has checked and accelerated the pulse of our emotion without our knowing it. Note that in these last words of Marcellus there is a deliberate brief emergence of the poetic into consciousness. When we hear the lines

> *But, look, the morn, in russet mantle clad,*
> *Walks o'er the dew of yon high eastern hill,*

we are lifted for a moment beyond character, but with no sense of unfitness of the words coming, and at this moment, from the lips of Horatio. The transitions in the scene obey laws of the music of dramatic poetry. Note that the two lines of Horatio which I have quoted twice are preceded by a line of the simplest speech which might be either verse or prose:

> *So have I heard and do in part believe it,*

and that he follows them abruptly with a half line which is hardly more than a stage direction:

> *Break we our watch up.*

It would be interesting to pursue, by a similar analysis, this problem of the double pattern in great poetic drama – the pattern which may be examined from the point of view of stagecraft or from that of the music. But I think that the examination of this one scene is enough to show us that verse is not merely a formalization, or an added decoration, but that it intensifies the drama. It should indicate also the importance of the unconscious effect of the verse upon us. And lastly, I do not think that this effect is felt only by those members of an audience who 'like poetry' but also by those who go for the play alone. By the people who do not like poetry, I mean those who cannot sit down with a book of poetry and enjoy reading it: these people also, when they go to a play in verse, should be affected by the poetry. And these are the audiences whom the writer of such a play ought to keep in mind.

At this point I might say a word about those plays which we call *poetic*, though they are written in prose. The plays of John Millington Synge form rather a special case, because they are based upon the idiom of a rural people whose speech is naturally poetic, both in imagery and in rhythm. I believe that he even incorporated phrases which he had heard from these country people of Ireland. The language of Synge is not available except for plays set among that same people. We can draw more general conclusions from the plays in prose (so much admired in my youth, and now hardly even read) by Maeterlinck. These plays are in a different way restricted in their subject matter; and to say that the characterization in them is dim is an understatement. I do not deny that they have some poetic quality. But in order to be poetic in prose, a dramatist has to be so consistently poetic that his scope is very limited. Synge wrote plays about characters whose originals in life talked poetically, so he could make them talk poetry and remain real people. The poetic prose dramatist who has not this advantage, has to be too poetic. The poetic drama in prose is more limited by poetic convention or by our conventions as to what subject matter is poetic, than is the poetic drama in verse. A really dramatic verse can be employed, as Shakespeare employed it, to say the most matter-of-fact things.

Yeats is a very different case, from Maeterlinck or Synge. A study of his development as a dramatist would show, I think, the great distance he went, and the triumph of his last plays. In his first period, he wrote plays in verse about subjects conventionally accepted as suitable for verse, in a metric which – though even at that early stage having the personal Yeats rhythm – is not really a form of speech quite suitable for anybody except mythical kings and queens. His middle-period *Plays for Dancers* are very beautiful, but they do not solve any problem for the dramatist in verse:
137

they are poetic prose plays with important interludes in verse. It was only in his last play *Purgatory* that he solved his problem of speech in verse, and laid all his successors under obligation to him.

II

Now, I am going to venture to make some observations based on my own experience, which will lead me to comment on my intentions, failures, and partial successes, in my own plays. I do this in the belief that any explorer or experimenter in new territory may, by putting on record a kind of journal of his explorations, say something of use to those who follow him into the same regions and who will perhaps go farther.

The first thing of any importance that I discovered, was that a writer who has worked for years, and achieved some success, in writing other kinds of verse, has to approach the writing of a verse play in a different frame of mind from that to which he has been accustomed in his previous work. In writing other verse, I think that one is writing, so to speak, in terms of one's own voice: the way it sounds when you read it to yourself is the test. For it is yourself speaking. The question of communication, of what the reader will get from it, is not paramount: if your poem is right to you, you can only hope that the readers will eventually come to accept it. The poem can wait a little while; the approval of a few sympathetic and judicious critics is enough to begin with; and it is for future readers to meet the poet more than half way. But in the theatre, the problem of communication presents itself immediately. You are deliberately writing verse for other voices, not for your own, and you do not know whose voices they will be. You are aiming to write lines which will have an immediate effect upon an unknown and unprepared audience, to be interpreted to that audience by unknown actors rehearsed by an unknown producer. And the unknown audience cannot be expected to show any indulgence towards the poet. The poet cannot afford to write his play merely for his admirers, those who know his non-dramatic work and are prepared to receive favourably anything he puts his name to. He must write with an audience in view which knows nothing and cares nothing, about any previous success he may have had before he ventured into the theatre. Hence one finds out that many of the things one likes to do, and knows how to do, are out of place; and that every line must be judged by a new law, that of dramatic relevance.

When I wrote *Murder in the Cathedral* I had the advantage for a beginner, of an occasion which called for a subject generally admitted to be suitable for verse. Verse plays, it has been generally held, should either take their subject matter from some mythology, or else should be about some remote historical period, far enough away from the present for the characters not to need to be recognizable as human beings, and therefore for them to be licensed to talk in verse. Picturesque period costume renders verse much more acceptable. Furthermore, my play was to be produced for a rather special kind of audience – an audience of those serious people who go to 'festivals' and expect to have to put up with poetry – though perhaps on this occasion some of them were not quite prepared for what they got. And finally it was a religious play, and people who go deliberately to a religious play at a religious festival expect to be patiently bored and to satisfy themselves with the feeling that they have done something meritorious. So the path was made easy.

It was only when I put my mind to thinking what sort of play I wanted to do next, that I realized that in *Murder in the Cathedral* I had not solved any general problem; but that from my point of view the play was a dead end. For one thing, the problem of language which that play had presented to me was a special problem. Fortunately, I did not have to write in the idiom of the twelfth century, because that idiom, even if I knew Norman French and Anglo-Saxon, would have been unintelligible. But the vocabulary and style could not be exactly those of modern conversation – as in some modern French plays using the plot and personages of Greek drama – because I had to take my audience back to an historical event; and they could not afford to be archaic, first because archaism would only have suggested the wrong period, and second because I wanted to bring home to the audience the contemporary relevance of the situation. The style therefore had to be *neutral*, committed neither to the present nor to the past. As for the versification, I was only aware at this stage that the essential was to avoid any echo of Shakespeare, for I was persuaded that the primary failure of nineteenth-century poets when they wrote for the theatre (and most of the greatest English poets had tried their hand at drama) was not in their theatrical technique, but in their dramatic language; and that this was due largely to their limitation to a strict blank verse which, after extensive use for non-dramatic poetry, had lost the flexibility which blank verse must have if it is to give the effect of conversation. The rhythm of regular blank verse had become too remote from the movement of modern speech. Therefore what I kept in mind was the versification of *Everyman*, hoping that anything unusual in the sound of it would be, on the whole, advantageous. An avoidance of too much iambic, some use of alliteration, and occasional unexpected rhyme, helped to distinguish the versification from that of the nineteenth century.

The versification of the dialogue in *Murder in the Cathedral* has therefore, in my opinion, only a *negative* merit: it succeeded in avoiding what had to be avoided, but it arrived at no positive novelty: in short, in so far as it solved the problem of speech in verse for writing today, it solved it for this play only, and provided me with no clue to the verse I should use in another kind of play. Here, then, were two problems left unsolved: that of the idiom and that of the metric (it is really one and the same problem), for general use in any play I might want to write in future. I next became aware of my reasons for depending, in that play, so heavily upon the assistance of the chorus. There were two reasons for this, which in the circumstances justified it. The first was that the essential action of the play – both the historical facts and the matter which I invented – was somewhat limited. A man comes home, foreseeing that he will be killed, and he is killed. I did not want to increase the number of characters, I did not want to write a chronicle of twelfth-century politics, nor did I want to tamper unscrupulously with the meagre records as Tennyson did (in introducing Fair Rosamund, and in suggesting that Becket had been crossed in love in early youth). I wanted to concentrate on death and martyrdom. The introduction of a chorus of excited and sometimes hysterical women, reflecting in their emotion the significance of the action, helped wonderfully. The second reason was this: that a poet writing for the first time for the stage, is much more at home in choral verse than in dramatic dialogue. This, I felt sure, was something I could do, and perhaps the dramatic weaknesses would be somewhat covered up by the cries of the women. The use of a chorus strengthened the power, and concealed the defects of my theatrical technique. For this reason I decided that next time I would try to integrate the chorus more closely into the play.

I wanted to find out also, whether I could learn to dispense altogether with the use of prose. The two prose passages in *Murder in the Cathedral* could not have been written in verse. Certainly, with the kind of dialogue verse which I used in that play, the audience would have been uncomfortably aware that it was verse they were hearing. A sermon cast in verse is too unusual an experience for even the most regular churchgoers: nobody could have responded to it as a sermon at all. And in the speeches of the knights, who are quite aware that they are addressing an audience of people living eight hundred years after they themselves are dead, the use of platform prose is intended of course to have a special effect: to shock the audience out of their complacency. But this is a kind of trick: that is, a device tolerable only in one play and of no use for any other. I may, for aught I know, have been slightly under the influence of *St. Joan.*

I do not wish to give you the impression that I would rule out of dramatic poetry these three things: historical or mythological subject-matter, the chorus, and traditional blank verse. I do not wish to lay down any law that the only suitable characters and situations are those of modern life, or that a verse play should consist of dialogue only, or that a wholly new versification is necessary. I am only tracing out the route of exploration of one writer, and that one myself. If the poetic drama is to reconquer its place, it must, in my opinion, enter into overt competition with prose drama. As I have said, people are prepared to put up with verse from the lips of personages dressed in the fashion of some distant age; therefore they should be made to hear it from people dressed like ourselves, living in houses and apartments like ours, and using telephones and motor cars and radio sets. Audiences are prepared to accept poetry recited by a chorus, for that is a kind of poetry recital, which it does them credit to enjoy. And audiences (those who go to a verse play because it is in verse) expect poetry to be in rhythms which have lost touch with colloquial speech. What we have to do is to bring poetry into the world in which the audience lives and to which it returns when it leaves the theatre; not to transport the audience into some imaginary world totally unlike its own, an unreal world in which poetry is tolerated. What I should hope might be achieved, by a generation of dramatists having the benefit of our experience, is that the audience should find, at the moment of awareness that it is hearing poetry, that it is saying to itself: '*I* could talk in poetry too!' Then we should not be transported into an artificial world; on the contrary, our own sordid, dreary daily world would be suddenly illuminated and transfigured.

I was determined, therefore, in my next play to take a theme of contemporary life, with characters of our own time living in our own world. *The Family Reunion* was the result. Here my first concern was the problem of the versification, to find a rhythm close to contemporary speech, in which the stresses could be made to come wherever we should naturally put them, in uttering the particular phrase on the particular occasion. What I worked out is substantially what I have continued to employ: a line of varying length and varying number of syllables, with a caesura and three stresses. The caesura and the stresses may come at different places, almost anywhere in the line; the stresses may be close together or well separated by light syllables; the only rule being that there must be one stress on one side of the caesura and two on the other. In retrospect, I soon saw that I had given my attention to versification, at the expense of plot and character. I had, indeed, made some progress in dispensing with the chorus; but the device of using four of the minor personages, representing the Family, sometimes as individual character parts and sometimes collectively as chorus, does not seem to me very satisfactory. For one thing, the immediate transition from individual, characterized part to membership of a chorus is asking too much of the actors: it is a very difficult transition to accomplish. For another thing, it seemed to me another trick, one which, even if successful, could not have been applicable in another play. Furthermore, I had in two passages used the device of a lyrical duet further isolated from the rest of the dialogue by being written in shorter lines with only two stresses. These passages are in a sense 'beyond character', the speakers have to be presented as falling into a kind of trance-like state in order to speak them. But they are so remote from the necessity of the action that they are hardly more than passages of poetry which might be spoken by anybody; they are too much like operatic arias. The member of the audience, if he enjoys this sort of thing, is putting up with a suspension of the action in order to enjoy a poetic fantasia: these passages are really less related to the action than are the choruses in *Murder in the Cathedral*.

I observed that when Shakespeare, in one of his mature plays, introduced what might seem a purely poetic line or passage, it never interrupts the action, or is out of character, but on the contrary, in some mysterious way supports both action and character. When Macbeth speaks his so often quoted words beginning

To-morrow and to-morrow and to-morrow,

or when Othello, confronted at night with his angry father-in-law and friends, utters the beautiful line

Keep up your bright swords, for the dew will rust them,

we do not feel that Shakespeare has thought of lines which are beautiful poetry and wishes to fit them in somehow, or that he has for the moment come to the end of his dramatic inspiration and has turned to poetry to fill up with. The lines are surprising, and yet they fit in with the character; or else we are compelled to adjust our conception of the character in such a way that the lines will be appropriate to it. The lines spoken by Macbeth reveal the weariness of the weak man who had been forced by his wife to realize his own half-hearted desires and her ambitions, and who, with her death, is left without the motive to continue. The line of

142

Othello expresses irony, dignity, and fearlessness; and incidentally reminds us of the time of night in which the scene takes place. Only poetry could do this; but it is *dramatic* poetry: that is, it does not interrupt but intensifies the dramatic situation.

It was not only because of the introduction of passages which called too much attention to themselves as poetry, and could not be dramatically justified, that I found *The Family Reunion* defective: there were two weaknesses which came to strike me as more serious still. The first was, that I had employed far too much of the strictly limited time allowed to a dramatist, in presenting a situation, and not left myself enough time, or provided myself with enough material, for developing it in action. I had written what was, on the whole, a good first act; except that for a first act it was much too long. When the curtain rises again, the audience is expecting, as it has a right to expect, that something is going to happen. Instead, it finds itself treated to a further exploration of the background: in other words, to what ought to have been given much earlier if at all. The beginning of the second act presents much the most difficult problem to producer and cast: for the audience's attention is beginning to wander. And then, after what must seem to the audience an interminable time of preparation, the conclusion comes so abruptly that we are, after all, unready for it. This was an elementary fault in mechanics.

But the deepest flaw of all, was in a failure of adjustment between the Greek story and the modern situation. I should either have stuck closer to Aeschylus or else taken a great deal more liberty with his myth. One evidence of this is the appearance of those ill-fated figures, the Furies. They must, in future, be omitted from the cast, and be understood to be visible only to certain of my characters, and not to the audience. We tried every possible manner of presenting them. We put them on the stage, and they looked like uninvited guests who had strayed in from a fancy dress ball. We concealed them behind gauze, and they suggested a still out of a Walt Disney film. We made them dimmer, and they looked like shrubbery just outside the window. I have seen other expedients tried: I have seen them signalling from across the garden, or swarming on to the stage like a football team, and they are never right. They never succeed in being either Greek goddesses or modern spooks. But their failure is merely a symptom of the failure to adjust the ancient with the modern.

A more serious evidence is that we are left in a divided frame of mind, not knowing whether to consider the play the tragedy of the mother or the salvation of the son. The two situations are not reconciled. I find a confirmation of this in the fact that my sympathies now have come to be all with the mother, who seems to me,

143

except perhaps for the chauffeur, the only complete human being in the play; and my hero now strikes me as an insufferable prig.

Well, I had made some progress in learning how to write the first act of a play, and I had – the one thing of which I felt sure – made a good deal of progress in finding a form of versification and an idiom which would serve all my purposes, without recourse to prose, and be capable of unbroken transition between the most intense speech and the most relaxed dialogue. You will understand, after my making these criticisms of *The Family Reunion*, some of the errors that I endeavoured to avoid in designing *The Cocktail Party*. To begin with, no chorus, and no ghosts. I was still inclined to go to a Greek dramatist for my theme, but I was determined to do so merely as a point of departure, and to conceal the origins so well that nobody would identify them until I pointed them out myself. In this at least I have been successful; for no one of my acquaintance (and no dramatic critics) recognized the source of my story in the *Alcestis* of Euripides. In fact, I have had to go into detailed explanation to convince them – I mean, of course, those who were familiar with the plot of that play – of the genuineness of the inspiration. But those who were at first disturbed by the eccentric behaviour of my unknown guest, and his apparently intemperate habits and tendency to burst into song, have found some consolation in having their attention called to the behaviour of Heracles in Euripides' play.

In the second place, I laid down for myself the ascetic rule to avoid poetry which could not stand the test of strict dramatic utility: with such success, indeed, that it is perhaps an open question whether there is any poetry in the play at all. And finally, I tried to keep in mind that in a play, from time to time, something should happen; that the audience should be kept in the constant expectation that something is going to happen; and that, when it does happen, it should be different, but not too different, from what the audience had been led to expect.

I have not yet got to the end of my investigation of the weaknesses of this play, but I hope and expect to find more than those of which I am yet aware. I say 'hope' because while one can never repeat a success, and therefore must always try to find something different, even if less popular, to do, the desire to write something which will be free of the defects of one's last work is a very powerful and useful incentive. I am aware that the last act of my play only just escapes, if indeed it does escape, the accusation of being not a last act but an epilogue; and I am determined to do something different, if I can, in this respect. I also believe that while the self-education of a poet trying to write for the theatre seems to require a long period of disciplining his poetry, and putting it, so to speak, on a very thin diet in order to adapt it to the needs of the stage he may find that later, when (and if) the understanding of theatrical technique has become second nature, he can dare to make more liberal use of poetry and take greater liberties with ordinary colloquial speech. I base this belief on the evolution of Shakespeare, and on some study of the language in his late plays.

In devoting so much time to an examination of my own plays, I have, I believe, been animated by a better motive than egotism. It seems to me that if we are to have a poetic drama, it is more likely to come from poets learning how to write plays, than from skilful prose dramatists learning to write poetry. That some poets can learn how to write plays, and write good ones, may be only a hope, but I believe a not unreasonable hope; but that a man who has started by writing successful prose plays should then learn how to write good poetry, seems to me extremely unlikely. And, under present-day conditions, and until the verse play is recognized by the larger public as a possible source of entertainment, the poet is likely to get his first opportunity to work for the stage only after making some sort of reputation for himself as the author of other kinds of verse. I have therefore wished to put on record, for what it may be worth to others, some account of the difficulties I have encountered, and the mistakes into which I have fallen, and the weaknesses I have had to try to overcome.

I should not like to close without attempting to set before you, though only a dim outline, the ideal towards which poetic drama should strive. It is an unattainable ideal: and that is why it interests me, for it provides an incentive towards further experiment and exploration, beyond any goal which there is prospect of attaining. It is a function of all art to give us some perception of an order in life, by imposing an order upon it. The painter works by selection, combination, and emphasis among the elements of the visible world; the musician in the world of sound. It seems to me that beyond the nameable, classifiable emotions and motives of our conscious life when directed towards action – the part of life which prose drama is wholly adequate to express – there is a fringe of indefinite extent, of feeling which we can only detect, so to speak, out of the corner of the eye and can never completely focus; of feeling of which we are only aware in a kind of temporary detachment from action. There are great prose dramatists – such as Ibsen and Chekhov – who have at times done things of which I would not otherwise have supposed prose to be capable, but who seem to me, in spite of their success, to have been hampered in expression by writing in prose. This peculiar range of sensibility can be expressed by dramatic poetry, at its moments of greatest intensity. At such moments, we touch the border of those feelings which only music can express. We can never emulate music, because to arrive at the condition of music would be the annihilation of poetry, and especially of dramatic poetry. Nevertheless, I have before my eyes a kind of mirage of the perfection of verse drama, which would be a design of human action and of words, such as to present at once the two aspects of dramatic and of musical order. It seems to me that Shakespeare achieved this at least in certain scenes – even rather early, for there is the balcony scene of *Romeo and Juliet* – and that this was what he was striving towards in his late plays. To go as far in this direction as it is possible to go, without losing that contact with the ordinary everyday world with which drama must come to terms, seems to me the proper aim of dramatic poetry. For it is ultimately the function of art, in imposing a credible order upon ordinary reality, and thereby eliciting some perception of an order *in* reality, to bring us to a condition of serenity, stillness, and reconciliation; and then leave us, as Virgil left Dante, to proceed toward a region where that guide can avail us no farther.

NOTE TO 'POETRY AND DRAMA'

As I explained in my Preface, the passage in this essay analysing the first scene of *Hamlet* was taken from a lecture delivered some years previously at Edinburgh University. From the same Edinburgh lecture I have extracted the following note on the balcony scene in *Romeo and Juliet*:

In Romeo's beginning, there is still some artificiality:

> *Two of the fairest stars in all the heaven,*
> *Having some business, do intreat her eyes*
> *To twinkle in their spheres till they return.*

For it seems unlikely that a man standing below in the garden, even on a very bright moonlight night, would see the eyes of the lady above flashing so brilliantly as to justify such a comparison. Yet one is aware, from the beginning of this scene, that there is a musical pattern coming, as surprising in its kind as that in the early work of Beethoven. The arrangement of voices – Juliet has three single lines, followed by Romeo's three, four and five, followed by her longer speech – is very remarkable. In this pattern, one feels that it is Juliet's voice that has the leading part: to her voice is assigned the dominant phrase of the whole duet:

> *My bounty is as boundless as the sea,*
> *My love as deep: the more I give to thee*
> *The more I have, for both are infinite.*

And to Juliet is given the key-word 'lightning', which occurs again in the play, and is significant of the sudden and disastrous power of her passion, when she says

> *'Tis like the lightning, which doth cease to be*
> *Ere one can say 'it lightens'.*

In this scene, Shakespeare achieves a perfection of verse which, being perfection, neither he nor anyone else could excel – for this particular purpose. The stiffness, the artificiality, the poetic decoration, of his early verse has finally given place to a simplification to the language of natural speech, and this language of conversation again raised to great poetry, and to great poetry which is essentially dramatic: for the scene has a structure of which each line is an essential part.

from EZRA POUND:
HIS METRIC AND POETRY

...Pound is not one of those poets who make no demands of the reader; and the casual reader of verse, disconcerted by the difference between Pound's poetry and that on which his taste has been trained, attributes his own difficulties to excessive scholarship on the part of the author. 'This', he will say of some of the poems in Provençal form or on Provençal subjects, 'is archaeology; it requires knowledge on the part of its reader, and true poetry does not require such knowledge.' But to display knowledge is not the same thing as to expect it on the part of the reader; and of this sort of pedantry Pound is quite free. He is, it is true, one of the most learned of poets. In America he had taken up the study of Romance Languages with the intention of teaching. After work in Spain and Italy, after pursuing the Provençal verb from Milan to Freiburg, he deserted the thesis on Lope de Vega and the Ph.D. and the professorial chair, and elected to remain in Europe. Mr. Pound has spoken out his mind from time to time on the subject of scholarship in American universities, its deadness, its isolation from genuine appreciation, and the active creative life of literature. He has always been ready to battle against pedantry. As for his own learning, he has studied poetry carefully, and has made use of his study in his own verse. *Personae* and *Exultations* show his talent for turning his studies to account. He was supersaturated in Provence; he had tramped over most of the country; and the life of the courts where the Troubadours thronged was part of his own life to him. Yet, though *Personae* and *Exultations* do exact something from the reader, they do not require a knowledge of Provençal or of Spanish or Italian. Very few people know the Arthurian legends well, or even Malory (if they did they might realize that the *Idylls of the King* are hardly more important than a parody, or a 'Chaucer retold for Children'); but no one accuses

149

Tennyson of needing footnotes, or of superciliousness toward the uninstructed. The difference is merely in what people are prepared for; most readers could no more relate the myth of Atys correctly than they could give a biography of Bertrand de Born. It is hardly too much to say that there is no poem in these volumes of Mr. Pound which needs fuller explanation than he gives himself. What the poems do require is a trained ear, or at least the willingness to be trained.

The metres and the use of language are unfamiliar. There are certain traces of modern influence. We cannot agree with Mr. Scott James that among these are 'W. E. Henley, Kipling, Chatterton, and especially Walt Whitman' – least of all Walt Whitman. Probably there are only two: Yeats and Browning. Yeats in 'La Fraisne', in *Personae*, for instance, in the attitude and somewhat in the vocabulary:

> *I wrapped my tears in an ellum leaf*
> *And left them under a stone,*
> *And now men call me mad because I have thrown*
> *All folly from me, putting it aside*
> *To leave the old barren ways of men . . .*

For Browning, Mr. Pound has always professed strong admiration (see 'Mesmerism' in *Personae*); there are traces of him in 'Cino' and 'Famam Librosque Cano', in the same volume. But it is more profitable to comment upon the variety of metres and the original use of language.

Ezra Pound has been fathered with vers libre in English, with all its vices and virtues. The term is a loose one – any verse is called 'free' by people whose ears are not accustomed to it – in the second place, Pound's use of this medium has shown the temperance of the artist, and his belief in it as a vehicle is not that of the fanatic. He has said himself that when one has the proper material for a sonnet, one should use the sonnet form; but that it happens very rarely to any poet to find himself in possession of just the block of stuff which can perfectly be modelled into the sonnet. It is true that up to very recently it was impossible to get free verse printed in any periodical except those in which Pound had influence; and that now it is possible to print free verse (second, third or tenth-rate) in almost any American magazine. Who is responsible for the bad free verse is a question of no importance, inasmuch as its authors would have written bad verse in any form; Pound has at least the right to be judged by the success or failure of his own. Pound's vers libre is such as is only possible for a poet who has worked tirelessly with rigid forms and different systems of metric. . . .

from HENRY JAMES

... He was a critic who preyed not upon ideas, but upon living beings. It is criticism which is in a very high sense creative. The characters, the best of them, are each a distinct success of creation: Daisy Miller's small brother is one of these. Done in a clean, flat drawing, each is extracted out of a reality of its own, substantial enough; everything given is true for that individual; but what is given is chosen with great art for its place in a general scheme. The general scheme is not one character, nor a group of characters in a plot or merely in a crowd. The focus is a situation, a relation, an atmosphere, to which the characters pay tribute, but being allowed to give only what the writer wants. The real hero, in any of James's stories, is a social entity of which men and women are constituents. It is, in *The Europeans*, that particular conjunction of people at the Wentworth house, a situation in which several memorable scenes are merely timeless parts, only occurring necessarily in succession. In this aspect, you can say that James is dramatic; as what Pinero and Mr. Jones used to do for a large public, James does for the intelligent. It is in the chemistry of these subtle substances, these curious precipitates and explosive gases which are suddenly formed by the contact of mind with mind, that James is unequalled. Compared with James's, other novelists' characters seem to be only accidentally in the same book. Naturally, there is something terrible, as disconcerting as a quicksand, in this discovery, though it only becomes absolutely dominant in such stories as *The Turn of the Screw*. It is partly foretold in Hawthorne, but James carried it much farther. And it makes the reader, as well as the personae, uneasily the victim of a merciless clairvoyance.

James's critical genius comes out most tellingly in his mastery over, his baffling escape from, Ideas; a mastery and an escape which are perhaps the last test of a superior intelligence. He had a mind so fine that no idea could violate it. Englishmen, with their uncritical admiration (in the present age) for France, like to refer to France as the Home of Ideas; a phrase which, if we could twist it into truth, or at least a compliment, ought to mean that in

France ideas are very severely looked after; not allowed to stray, but preserved for the inspection of civic pride in a Jardin des Plantes, and frugally dispatched on occasions of public necessity. England, on the other hand, if it is not the Home of Ideas, has at least become infested with them in about the space of time within which Australia has been overrun by rabbits. In England ideas run wild and pasture on the emotions; instead of thinking with our feelings (a very different thing) we corrupt our feelings with ideas; we produce the political, the emotional idea, evading sensation and thought. George Meredith (the disciple of Carlyle) was fertile in ideas; his epigrams are a facile substitute for observation and inference. Mr. Chesterton's brain swarms with ideas; I see no evidence that it thinks. James in his novels is like the best French critics in maintaining a point of view, a viewpoint untouched by the parasite idea. He is the most intelligent man of his generation. . . .

from PHILIP MASSINGER

... We must employ Mr. Cruickshank's judgments; and perhaps
the most important judgment to which he has committed himself
is this:
    'Massinger, in his grasp of stagecraft, his flexible metre, his
desire in the sphere of ethics to exploit both vice and virtue, is
typical of an age which had much culture, but which, without
being exactly corrupt, lacked moral fibre.'
    Here, in fact, is our text: to elucidate this sentence would be to
account for Massinger. We begin vaguely with good taste, by a
recognition that Massinger is inferior: can we trace this inferiority,
dissolve it, and have left any element of merit?
    We turn first to the parallel quotations from Massinger and
Shakespeare collocated by Mr. Cruickshank to make manifest
Massinger's indebtedness. One of the surest of tests is the way in
which a poet borrows. Immature poets imitate; mature poets
steal; bad poets deface what they take, and good poets make it
into something better, or at least something different. The good
poet welds his theft into a whole of feeling which is unique, utterly
different from that from which it was torn; the bad poet throws it
into something which has no cohesion. A good poet will usually
borrow from authors remote in time, or alien in language, or
diverse in interest. Chapman borrowed from Seneca; Shakespeare and Webster from Montaigne. The two great followers of
Shakespeare, Webster and Tourneur, in their mature work do not
borrow from him; he is too close to them to be of use to them in
this way. Massinger, as Mr. Cruickshank shows, borrows from
Shakespeare a good deal. Let us profit by some of the quotations
with which he has provided us:

> *Can I call back yesterday, with all their aids*
> *That bow unto my sceptre? or restore*

My mind to that tranquillity and peace
It then enjoyed?

MASSINGER

Not poppy, nor mandragora,
Nor all the drowsy syrops of the world
Shall ever medicine thee to that sweet sleep
Which thou owedst yesterday.

SHAKESPEARE

Massinger's is a general rhetorical question, the language just and pure, but colourless. Shakespeare's has particular significance; and the adjective 'drowsy' and the verb 'medicine' infuse a precise vigour. This is, on Massinger's part, an echo, rather than an imitation or a plagiarism – the basest, because least conscious form of borrowing. 'Drowsy syrop' is a condensation of meaning frequent in Shakespeare, but rare in Massinger.

Thou didst not borrow of Vice her indirect,
Crooked, and abject means.

MASSINGER

God knows, my son,
By what by-paths and indirect crook'd ways
I met this crown.

SHAKESPEARE

Here, again, Massinger gives the general forensic statement, Shakespeare the particular image. 'Indirect crook'd' is forceful in Shakespeare; a mere pleonasm in Massinger. 'Crook'd ways' is a metaphor; Massinger's phrase only the ghost of a metaphor.

And now, in the evening,
When thou should'st pass with honour to thy rest,
Wilt thou fall like a meteor?

MASSINGER

I shall fall
Like a bright exhalation in the evening,
And no man see me more.

SHAKESPEARE

Here the lines of Massinger have their own beauty. Still, a 'bright exhalation' appears to the eye and makes us catch our breath in the evening; 'meteor' is a dim simile; the word is worn.

What you deliver to me shall be lock'd up
In a strong cabinet, of which you yourself
Shall keep the key.

MASSINGER

'Tis in my memory locked,
And you yourself shall keep the key of it.

SHAKESPEARE

In the preceding passage Massinger had squeezed his simile to death, here he drags it round the city at his heels; and how swift Shakespeare's figure is! We may add two more passages, not given by our commentator; here the model is Webster. They occur on the same page, an artless confession.

Here he comes,
His nose held up; he hath something in the wind,

is hardly comparable to 'the Cardinal lifts up his nose like a foul porpoise before a storm', and when we come upon

as tann'd galley-slaves
Pay such as do redeem them from the oar

it is unnecessary to turn up the great lines in the *Duchess of Malfy*. Massinger fancied this galley-slave; for he comes with his oar again in the *Bondman*:

Never did galley-slave shake off his chains,
Or looked on his redemption from the oar. . . .

Now these are mature plays; and the *Roman Actor* (from which we have drawn the two previous extracts) is said to have been the preferred play of its author.

We may conclude directly from these quotations that Massinger's feeling for language had outstripped his feeling for things; that his eye and his vocabulary were not in co-operation. One of the greatest distinctions of several of his elder contemporaries – we name Middleton, Webster, Tourneur – is a gift for combining, for fusing into a single phrase, two or more diverse impressions.

. . . in her strong toil of grace

of Shakespeare is such a fusion; the metaphor identified itself with what suggests it; the resultant is one and is unique:

155

Does the silk worm expend *her* yellow labours? . . .
Why does yon fellow falsify highways
And lays his life between the judge's lips
To refine *such a one? keeps horse and men*
To beat their valours *for her?*

Let the common sewer take it from distinction. . . .
Lust and forgetfulness have been amongst us. . . .

These lines of Tourneur and of Middleton exhibit that perpetual slight alteration of language, words perpetually juxtaposed in new and sudden combinations, meanings perpetually *eingeschachtelt* into meanings, which evidences a very high development of the senses, a development of the English language which we have perhaps never equalled. And, indeed, with the end of Chapman, Middleton, Webster, Tourneur, Donne we end a period when the intellect was immediately at the tips of the senses. Sensation became word and word was sensation. The next period is the period of Milton (though still with a Marvell in it); and this period is initiated by Massinger.

It is not that the word becomes less exact. Massinger is, in a wholly eulogistic sense, choice and correct. And the decay of the senses is not inconsistent with a greater sophistication of language. But every vital development in language is a development of feeling as well. The verse of Shakespeare and the major Shakespearian dramatists is an innovation of this kind, a true mutation of species. The verse practised by Massinger is a different verse from that of his predecessors; but it is not a development based on, or resulting from, a new way of feeling. On the contrary, it seems to lead us away from feeling altogether.

We mean that Massinger must be placed as much at the beginning of one period as at the end of another. A certain Boyle, quoted by Mr. Cruickshank, says that Milton's blank verse owes much to the study of Massinger's.

In the indefinable touches which make up the music of a verse [says Boyle], in the artistic distribution of pauses, and in the unerring choice and grouping of just those words which strike the ear as the perfection of harmony, there are, if we leave Cyril Tourneur's *Atheist's Tragedy* out of the question, only two masters in the drama, Shakespeare in his latest period and Massinger.

This Boyle must have had a singular ear to have preferred Tourneur's secondary work to his *Revenger's Tragedy*, and one must think that he had never glanced at Ford. But though the
156

appraisal be ludicrous, the praise is not undeserved. Mr. Cruickshank has given us an excellent example of Massinger's syntax:

> *What though my father*
> *Writ man before he was so, and confirm'd it,*
> *By numbering that day no part of his life*
> *In which he did not service to his country;*
> *Was he to be free therefore from the laws*
> *And ceremonious form in your decrees?*
> *Or else because he did as much as man*
> *In those three memorable overthrows,*
> *At Granson, Morat, Nancy, where his master,*
> *The warlike Charalois, with whose misfortunes*
> *I bear his name, lost treasure, men, and life,*
> *To be excused from payment of those sums*
> *Which (his own patrimony spent) his zeal*
> *To serve his country forced him to take up?*

It is impossible to deny the masterly construction of this passage; perhaps there is not one living poet who could do the like. It is impossible to deny the originality. The language is pure and correct, free from muddiness or turbidity. Massinger does not confuse metaphors, or heap them one upon another. He is lucid, though not easy. But if Massinger's age, 'without being exactly corrupt, lacks moral fibre', Massinger's verse, without being exactly corrupt, suffers from cerebral anaemia. To say that an involved style is necessarily a bad style would be preposterous. But such a style should follow the involutions of a mode of perceiving, registering, and digesting impressions which is also involved. It is to be feared that the feeling of Massinger is simple and overlaid with received ideas. Had Massinger had a nervous system as refined as that of Middleton, Tourneur, Webster, or Ford, his style would be a triumph. But such a nature was not at hand, and Massinger precedes, not another Shakespeare, but Milton.

Massinger is, in fact, at a further remove from Shakespeare than that other precursor of Milton – John Fletcher. Fletcher was above all an opportunist, in his verse, in his momentary effects, never quite a pastiche; in his structure ready to sacrifice everything to the single scene. To Fletcher, because he was more intelligent, less will be forgiven. Fletcher had a cunning guess at feelings, and betrayed them; Massinger was unconscious and innocent. As an artisan of the theatre he is not inferior to Fletcher, and his best tragedies have an honester unity than *Bonduca*. But the unity is superficial. In the *Roman Actor* the development of

157

parts is out of all proportion to the central theme; in the *Un-natural Combat*, in spite of the deft handling of suspense and the quick shift from climax to a new suspense, the first part of the play is the hatred of Malefort for his son and the second part is his passion for his daughter. It is theatrical skill, not an artistic conscience arranging emotions, that holds the two parts together. In the *Duke of Milan* the appearance of Sforza at the Court of his conqueror only delays the action, or rather breaks the emotional rhythm. And we have named three of Massinger's best.

A dramatist who so skilfully welds together parts which have no reason for being together, who fabricates plays so well knit and so remote from unity, we should expect to exhibit the same synthetic cunning in character. Mr. Cruickshank, Coleridge, and Leslie Stephen are pretty well agreed that Massinger is no master of characterization. You can, in fact, put together heterogeneous parts to form a lively play; but a character, to be living, must be conceived from some emotional unity. A character is not to be composed of scattered observations of human nature, but of parts which are felt together. Hence it is that although Massinger's failure to draw a moving character is no greater than his failure to make a whole play, and probably springs from the same defective sensitiveness, yet the failure in character is more conspicuous and more disastrous. A 'living' character is not necessarily 'true to life'. It is a person whom we can see and hear, whether he be true or false to human nature as we know it. What the creator of character needs is not so much knowledge of motives as keen sensibility; the dramatist need not understand people; but he must be exceptionally aware of them. This awareness was not given to Massinger. He inherits the traditions of conduct, female chastity, hymeneal sanctity, the fashion of honour, without either criticizing or informing them from his own experience. In the earlier drama these conventions are merely a framework, or an alloy necessary for working the metal; the metal itself consisted of unique emotions resulting inevitably from the circumstances, resulting or inhering as inevitably as the properties of a chemical compound. Middleton's heroine, for instance, in *The Changeling*, exclaims in the well-known words:

> *Why, 'tis impossible thou canst be so wicked,*
> *To shelter such a cunning cruelty*
> *To make his death the murderer of my honour!*

The word 'honour' in such a situation is out of date, but the emotion of Beatrice at that moment, given the conditions, is as permanent and substantial as anything in human nature. The emotion of Othello in Act V. is the emotion of a man who discovers that the worst part of his own soul has been exploited by someone more clever than he; it is this emotion carried by the writer to a very high degree of intensity. Even in so late and so decayed a drama as that of Ford, the framework of emotions and morals of the time is only the vehicle for statements of feeling which are unique and imperishable: Ford's and Ford's only.

What may be considered corrupt or decadent in the morals of Massinger is not an alteration or diminution in morals; it is simply the disappearance of all the personal and real emotions which this morality supported and into which it introduced a kind of order. As soon as the emotions disappear the morality which ordered it appears hideous. Puritanism itself became repulsive only when it appeared as the survival of a restraint after the feelings which it restrained had gone. When Massinger's ladies resist temptation they do not appear to undergo any important emotion; they merely know what is expected of them; they manifest themselves to us as lubricious prudes. Any age has its conventions; and any age might appear absurd when its conventions get into the hands of a man like Massinger – a man, we mean, of so exceptionally superior a literary talent as Massinger's, and so paltry an imagination. The Elizabethan morality was an important convention; important because it was not consciously of one social class alone, because it provided a framework for emotions to which all classes could respond, and it hindered no feeling. It was not hypocritical, and it did not suppress; its dark corners are haunted by the ghost of Mary Fitton and perhaps greater. It is a subject which has not been sufficiently investigated. Fletcher and Massinger rendered it ridiculous; not by not believing it, but because they were men of great talents who could not vivify it; because they could not fit into it passionate, complete human characters.

The tragedy of Massinger is interesting chiefly according to the definition given before; the highest degree of verbal excellence compatible with the most rudimentary development of the senses. Massinger succeeds better in something which is not tragedy; in the romantic comedy. *A Very Woman* deserves all the praise that Swinburne, with his almost unerring gift of selection, has bestowed upon it. The probable collaboration of Fletcher had the happiest result; for certainly that admirable comic personage, the tipsy Borachia, is handled with more humour than we expect of Massinger. It is a play which would be enjoyable on the stage. The form, however, of romantic comedy is itself inferior and decadent. There is an inflexibility about the poetic drama which is by no means a matter of classical, or neoclassical, or pseudo-

159

classical law. The poetic drama might develop forms highly different from those of Greece or England, India or Japan. Conceded the utmost freedom, the romantic drama would yet remain inferior. The poetic drama must have an emotional unity, let the emotion be whatever you like. It must have a dominant tone; and if this be strong enough, the most heterogeneous emotions may be made to reinforce it. The romantic comedy is a skilful concoction of inconsistent emotion, a *revue* of emotion. *A Very Woman* is surpassingly well plotted. The debility of romantic drama does not depend upon extravagant setting, or preposterous events, or inconceivable coincidences: all these might be found in a serious tragedy or comedy. It consists in an internal incoherence of feelings, a concatenation of emotions which signifies nothing.

From this type of play, so eloquent of emotional disorder, there was no swing back of the pendulum. Changes never come by a simple reinfusion into the form which the life has just left. The romantic drama was not a new form. Massinger dealt not with emotions so much as with the social abstractions of emotions, more generalized and therefore more quickly and easily interchangeable within the confines of a single action. He was not guided by direct communications through the nerves. Romantic drama tended, accordingly, toward what is sometimes called the 'typical', but which is not the truly typical; for the *typical* figure in a drama is always particularized – an individual. The tendency of the romantic drama was towards a form which continued it in removing its more conspicuous vices, was towards a more severe external order. This form was the Heroic Drama. We look into Dryden's 'Essay on Heroic Plays', and we find that 'love and valour ought to be the subject of an heroic poem'. Massinger, in his destruction of the old drama, had prepared the way for Dryden. The intellect had perhaps exhausted the old conventions. It was not able to supply the impoverishment of feeling. . . .

ANDREW MARVELL

The tercentenary of the former member for Hull deserves not only the celebration proposed by that favoured borough, but a little serious reflection upon his writing. That is an act of piety, which is very different from the resurrection of a deceased reputation. Marvell has stood high for some years; his best poems are not very many, and not only must be well known, from the *Golden Treasury* and the *Oxford Book of English Verse*, but must also have been enjoyed by numerous readers. His grave needs neither rose nor rue nor laurel; there is no imaginary justice to be done; we may think about him, if there be need for thinking, for our own benefit, not his. To bring the poet back to life – the great, the perennial, task of criticism – is in this case to squeeze the drops of the essence of two or three poems; even confining ourselves to these, we may find some precious liquor unknown to the present age. Not to determine rank, but to isolate this quality, is the critical labour. The fact that of all Marvell's verse, which is itself not a great quantity, the really valuable part consists of a very few poems indicates that the unknown quality of which we speak is probably a literary rather than a personal quality; or, more truly, that it is a quality of a civilization, of a traditional habit of life. A poet like Donne, or like Baudelaire or Laforgue, may almost be considered the inventor of an attitude, a system of feeling or of morals. Donne is difficult to analyse: what appears at one time a curious personal point of view may at another time appear rather the precise concentration of a kind of feeling diffused in the air about him. Donne and his shroud, the shroud and his motive for wearing it, are inseparable, but they are not the same thing. The seventeenth century sometimes seems for more than a moment to gather up and to digest into its art all the experience of the human mind which (from the same point of view) the later centuries seem to have been partly engaged in repudiating. But Donne would have been an individual at any time and place; Marvell's best verse is the product of European, that is to say Latin, culture.

Out of that high style developed from Marlowe through Jonson (for Shakespeare does not lend himself to these genealogies) the seventeenth century separated two qualities: wit and magniloquence. Neither is as simple or as apprehensible as its name seems to imply, and the two are not in practice antithetical; both are conscious and cultivated, and the mind which cultivates one may cultivate the other. The actual poetry, of Marvell, of Cowley, of Milton, and of others, is a blend in varying proportions. And we must be on guard not to employ the terms with too wide a comprehension; for like the other fluid terms with which literary criticism deals, the meaning alters with the age, and for precision we must rely to some degree upon the literacy and good taste of the reader. The wit of the Caroline poets is not the wit of Shakespeare, and it is not the wit of Dryden, the great master of contempt, or of Pope, the great master of hatred, or of Swift, the great master of disgust. What is meant is some quality which is common to the songs in *Comus* and Cowley's Anacreontics and Marvell's Horatian Ode. It is more than a technical accomplishment, or the vocabulary and syntax of an epoch; it is, what we have designated tentatively as wit, a tough reasonableness beneath the slight lyric grace. You cannot find it in Shelley or Keats or Wordsworth; you cannot find more than an echo of it in Landor; still less in Tennyson or Browning; and among contemporaries Mr. Yeats is an Irishman and Mr. Hardy is a modern Englishman – that is to say, Mr. Hardy is without it and Mr. Yeats is outside of the tradition altogether. On the other hand, as it certainly exists in Lafontaine, there is a large part of it in Gautier. And of the magniloquence, the deliberate exploitation of the possibilities of magnificence in language which Milton used and abused, there is also use and even abuse in the poetry of Baudelaire.

Wit is not a quality that we are accustomed to associate with 'Puritan' literature, with Milton or with Marvell. But if so, we are at fault partly in our conception of wit and partly in our generalizations about the Puritans. And if the wit of Dryden or of Pope is not the only kind of wit in the language the rest is not merely a little merriment or a little levity or a little impropriety or a little epigram. And, on the other hand, the sense in which a man like Marvell is a 'Puritan' is restricted. The persons who opposed Charles I and the persons who supported the Commonwealth were not all of the flock of Zeal-of-the-land Busy or the United Grand Junction Ebenezer Temperance Association. Many of them were gentlemen of the time who merely believed, with considerable show of reason, that government by a Parliament of gentlemen was better than government by a Stuart; though they were, to that extent, Liberal Practitioners, they could hardly foresee the tea-meeting and the Dissidence of Dissent. Being men of education and culture, even of travel, some of them were exposed to that spirit of the age which was coming to be the French spirit of the age. This spirit, curiously enough, was quite opposed to the tendencies latent or the forces active in Puritanism; the contest does great damage to the poetry of Milton; Marvell, an active servant of the public, but a lukewarm partisan, and a poet on a smaller scale, is far less injured by it. His line on the statue of Charles II, 'It is such a King as no chisel can mend', may be set off against his criticism of the Great Rebellion: 'Men . . . ought and might have trusted the King'. Marvell, therefore, more a man of the century than a Puritan, speaks more clearly and unequivocally with the voice of his literary age than does Milton.

This voice speaks out uncommonly strong in the *Coy Mistress*. The theme is one of the great traditional commonplaces of European literature. It is the theme of *O mistress mine*, of *Gather ye rosebuds*, of *Go, lovely rose*; it is in the savage austerity of Lucretius and the intense levity of Catullus. Where the wit of Marvell renews the theme is in the variety and order of the images. In the first of the three paragraphs Marvell plays with a fancy which begins by pleasing and leads to astonishment.

> *Had we but world enough and time,*
> *This coyness, lady, were no crime,*
> *. . . I would*
> *Love you ten years before the Flood,*
> *And you should, if you please, refuse*
> *Till the conversion of the Jews;*
> *My vegetable love should grow*
> *Vaster than empires and more slow. . . .*

We notice the high speed, the succession of concentrated images, each magnifying the original fancy. When this process has been carried to the end and summed up, the poem turns suddenly with that surprise which has been one of the most important means of poetic effect since Homer:

> *But at my back I always hear*
> *Time's wingèd chariot hurrying near,*
> *And yonder all before us lie*
> *Deserts of vast eternity.*

A whole civilization resides in these lines:

> *Pallida Mors æquo pulsat pede pauperum tabernas,*
> *Regumque turris. . . .*

And not only Horace but Catullus himself:

> *Nobis, cum semel occidit brevis lux,*
> *Nox est perpetua una dormienda.*

The verse of Marvell has not the grand reverberation of Catullus's Latin; but the image of Marvell is certainly more comprehensive and penetrates greater depths than Horace's.

A modern poet, had he reached the height, would very likely have closed on this moral reflection. But the three strophes of Marvell's poem have something like a syllogistic relation to each other. After a close approach to the mood of Donne,

> *then worms shall try*
> *That long-preserved virginity . . .*
> *The grave's a fine and private place,*
> *But none, I think, do there embrace,*

the conclusion,

> *Let us roll all our strength and all*
> *Our sweetness up into one ball,*
> *And tear our pleasures with rough strife,*
> *Thorough the iron gates of life.*

It will hardly be denied that this poem contains wit; but it may not be evident that this wit forms the crescendo and diminuendo of a scale of great imaginative power. The wit is not only combined with, but fused into, the imagination. We can easily recognize a witty fancy in the successive images ('my *vegetable* love', 'till the conversion of the Jews'), but this fancy is not indulged, as it sometimes is by Cowley or Cleveland, for its own sake. It is structural decoration of a serious idea. In this it is superior to the fancy of *L'Allegro, Il Penseroso*, or the lighter and less successful poems of Keats. In fact, this alliance of levity and seriousness (by which the seriousness is intensified) is a characteristic of the sort of wit we are trying to identify. It is found in

> *Le squelette était invisible*
> *Au temps heureux de l'art païen!*

of Gautier, and in the *dandysme* of Baudelaire and Laforgue. It is in the poem of Catullus which has been quoted, and in the variation by Ben Jonson:

Cannot we delude the eyes
Of a few poor household spies?
'Tis no sin love's fruits to steal;
But the sweet thefts to reveal,
To be taken, to be seen,
These have crimes accounted been.

It is in Propertius and Ovid. It is a quality of a sophisticated literature; a quality which expands in English literature just at the moment before the English mind altered; it is not a quality which we should expect Puritanism to encourage. When we come to Gray and Collins, the sophistication remains only in the language, and has disappeared from the feeling. Gray and Collins were masters, but they had lost that hold on human values, that firm grasp of human experience, which is a formidable achievement of the Elizabethan and Jacobean poets. This wisdom, cynical perhaps but untired (in Shakespeare, a terrifying clairvoyance), leads toward, and is only completed by, the religious comprehension; it leads to the point of the *Ainsi tout leur a craqué dans la main* of Bouvard and Pécuchet.

The difference between imagination and fancy, in view of this poetry of wit, is a very narrow one. Obviously, an image which is immediately and unintentionally ridiculous is merely a fancy. In the poem *Upon Appleton House*, Marvell falls in with one of these undesirable images, describing the attitude of the house toward its master:

Yet thus the leaden house does sweat,
And scarce endures the master great;
But, where he comes, the swelling hall
Stirs, and the square grows spherical;

which, whatever its intention, is more absurd than it was intended to be. Marvell also falls into the even commoner error of images which are over-developed or distracting; which support nothing but their own misshapen bodies:

And now the salmon-fishers moist
Their leathern boats begin to hoist;
And, like Antipodes in shoes,
Have shod their heads in their canoes.

Of this sort of image a choice collection may be found in Johnson's *Life of Cowley*. But the images in the *Coy Mistress* are not only witty, but satisfy the elucidation of Imagination given by Coleridge:

165

This power . . . reveals itself in the balance or reconcilement of opposite or discordant qualities: of sameness, with difference; of the general, with the concrete; the idea with the image; the individual with the representative; the sense of novelty and freshness with old and familiar objects; a more than usual state of emotion with more than usual order; judgment ever awake and steady self-possession with enthusiasm and feeling profound or vehement. . . .

Coleridge's statement applies also to the following verses, which are selected because of their similarity, and because they illustrate the marked caesura which Marvell often introduces in a short line:

> *The tawny mowers enter next,*
> *Who seem like Israelites to be*
> *Walking on foot through a green sea. . . .*

> *And now the meadows fresher dyed,*
> *Whose grass, with moister colour dashed,*
> *Seems as green silks but newly washed. . . .*

> *He hangs in shades the orange bright,*
> *Like golden lamps in a green night. . . .*

> *Annihilating all that's made*
> *To a green thought in a green shade. . . .*

> *Had it lived long, it would have been*
> *Lilies without, roses within.*

The whole poem, from which the last of these quotations is drawn (*The Nymph and the Fawn*), is built upon a very slight foundation, and we can imagine what some of our modern practitioners of slight themes would have made of it. But we need not descend to an invidious contemporaneity to point the difference. Here are six lines from *The Nymph and the Fawn*:

> *I have a garden of my own,*
> *But so with roses overgrown*
> *And lilies, that you would it guess*
> *To be a little wilderness;*
> *And all the spring-time of the year*
> *It only lovèd to be there.*

And here are five lines from *The Nymph's Song to Hylas* in the *Life and Death of Jason*, by William Morris:

I know a little garden close
Set thick with lily and red rose.
Where I would wander if I might
From dewy dawn to dewy night,
And have one with me wandering.

So far the resemblance is more striking than the difference, although we might just notice the vagueness of allusion in the last line to some indefinite person, form, or phantom, compared with the more explicit reference of emotion to object which we should expect from Marvell. But in the latter part of the poem Morris divaricates widely:

Yet tottering as I am, and weak,
Still have I left a little breath
To seek within the jaws of death
An entrance to that happy place;
To seek the unforgotten face
Once seen, once kissed, once reft from me
Anigh the murmuring of the sea.

Here the resemblance, if there is any, is to the latter part of *The Coy Mistress*. As for the difference, it could not be more pronounced. The effect of Morris's charming poem depends upon the mistiness of the feeling and the vagueness of its object; the effect of Marvell's upon its bright, hard precision. And this precision is not due to the fact that Marvell is concerned with cruder or simpler or more carnal emotions. The emotion of Morris is not more refined or more spiritual; it is merely more vague: if anyone doubts whether the more refined or spiritual emotion can be precise, he should study the treatment of the varieties of discarnate emotion in the *Paradiso*. A curious result of the comparison of Morris's poem with Marvell's is that the former, though it appears to be more serious, is found to be the slighter; and Marvell's *Nymph and the Fawn*, appearing more slight, is the more serious.

So weeps the wounded balsam; so
The holy frankincense doth flow;
The brotherless Heliades
Melt in such amber tears as these.

These verses have the suggestiveness of true poetry; and the verses of Morris, which are nothing if not an attempt to suggest, really suggest nothing; and we are inclined to infer that the suggestiveness is the aura around a bright clear centre, that you cannot have the aura alone. The day-dreamy feeling of Morris is essentially a slight thing; Marvell takes a slight affair, the feeling of a girl for her pet, and gives it a connection with that inexhaustible and terrible nebula of emotion which surrounds all our exact and practical passions and mingles with them. Again, Marvell does this in a poem which, because of its formal pastoral machinery, may appear a trifling object:

CLORINDA. *Near this, a fountain's liquid bell*
Tinkles within the concave shell.
DAMON. *Might a soul bathe there and be clean,*
Or slake its drought?

where we find that a metaphor has suddenly rapt us to the image of spiritual purgation. There is here the element of *surprise*, as when Villon says:

Necessité faict gens mesprendre
Et faim saillir le loup des boys,

the surprise which Poe considered of the highest importance, and also the restraint and quietness of tone which makes the surprise possible. And in the verses of Marvell which have been quoted there is the making the familiar strange, and the strange familiar, which Coleridge attributed to good poetry.

The effort to construct a dream world, which alters English poetry so greatly in the nineteenth century, a dream world utterly different from the visionary realities of the *Vita Nuova* or of the poetry of Dante's contemporaries, is a problem of which various explanations may no doubt be found; in any case, the result makes a poet of the nineteenth century, of the same size as Marvell, a more trivial and less serious figure. Marvell is no greater personality than William Morris, but he had something much more solid behind him: he had the vast and penetrating influence of Ben Jonson. Jonson never wrote anything purer than Marvell's *Horatian Ode*; this ode has that same quality of wit which was diffused over the whole Elizabethan product and concentrated in the work of Jonson. And, as was said before, this wit which pervades the poetry of Marvell is more Latin, more refined, than anything that succeeded it. The great danger, as well as the greatest interest and excitement, of English prose and verse, compared with French, is that it permits and justifies an exaggeration of particular qualities to the exclusion of others. Dryden was great in wit, as Milton in magniloquence; but the former, by isolating this quality and making it by itself into great poetry, and the latter, by coming to dispense with it altogether, may perhaps have injured the language. In Dryden wit becomes almost fun, and thereby loses some contact with reality; becomes pure fun, which French wit almost never is.

> *The midwife placed her hand on his thick skull,*
> *With this prophetic blessing:* Be thou dull. . . .

> *A numerous host of dreaming saints succeed,*
> *Of the true old enthusiastic breed.*

This is audacious and splendid; it belongs to satire beside which Marvell's Satires are random babbling, but it is perhaps as exaggerated as:

> *Oft he seems to hide his face,*
> *But unexpectedly returns,*
> *And to his faithful champion hath in place*
> *Bore witness gloriously; whence* Gaza mourns,
> *And all that band them to resist*
> *His uncontrollable intent.*

How oddly the sharp Dantesque phrase 'whence Gaza mourns' springs out from the brilliant contortions of Milton's sentence!

> *Who from his private gardens, where*
> *He lived reservèd and austere,*
> *(As if his highest plot*
> *To plant the bergamot)*

> *Could by industrious valour climb*
> *To ruin the great work of Time,*
> *And cast the kingdoms old*
> *Into another mold;*

> .   .   .   .

> *The Pict no shelter now shall find*
> *Within his parti-coloured mind,*
> *But, from this valour sad,*
> *Shrink underneath the plaid:*

There is here an equipoise, a balance and proportion of tones, which, while it cannot raise Marvell to the level of Dryden or Milton, extorts an approval which these poets do not receive from us, and bestows a pleasure at least different in kind from any they can often give. It is what makes Marvell a classic; or classic in a sense in which Gray and Collins are not; for the latter, with all their accredited purity, are comparatively poor in shades of feeling to contrast and unite.

We are baffled in the attempt to translate the quality indicated by the dim and antiquated term wit into the equally unsatisfactory nomenclature of our own time. Even Cowley is only able to define it by negatives:

> *Comely in thousand shapes appears;*
> *Yonder we saw it plain ; and here 'tis now,*
> *Like spirits in a place, we know not how.*

It has passed out of our critical coinage altogether, and no new term has been struck to replace it; the quality seldom exists, and is never recognized.

> *In a true piece of Wit all things must be*
> *Yet all things there agree;*
> *As in the Ark, join'd without force or strife,*
> *All creatures dwelt, all creatures that had life.*
> *Or as the primitive forms of all*
> *(If we compare great things with small)*
> *Which, without discord or confusion, lie*
> *In that strange mirror of the Deity.*

So far Cowley has spoken well. But if we are to attempt even no more than Cowley, we, placed in a retrospective attitude, must risk much more than anxious generalizations. With our eye still on Marvell, we can say that wit is not erudition; it is sometimes stifled by erudition, as in much of Milton. It is not cynicism, though it has a kind of toughness which may be confused with cynicism by the tender-minded. It is confused with erudition because it belongs to an educated mind, rich in generations of experience; and it is confused with cynicism because it implies a constant inspection and criticism of experience. It involves, probably, a recognition, implicit in the expression of every experience, of other kinds of experience which are possible, which we find as clearly in the greatest as in poets like Marvell. Such a general statement may seem to take us a long way from *The Nymph and the Fawn*, or even from the *Horatian Ode*; but it is perhaps justified by the desire to account for that precise taste of Marvell's which finds for him the proper degree of seriousness for every subject which he treats. His errors of taste, when he trespasses, are not sins against this virtue; they are conceits, distended

170

metaphors and similes, but they never consist in taking a subject too seriously or too lightly. This virtue of wit is not a peculiar quality of minor poets, or of the minor poets of one age or of one school; it is an intellectual quality which perhaps only becomes noticeable by itself, in the work of lesser poets. Furthermore, it is absent from the work of Wordsworth, Shelley, and Keats, on whose poetry nineteenth-century criticism has unconsciously been based. To the best of their poetry wit is irrelevant:

> *Art thou pale for weariness*
> *Of climbing heaven and gazing on the earth,*
> *Wandering companionless*
> *Among the stars that have a different birth,*
> *And ever changing, like a joyless eye,*
> *That finds no object worth its constancy?*

We should find it difficult to draw any useful comparison between these lines of Shelley and anything by Marvell. But later poets, who would have been the better for Marvell's quality, were without it; even Browning seems oddly immature, in some way, beside Marvell. And nowadays we find occasionally good irony, or satire, which lack wit's internal equilibrium, because their voices are essentially protests against some outside sentimentality or stupidity; or we find serious poets who seem afraid of acquiring wit, lest they lose intensity. The quality which Marvell had, this modest and certainly impersonal virtue – whether we call it wit or reason, or even urbanity – we have patently failed to define. By whatever name we call it, and however we define that name, it is something precious and needed and apparently extinct; it is what should preserve the reputation of Marvell. *C'était une belle âme, comme on ne fait plus à Londres.*

MARIE LLOYD

It requires some effort to understand why one person, among many who do a thing with accomplished skill, should be greater than the others; and it is not always easy to distinguish superiority from great popularity, when the two go together. Although I have always admired the genius of Marie Lloyd I do not think that I always appreciated its uniqueness; I certainly did not realize that her death would strike me as the important event that it was. Marie Lloyd was the greatest music-hall artist of her time in England: she was also the most popular. And popularity in her case was not merely evidence of her accomplishment; it was something more than success. It is evidence of the extent to which she represented and expressed that part of the English nation which has perhaps the greatest vitality and interest.

Among all of that small number of music-hall performers, whose names are familiar to what is called the lower class, Marie Lloyd had far the strongest hold on popular affection. The attitude of audiences toward Marie Lloyd was different from their attitude toward any other of their favourites of that day, and this difference represents the difference in her art. Marie Lloyd's audiences were invariably sympathetic, and it was through this sympathy that she controlled them. Among living music-hall artists none can better control an audience than Nellie Wallace. I have seen Nellie Wallace interrupted by jeering or hostile comment from a boxful of Eastenders; I have seen her, hardly pausing in her act, make some quick retort that silenced her tormentors for the rest of the evening. But I have never known Marie Lloyd to be confronted by this kind of hostility; in any case, the feeling of the vast majority of the audience was so manifestly on her side, that no objector would have dared to lift his voice. And the difference is this: that whereas other comedians amuse their audiences as much and sometimes more than Marie Lloyd, no other comedian succeeded so well in giving expression to the life of that audience, in raising it to a kind of art. It was, I think, this capacity for expressing the soul of the people that made Marie Lloyd unique, and that made her audiences, even when they joined in the chorus, not so much hilarious as happy.

In the details of acting Marie Lloyd was perhaps the most perfect, in her own style, of British actresses. There are no cinema records of her; she never descended to this form of money-making; it is to be regretted, however, that there is no film of her to preserve for the recollection of her admirers the perfect expressiveness of her smallest gestures. But it is less in the accomplishment of her act than in what she made it, that she differed from other comedians. There was nothing about her of the grotesque; none of her comic appeal was due to exaggeration; it was all a matter of selection and concentration. The most remarkable of the survivors of the music-hall stage, to my mind, are Nellie Wallace and Little Tich;[1] but each of these is a kind of grotesque; their acts are an orgy of parody of the human race. For this reason, the appreciation of these artists requires less knowledge of the environment. To appreciate, for instance, the last turn in which Marie Lloyd appeared, one ought to know what objects a middle-aged woman of the char-woman class would carry in her bag; exactly how she would go through her bag in search of something; and exactly the tone of voice in which she would enumerate the objects she found in it. This was only part of the acting in Marie Lloyd's last song, 'One of the Ruins that Cromwell Knocked Abaht a Bit'.

Marie Lloyd's art will, I hope, be discussed by more competent critics of the theatre than I. My own chief point is that I consider her superiority over other performers to be in a way a moral superiority: it was her understanding of the people and sympathy with them, and the people's recognition of the fact that she embodied the virtues which they genuinely most respected in private life, that raised her to the position she occupied at her death. And her death is itself a significant moment in English history. I have called her the expressive figure of the lower classes. There is no such expressive figure for any other class. The middle classes have no such idol: the middle classes are morally corrupt. That is to say, their own life fails to find a Marie Lloyd to express it; nor have they any independent virtues which might give them as a conscious class any dignity. The middle classes, in England as elsewhere, under democracy, are morally dependent upon the aristocracy, and the aristocracy are subordinate to the middle class, which is gradually absorbing and destroying them. The lower class still exists; but perhaps it will not exist for long. In the music-hall comedians they find the expression and dignity of their own lives; and this is not found in the most elaborate and expensive revue. In England, at any rate, the revue expresses

[1] Without prejudice to the younger generation.

almost nothing. With the decay of the music-hall, with the encroachment of the cheap and rapid-breeding cinema, the lower classes will tend to drop into the same state of protoplasm as the bourgeoisie. The working man who went to the music-hall and saw Marie Lloyd and joined in the chorus was himself performing part of the act; he was engaged in that collaboration of the audience with the artist which is necessary in all art and most obviously in dramatic art. He will now go to the cinema, where his mind is lulled by continuous senseless music and continuous action too rapid for the brain to act upon, and will receive, without giving, in that same listless apathy with which the middle and upper classes regard any entertainment of the nature of art. He will also have lost some of his interest in life. Perhaps this will be the only solution. In an interesting essay in the volume of *Essays on the Depopulation of Melanesia*, the psychologist W. H. R. Rivers adduced evidence which has led him to believe that the natives of that unfortunate archipelago are dying out principally for the reason that the 'Civilization' forced upon them has deprived them of all interest in life. They are dying from pure boredom. When every theatre has been replaced by 100 cinemas, when every musical instrument has been replaced by 100 gramophones, when every horse has been replaced by 100 cheap motorcars, when electrical ingenuity has made it possible for every child to hear its bedtime stories from a loudspeaker, when applied science has done everything possible with the materials on this earth to make life as interesting as possible, it will not be surprising if the population of the entire civilized world rapidly follows the fate of the Melanesians.[1]

[1] These lines were written nine years ago [Ed. of 1932].

ULYSSES, ORDER, AND MYTH[1]

Mr. Joyce's book has been out long enough for no more general expression of praise, or expostulation with its detractors, to be necessary; and it has not been out long enough for any attempt at a complete measurement of its place and significance to be possible. All that one can usefully do at this time, and it is a great deal to do, for such a book, is to elucidate any aspect of the book – and the number of aspects is indefinite – which has not yet been fixed. I hold this book to be the most important expression which the present age has found; it is a book to which we are all indebted, and from which none of us can escape. These are postulates for anything that I have to say about it, and I have no wish to waste the reader's time by elaborating my eulogies; it has given me all the surprise, delight, and terror that I can require, and I will leave it at that.

Among all the criticisms I have seen of the book, I have seen nothing – unless we except, in its way, M. Valéry Larbaud's valuable paper which is rather an Introduction than a criticism – which seemed to me to appreciate the significance of the method employed – the parallel to the *Odyssey*, and the use of appropriate styles and symbols to each division. Yet one might expect this to be the first peculiarity to attract attention; but it has been treated as an amusing dodge, or scaffolding erected by the author for the purpose of disposing his realistic tale, of no interest in the completed structure. The criticism which Mr. Aldington directed upon *Ulysses* several years ago seems to me to fail by this oversight – but, as Mr. Aldington wrote before the complete work had appeared, fails more honourably than the attempts of those who had the whole book before them. Mr. Aldington treated Mr. Joyce as a prophet of chaos; and wailed at the flood of Dadaism which his prescient eye saw bursting forth at the tap of the magician's rod. Of course, the influence which Mr. Joyce's book may have is from my point of view an irrelevance. A very great book may have a very bad influence indeed; and a mediocre book

[1] This article appeared in *The Dial*, November, 1923.

may be in the event most salutary. The next generation is responsible for its own soul; a man of genius is responsible to his peers, not to a studio full of uneducated and undisciplined coxcombs. Still, Mr. Aldington's pathetic solicitude for the half-witted seems to me to carry certain implications about the nature of the book itself to which I cannot assent; and this is the important issue. He finds the book, if I understand him, to be an invitation to chaos, and an expression of feelings which are perverse, partial, and a distortion of reality. But unless I quote Mr. Aldington's words I am likely to falsify. 'I say, moreover,' he says,[1] 'that when Mr. Joyce, with his marvellous gifts, uses them to disgust us with mankind, he is doing something which is false and a libel on humanity.' It is somewhat similar to the opinion of the urbane Thackeray upon Swift. 'As for the moral, I think it horrible, shameful, unmanly, blasphemous: and giant and great as this Dean is, I say we should hoot him.' (This, of the conclusion of the Voyage to the Houyhnhnms – which seems to me one of the greatest triumphs that the human soul has ever achieved. It is true that Thackeray later pays Swift one of the finest tributes that a man has ever given or received: 'So great a man he seems to me that thinking of him is like thinking of an empire falling.' And Mr. Aldington, in his time, is almost equally generous.)

Whether it is possible to libel humanity (in distinction to libel in the usual sense, which is libelling an individual or a group in contrast with the rest of humanity) is a question for philosophical societies to discuss; but of course if *Ulysses* were a 'libel' it would simply be a forged document, a powerless fraud, which would never have extracted from Mr. Aldington a moment's attention. I do not wish to linger over this point: the interesting question is that begged by Mr. Aldington when he refers to Mr. Joyce's 'great *undisciplined* talent'.

I think that Mr. Aldington and I are more or less agreed as to what we want in principle, and agreed to call it classicism. It is because of this agreement that I have chosen Mr. Aldington to attack on the present issue. We are agreed as to what we want, but not as to how to get it, or as to what contemporary writing exhibits a tendency in that direction. We agree, I hope, that 'classicism' is not an alternative to 'romanticism', as of political parties, Conservative and Liberal, Republican and Democrat, on a 'turn-the-rascals-out' platform. It is a goal toward which all good literature strives, so far as it is good, according to the possibilities of its place and time. One can be 'classical', in a sense, by turning away from nine-tenths of the material which lies at hand and selecting

[1] *English Review*, April, 1921.

only mummified stuff from a museum – like some contemporary writers, about whom one could say some nasty things in this connection, if it were worth while (Mr. Aldington is not one of them). Or one can be classical in tendency by doing the best one can with the material at hand. The confusion springs from the fact that the term is applied to literature and to the whole complex of interests and modes of behaviour and society of which literature is a part; and it has not the same bearing in both applications. It is much easier to be a classicist in literary criticism than in creative art – because in criticism you are responsible only for what you want, and in creation you are responsible for what you can do with material which you must simply accept. And in this material I include the emotions and feelings of the writer himself, which, for that writer, are simply material which he must accept – not virtues to be enlarged or vices to be diminished. The question, then, about Mr. Joyce, is: how much living material does he deal with, and how does he deal with it. deal with, not as a legislator or exhorter, but as an artist?

It is here that Mr. Joyce's parallel use of the *Odyssey* has a great importance. It has the importance of a scientific discovery. No one else has built a novel upon such a foundation before: it has never before been necessary. I am not begging the question in calling *Ulysses* a 'novel'; and if you call it an epic it will not matter. If it is not a novel, that is simply because the novel is a form which will no longer serve; it is because the novel, instead of being a form, was simply the expression of an age which had not sufficiently lost all form to feel the need of something stricter. Mr. Joyce has written one novel – the *Portrait*; Mr. Wyndham Lewis has written one novel – *Tarr*. I do not suppose that either of them will ever write another 'novel'. The novel ended with Flaubert and with James. It is, I think, because Mr. Joyce and Mr. Lewis, being 'in advance' of their time, felt a conscious or probably unconscious dissatisfaction with the form, that their novels are more formless than those of a dozen clever writers who are unaware of its obsolescence.

In using the myth, in manipulating a continuous parallel between contemporaneity and antiquity, Mr. Joyce is pursuing a method which others must pursue after him. They will not be imitators, any more than the scientist who uses the discoveries of an Einstein in pursuing his own, independent, further investigations. It is simply a way of controlling, of ordering, of giving a shape and a significance to the immense panorama of futility and anarchy which is contemporary history. It is a method already adumbrated by Mr. Yeats, and of the need for which I believe Mr. Yeats to have been the first contemporary to be conscious. It is a method for which the horoscope is auspicious. Psychology (such as it is, and whether our reaction to it be comic or serious), ethnology, and *The Golden Bough* have concurred to make possible what was impossible even a few years ago. Instead of narrative method, we may now use the mythical method. It is, I seriously believe, a step toward making the modern world possible for art, toward that order and form which Mr. Aldington so earnestly desires. And only those who have won their own discipline in secret and without aid, in a world which offers very little assistance to that end, can be of any use in furthering this advance.

LANCELOT ANDREWES

The Right Reverend Father in God, Lancelot Bishop of Winchester, died on September 25, 1626. During his lifetime he enjoyed a distinguished reputation for the excellence of his sermons, for the conduct of his diocese, for his ability in controversy displayed against Cardinal Bellarmine, and for the decorum and devotion of his private life. Some years after Andrewes's death Lord Clarendon, in his *History of the Rebellion*, expressed regret that Andrewes had not been chosen instead of Abbott to the Archbishopric of Canterbury, for thus affairs in England might have taken a different course. By authorities on the history of the English Church Andrewes is still accorded a high, perhaps the highest, place; among persons interested in devotion his *Private Prayers* are not unknown. But among those persons who read sermons, if they read them at all, as specimens of English prose, Andrewes is little known. His sermons are too well built to be readily quotable; they stick too closely to the point to be entertaining. Yet they rank with the finest English prose of their time, of any time. Before attempting to remove the remains of his reputation to a last resting place in the dreary cemetery of literature, it is desirable to remind the reader of Andrewes's position in history.

The Church of England is the creation not of the reign of Henry VIII or of the reign of Edward VI, but of the reign of Elizabeth. The *via media* which is the spirit of Anglicanism was the spirit of Elizabeth in all things; the last of the humble Welsh family of Tudor was the first and most complete incarnation of English policy. The taste or sensibility of Elizabeth, developed by her intuitive knowledge of the right policy for the hour and her ability to choose the right men to carry out that policy, determined the future of the English Church. In its persistence in finding a mean between Papacy and Presbytery the English Church under Elizabeth became something representative of the finest spirit of England of the time. It came to reflect not only the personality of Elizabeth herself, but the best community of her subjects of every rank. Other religious impulses, of varying

179

degrees of spiritual value, were to assert themselves with greater vehemence during the next two reigns. But the Church at the end of the reign of Elizabeth, and as developed in certain directions under the next reign, was a masterpiece of ecclesiastical states-manship. The same authority that made use of Gresham, and of Walsingham, and of Cecil, appointed Parker to the Archbishopric of Canterbury; the same authority was later to appoint Whitgift to the same office.

To the ordinary cultivated student of civilization the genesis of a Church is of little interest, and at all events we must not con-found the history of a Church with its spiritual meaning. To the ordinary observer the English Church in history means Hooker and Jeremy Taylor – and should mean Andrewes also: it means George Herbert, and it means the churches of Christopher Wren. This is not an error: a Church is to be judged by its intellectual fruits, by its influence on the sensibility of the most sensitive and on the intellect of the most intelligent, and it must be made real to the eye by monuments of artistic merit. The English Church has no literary monument equal to that of Dante, no intellectual monument equal to that of St. Thomas, no devotional monument equal to that of St. John of the Cross, no building so beautiful as the Cathedral of Modena or the basilica of St. Zeno in Verona. But there are those for whom the City churches are as precious as any of the four hundred odd churches in Rome which are in no danger of demolition, and for whom St. Paul's, in comparison with St. Peter's, is not lacking in decency; and the English devotional verse of the seventeenth century – admitting the one difficult case of conversion, that of Crashaw – finer than that of any other country or religious communion at the time.

The intellectual achievement and the prose style of Hooker and Andrewes came to complete the structure of the English Church as the philosophy of the thirteenth century crowns the Catholic Church. To make this statement is not to compare the *Laws of Ecclesiastical Polity* with the *Summa*. The seventeenth century was not an age in which the Churches occupied themselves with metaphysics, and none of the writings of the fathers of the English Church belongs to the category of speculative philosophy. But the achievement of Hooker and Andrewes was to make the English Church more worthy of intellectual assent. No religion can survive the judgment of history unless the best minds of its time have collaborated in its construction; if the Church of Elizabeth is worthy of the age of Shakespeare and Jonson, that is because of the work of Hooker and Andrewes.

The writings of both Hooker and Andrewes illustrate that determination to stick to essentials, that awareness of the needs of

180

the time, the desire for clarity and precision on matters of importance, and the indifference to matters indifferent, which was the general policy of Elizabeth. These characteristics are illustrated in the definition of the Church in the second book of the *Ecclesiastical Polity*. ('The Church of Christ which was from the beginning is and continueth until the end.') And in both Hooker and Andrewes – the latter the friend and intimate of Isaac Casaubon – we find also that breadth of culture, an ease with humanism and Renaissance learning, which helped to put them on terms of equality with their continental antagonists and to elevate their Church above the position of a local heretical sect. They were fathers of a national Church and they were Europeans. Compare a sermon of Andrewes with a sermon by another earlier master, Latimer. It is not merely that Andrewes knew Greek, or that Latimer was addressing a far less cultivated public, or that the sermons of Andrewes are peppered with allusion and quotation. It is rather that Latimer, the preacher of Henry VIII and Edward VI, is merely a Protestant; but the voice of Andrewes is the voice of a man who has a formed visible Church behind him, who speaks with the old authority and the new culture. It is the difference of negative and positive: Andrewes is the first great preacher of the English Catholic Church.

The sermons of Andrewes are not easy reading. They are only for the reader who can elevate himself to the subject. The most conspicuous qualities of the style are three: ordonnance, or arrangement and structure, precision in the use of words, and relevant intensity. The last remains to be defined. All of them are best elucidated by comparison with a prose which is much more widely known, but to which I believe that we must assign a lower place – that of Donne. Donne's sermons, or fragments from Donne's sermons, are certainly known to hundreds who have hardly heard of Andrewes; and they are known precisely for the reasons because of which they are inferior to those of Andrewes. In the introduction to an admirable selection of passages from Donne's sermons, which was published a few years ago by the Oxford Press, Mr. Logan Pearsall Smith, after 'trying to explain Donne's sermons and account for them in a satisfactory manner', observes:

And yet in these, as in his poems, there remains something baffling and enigmatic which still eludes our last analysis. Reading these old hortatory and dogmatic pages, the thought suggests itself that Donne is often saying something else, something poignant and personal, and yet, in the end, incommunicable to us.

We may cavil at the word 'incommunicable', and pause to ask

181

whether the incommunicable is not often the vague and un-
formed; but the statement is essentially right. About Donne there
hangs the shadow of the impure motive; and impure motives lend
their aid to a facile success. He is a little of the religious spell-
binder, the Reverend Billy Sunday of his time, the flesh-creeper,
the sorcerer of emotional orgy. We emphasize this aspect to the
point of the grotesque. Donne had a trained mind; but without
belittling the intensity or the profundity of his experience, we can
suggest that this experience was not perfectly controlled, and that
he lacked spiritual discipline.

But Bishop Andrewes is one of the community of the born
spiritual, one

> *che in questo mondo,*
> *contemplando, gustò di quella pace.*

Intellect and sensibility were in harmony; and hence arise the
particular qualities of his style. Those who would prove this
harmony would do well to examine, before proceeding to the
sermons, the volume of *Preces Privatæ*. This book, composed by
him for his private devotions, was printed only after his death; a
few manuscript copies may have been given away during his lifetime – one bears the name of William Laud. It appears to have
been written in Latin and translated by him into Greek; some of
it is in Hebrew; it has been several times translated into English.
The most recent edition is the translation of the late F. E.
Brightman, with an interesting introduction (Methuen, 1903).
They are almost wholly an arrangement of Biblical texts, and of
texts from elsewhere in Andrewes's immense theological reading.
Dr. Brightman has a paragraph of admirable criticism of these
prayers which deserves to be quoted in full:

But the structure is not merely an external scheme or framework: the
internal structure is as close as the external. Andrewes develops an idea
he has in his mind: every line tells and adds something. He does not
expatiate, but moves forward: if he repeats, it is because the repetition
has a real force of expression; if he accumulates, each new word or
phrase represents a new development, a substantive addition to what
he is saying. He assimilates his material and advances by means of it.
His quotation is not decoration or irrelevance, but the matter in which
he expresses what he wants to say. His single thoughts are no doubt
often suggested by the words he borrows, but the thoughts are made
his own, and the constructive force, the fire that fuses them, is his own.
And this internal, progressive, often poetic structure is marked out-
wardly. The editions have not always reproduced this feature of the
Preces, nor perhaps is it possible in any ordinary page to represent the

structure adequately; but in the manuscript the intention is clear enough. The prayers are arranged, not merely in paragraphs, but in lines advanced and recessed, so as in a measure to mark the inner structure and the steps and stages of the movement. Both in form and in matter Andrewes's prayers may often be described rather as hymns.

The first part of this excellent piece of criticism may be applied equally well to the prose of Andrewes's sermons. The prayers themselves, which, as Canon Brightman seems to hint, should take for Anglicans a place beside the Exercises of St. Ignatius and the works of St. François de Sales, illustrate the devotion to private prayer (Andrewes is said to have passed nearly five hours a day in prayer) and to public ritual which Andrewes bequeathed to William Laud; and his passion for order in religion is reflected in his passion for order in prose.

Readers who hesitate before the five large volumes of Andrewes's sermons in *The Library of Anglo-Catholic Theology* may find their introduction more easy through the *Seventeen Sermons on the Nativity*, which were published separately in a small volume by Griffith Farran Okeden and Welsh, in *The Ancient and Modern Library of Theological Literature*, and which can still be picked up here and there. It is an additional advantage that these sermons are all on the same subject, the Incarnation; they are the Christmas Day sermons preached before King James between 1605 and 1624. And in the sermons preached before King James, himself a theologian, Andrewes was not hampered as he sometimes was in addressing more popular audiences. His erudition had full play, and his erudition is essential to his originality.

Bishop Andrewes, as was hinted above, tried to confine himself in his sermons to the elucidation of what he considered essential in dogma; he said himself that in sixteen years he had never alluded to the question of predestination, to which the Puritans, following their continental brethren, attached so much importance. The Incarnation was to him an essential dogma, and we are able to compare seventeen developments of the same idea. Reading Andrewes on such a theme is like listening to a great Hellenist expounding a text of the *Posterior Analytics*: altering the punctuation, inserting or removing a comma or a semi-colon to make an obscure passage suddenly luminous, dwelling on a single word, comparing its use in its nearer and in its most remote contexts, purifying a disturbed or cryptic lecture-note into lucid profundity. To persons whose minds are habituated to feed on the vague jargon of our time, when we have a vocabulary for everything and exact ideas about nothing – when a word half understood, torn from its place in some alien or half-formed science, as of psychology, conceals from both writer and reader the meaninglessness of a statement, when all dogma is in doubt except the dogmas of sciences of which we have read in the news-papers, when the language of theology itself, under the influence of an undisciplined mysticism of popular philosophy, tends to become a language of tergiversation – Andrewes may seem pedantic and verbal. It is only when we have saturated ourselves in his prose, followed the movement of his thought, that we find his examination of words terminating in the ecstasy of assent. Andrewes takes a word and derives the world from it; squeezing and squeezing the word until it yields a full juice of meaning which we should never have supposed any word to possess. In this process the qualities which we have mentioned, of ordon-nance and precision, are exercised.

Take, almost at random, a passage from Andrewes's exposition of the text, 'For unto you is born this day in the city of David a Saviour, which is Christ the Lord'. (Luke ii. 11). Any passage that we can choose must be torn violently from its context.

Who is it? Three things are said of this Child by the Angel. (1) He is 'a Saviour'. (2) 'Which is Christ'. (3) 'Christ the Lord.' Three of his titles, well and orderly inferred one of another by good consequence. We cannot miss one of them; they be necessary all. Our method on earth is to begin with great; in heaven they begin with good first.

First, then, 'a Saviour'; that is His name, Jesus, *Soter*; and in that Name His benefit, *Salus*, 'saving health or salvation'. Such a name as the great Orator himself saith of it, *Soter, hoc quantum est? Ita magnum est ut latino uno verbo exprimi non possit.* 'This name Saviour is so great as no one word can express the force of it.'

But we are not so much to regard the *ecce* how great it is, as *gaudium* what joy is in it; that is the point we are to speak to. And for that, men may talk what they will, but sure there is no joy in the world to the joy of a man saved; no joy so great, no news so welcome, as to one ready to perish, in case of a lost man, to hear of one that will save him. In danger of perishing by sickness, to hear of one will make him well again; by sentence of the law, of one with a pardon to save his life; by enemies, of one that will rescue and set him in safety. Tell any of these, assure them but of a Saviour, it is the best news he ever heard in his life. There is joy in the name of a Saviour. And even this way, this Child is a Saviour too. *Potest hoc facere, sed hoc non est opus Ejus.* 'This He can do, but this is not His work'; a farther matter there is, a greater salvation He came for. And it may be we need not any of these; we are not presently sick, in no fear of the law, in no danger of enemies. And it may be, if we were, we fancy to ourselves to be relieved some other

184

way. But that which He came for, that saving we need all; and none but He can help us to it. We have therefore all cause to be glad for the Birth of this Saviour.

And then, after this succession of short sentences – no one is more master of the short sentence than Andrewes – in which the effort is to find the exact meaning and make that meaning live, he slightly but sufficiently alters the rhythm in proceeding more at large:

I know not how, but when we hear of saving or mention of a Saviour, presently our mind is carried to the saving of our skin, of our temporal state, of our bodily life, and farther saving we think not of. But there is another life not to be forgotten, and greater the dangers, and the destruction more to be feared than of this here, and it would be well sometimes we were remembered of it. Besides our skin and flesh a soul we have, and it is our better part by far, that also hath need of a Saviour; that hath her destruction out of which, that hath her destroyer from which she would be saved, and those would be thought on. Indeed our chief thought and care would be for that; how to escape the wrath, how to be saved from the destruction to come, whither our sins will certainly bring us. Sin it is will destroy us all.

In this extraordinary prose, which appears to repeat, to stand still, but is nevertheless proceeding in the most deliberate and orderly manner, there are often flashing phrases which never desert the memory. In an age of adventure and experiment in language, Andrewes is one of the most resourceful of authors in his devices for seizing the attention and impressing the memory. Phrases such as 'Christ is no wild-cat. What talk ye of twelve days?' or 'the word within a word, unable to speak a word', do not desert us; nor do the sentences in which, before extracting all the spiritual meaning of a text, Andrewes forces a concrete presence upon us.

Of the wise men come from the East:

It was no summer progress. A cold coming they had of it at this time of the year, just the worst time of the year to take a journey, and specially a long journey in. The ways deep, the weather sharp, the days short, the sun farthest off, *in solstitio brumali*, 'the very dead of winter'.

Of 'the Word made flesh' again:

I add yet farther; what flesh? The flesh of an infant. What, *Verbum infans*, the Word of an infant? The Word, and not be able to speak a word? How evil agreeth this! This He put up. How born, how entertained? In a stately palace, cradle of ivory, robes of estate? No;

but a stable for His palace, a manger for His cradle, poor clouts for His array.

He will not hesitate to hammer, to inflect, even to play upon a word for the sake of driving home its meaning:

Let us then make this so accepted a time in itself twice acceptable by our accepting, which He will acceptably take at our hands.

We can now better estimate what is this that we have called relevant intensity, for we have had enough of passages from Andrewes to recognize the extremity of his difference from Donne.

Everyone knows a passage from a sermon of Donne's, which is given by Mr. Pearsall Smith under the title of 'I am Not all Here'.

I am here speaking to you, and yet I consider by the way, in the same instant, what it is likely you will say to one another, when I have done, you are not all here neither; you are here now, hearing me, and yet you are thinking that you have heard a better sermon somewhere else of this text before; you are here, and yet you think you could have heard some other doctrine of downright *Predestination* and *Reprobation* roundly delivered somewhere else with more edification to you; you are here, and you remember yourselves that now yee think of it: This had been the fittest time, now, when everybody else is at church, to have made such and such a private visit; and because you would bee there, you are there,

after which Mr. Pearsall Smith very happily places the paragraph on 'Imperfect Prayers':

A memory of yesterday's pleasures, a feare of tomorrow's dangers, a straw under my knee, a noise in mine eare, a light in mine eye, an anything, a nothing, a fancy, a Chimera in my braine, troubles me in my prayer. So certainely is there nothing, nothing in spirituall things, perfect in this world.

These are thoughts which would never have come to Andrewes. When Andrewes begins his sermon, from beginning to end you are sure that he is wholly in his subject, unaware of anything else, that his emotion grows as he penetrates more deeply into his subject, that he is finally 'alone with the Alone', with the mystery which he is seeking to grasp more and more firmly. One is reminded of the words of Arnold about the preaching of Newman. Andrewes's emotion is purely contemplative; it is not personal, it is wholly evoked by the object of contemplation, to which it is adequate; his emotions wholly contained in and explained by its object. But with Donne there is always the something else, the 'baffling' of which Mr. Pearsall Smith speaks in his introduction. Donne is a 'personality' in a sense in which Andrewes is not: his sermons, one feels, are a 'means of self-expression'. He is constantly finding an object which shall be adequate to his feelings; Andrewes is wholly absorbed in the object and therefore responds with the adequate emotion. Andrewes has the *goût pour la vie spirituelle*, which is not native to Donne. On the other hand, it would be a great mistake to remember only that Donne was called to the priesthood by King James against his will, and that he accepted a benefice because he had no other way of making a living. Donne had a genuine taste both for theology and for religious emotion; but he belonged to that class of persons, of which there are always one or two examples in the modern world, who seek refuge in religion from the tumults of a strong emotional temperament which can find no complete satisfaction elsewhere. He is not wholly without kinship to Huysmans.

But Donne is not the less valuable, though he is the more dangerous for this reason. Of the two men, it may be said that Andrewes is the more mediaeval, because he is the more pure, and because his bond was with the Church, with tradition. His intellect was satisfied by theology and his sensibility by prayer and liturgy. Donne is the more modern – if we are careful to take this word exactly, without any implication of value, or any suggestion that we must have more sympathy with Donne than with Andrewes. Donne is much less the mystic; he is primarily interested in man. He is much less traditional. In his thought Donne has, on the one hand, much more in common with the Jesuits, and, on the other hand, much more in common with the Calvinists, than has Andrewes. Donne many times betrays the consequences of early Jesuit influence and of his later studies in Jesuit literature; in his cunning knowledge of the weaknesses of the human heart, his understanding of human sin, his skill in coaxing and persuading the attention of the variable human mind to Divine objects, and in a kind of smiling tolerance among his menaces of damnation. He is dangerous only for those who find in his sermons an indulgence of their sensibility, or for those who, fascinated by 'personality' in the romantic sense of the word – for those who find in 'personality' an ultimate value – forget that in the spiritual hierarchy there are places higher than that of Donne. Donne will certainly have always more readers than Andrewes, for the reason that his sermons can be read in detached passages and for the reason that they can be read by those who have no interest in the subject. He has many means of appeal, and appeals to many temperaments and minds, and, among others, to those capable of a certain wantonness of the spirit. Andrewes will never have many readers in any one generation, and his will never be the immortality of anthologies. Yet his prose is not inferior to that of any sermons in the language, unless it be some of Newman's. And even the larger public which does not read him may do well to remember his greatness in history – a place second to none in the history of the formation of the English Church.

from THOMAS MIDDLETON

... Between the tragedies and the comedies of Shakespeare, and certainly between the tragedies and the comedies of Jonson, we can establish a relation; we can see, for Shakespeare or Jonson, that each had in the end a personal point of view which can be called neither comic nor tragic. But with Middleton we can establish no such relation. He remains merely a name, a voice, the author of certain plays, which are all of them great plays. He has no point of view, is neither sentimental nor cynical; he is neither resigned, nor disillusioned, nor romantic; he has no message. He is merely the name which associates six or seven great plays.

For there is no doubt about *The Changeling*. Like all of the plays attributed to Middleton, it is long-winded and tiresome; the characters talk too much, and then suddenly stop talking and act; they are real and impelled irresistibly by the fundamental motions of humanity to good or evil. This mixture of tedious discourse and sudden reality is everywhere in the work of Middleton, in his comedy also. In *The Roaring Girl* we read with toil through a mass of cheap conventional intrigue, and suddenly realize that we are, and have been for some time without knowing it, observing a real and unique human being. In reading *The Changeling* we may think, till almost the end of the play, that we have been concerned merely with a fantastic Elizabethan morality, and then discover that we are looking on at a dispassionate exposure of fundamental passions of any time and any place. The usual opinion remains the just judgment: *The Changeling* is Middleton's greatest play. The morality of the convention seems to us absurd. To many intelligent readers this play has only an historical interest, and serves only to illustrate the moral taboos of the Elizabethans. The heroine is a young woman who, in order to dispose of a fiancé to whom she is indifferent, so that she may marry the man she loves, accepts the offer of an adventurer to murder the affianced, at the price (as she finds in due course) of becoming the murderer's mistress. Such a plot is, to a modern mind, absurd; and the consequent tragedy seems a fuss about nothing. But *The Changeling* is not merely contingent for its effect upon our acceptance of

Elizabethan good form or convention; it is, in fact, no more dependent upon the convention of its epoch than a play like *A Doll's House*. Underneath the convention there is the stratum of truth permanent in human nature. The tragedy of *The Changeling* is an eternal tragedy, as permanent as *Œdipus* or *Antony and Cleopatra*; it is the tragedy of the not naturally bad but irresponsible and undeveloped nature, caught in the consequences of its own action. In every age and in every civilization there are instances of the same things the unmoral nature, suddenly trapped in the inexorable toil: of morality – of morality not made by man but by Nature – and forced to take the consequences of an act which it had planned light-heartedly. Beatrice is not a moral creature; she becomes moral only by becoming damned. Our conventions are not the same as those which Middleton assumed for his play. But the possibility of that frightful discovery of morality remains permanent.

The words in which Middleton expresses his tragedy are as great as the tragedy. The process through which Beatrice, having decided that De Flores is the instrument for her purpose, passes from aversion to habituation, remains a permanent commentary on human nature. The directness and precision of De Flores are masterly, as is also the virtuousness of Beatrice on first realizing his motives –

> *Why, 'tis impossible thou canst be so wicked,*
> *Or shelter such a cunning cruelty,*
> *To make his death the murderer of my honour!*
> *Thy language is so bold and vicious,*
> *I cannot see which way I can forgive it*
> *With any modesty*

– a passage which ends with the really great lines of De Flores, lines of which Shakespeare or Sophocles might have been proud:

> *Can you weep Fate from its determined purpose?*
> *So soon may you weep me.*

But what constitutes the essence of the tragedy is something which has not been sufficiently remarked; it is the *habituation* of Beatrice to her sin; it becomes no longer merely sin but custom. Such is the essence of the tragedy of *Macbeth* – the habituation to crime. And in the end Beatrice, having been so long the enforced conspirator of De Flores, becomes (and this is permanently true to human nature) more *his* partner, *his* mate, than the mate and partner of the man for the love of whom she consented to the crime. Her lover disappears not only from the scene but from her own imagination. When she says of De Flores,

A wondrous necessary man, my lord,

her praise is more than half sincere; and at the end she belongs far more to De Flores – towards whom, at the beginning, she felt strong physical repulsion – than to her lover Alsemero. It is De Flores, in the end, to whom she belongs as Francesca to Paolo:

Beneath the stars, upon yon meteor
Ever hung my fate, 'mongst things corruptible;
I ne'er could pluck it from him; my loathing
Was prophet to the rest, but ne'er believed.

And De Flores's cry is perfectly sincere and in character:

I loved this woman in spite of her heart;
Her love I earned out of Piracquo's murder . . .
Yes, and her honour's prize
Was my reward; I thank life for nothing
But that pleasure; it was so sweet to me,
That I have drunk up all, left none behind
For any man to pledge me.

The tragedy of Beatrice is not that she has lost Alsemero, for whose possession she played; it is that she has won De Flores. Such tragedies are not limited to Elizabethan times: they happen every day and perpetually. The greatest tragedies are occupied with great and permanent moral conflicts: the great tragedies of Æschylus, of Sophocles, of Corneille, of Racine, of Shakespeare have the same burden. In poetry, in dramatic technique, *The Changeling* is inferior to the best plays of Webster. But in the moral essence of tragedy it is safe to say that in this play Middleton is surpassed by one Elizabethan alone, and that is Shakespeare. In some respects in which Elizabethan tragedy can be compared to French or to Greek tragedy *The Changeling* stands above every tragic play of its time, except those of Shakespeare.

The genius which blazed in *The Changeling* was fitful but not accidental. The best tragedy after *The Changeling* is *Women Beware Women*. The thesis of the play, as the title indicates, is more arbitrary and less fundamental. The play itself, although less disfigured by ribaldry or clowning, is more tedious. Middleton sinks himself in conventional moralizing of the epoch; so that, if we are impatient, we decide that he gives merely a document of

Elizabethan humbug – and then suddenly a personage will blaze out in genuine fire of vituperation. The wickedness of the personages in *Women Beware Women* is conventional wickedness of the stage of the time; yet slowly the exasperation of Bianca, the wife who married beneath her, beneath the ambitions to which she was entitled, emerges from the negative; slowly the real human passions emerge from the mesh of interest in which they begin. And here again Middleton, in writing what appears on the surface a conventional picture-palace Italian melodrama of the time, has caught permanent human feelings. And in this play Middleton shows his interest – more than any of his contemporaries – in innuendo and double meanings; and makes use of that game of chess, which he was to use more openly and directly for satire in that perfect piece of literary political art, *A Game at Chess*. The irony could not be improved upon:

> *Did I not say my duke would fetch you o'er, Widow?*
> *I think you spoke in earnest when you said it, madam.*
> *And my black king makes all the haste he can too.*
> *Well, madam, we may meet with him in time yet.*
> *I've given thee blind mate twice.*

There is hardly anything truer in Elizabethan drama than Bianca's gradual self-will and self-importance in consequence of her courtship by the Duke:

> *Troth, you speak wondrous well for your old house here;*
> *'Twill shortly fall down at your feet to thank you,*
> *Or stoop, when you go to bed, like a good child,*
> *To ask you blessing.*

In spite of all the long-winded speeches, in spite of all the conventional Italianate horrors, Bianca remains, like Beatrice in *The Changeling*, a real woman; as real, indeed, as any woman of Elizabethan tragedy. Bianca is a woman of the type who is purely moved by vanity.

But if Middleton understood woman in tragedy better than any of the Elizabethans – better than the creator of the Duchess of Malfy, better than Marlowe, better than Tourneur, or Shirley, or Fletcher, better than any of them except Shakespeare alone – he was also able, in his comedy, to present a finer woman than any of them. *The Roaring Girl* has no apparent relation to Middleton's tragedies, yet it is agreed to be primarily the work of Middleton. It is typical of the comedies of Middleton, and it is the best. In his tragedies Middleton employs all the Italianate horrors of his time, and obviously for the purpose of pleasing the taste of his time; yet underneath we feel always a quiet and undisturbed vision of things as they are and not 'another thing'. So in his comedies. The comedies are long-winded; the fathers are heavy fathers, and rant as heavy fathers should; the sons are wild and wanton sons, and perform all the pranks to be expected of them; the machinery is the usual Elizabethan machinery; Middleton is solicitous to please his audience with what they expect; but there is underneath the same steady impersonal passionless observation of human nature. *The Roaring Girl* is as artificial as any comedy of the time; its plot creaks loudly; yet the Girl herself is always real. She may rant, she may behave preposterously, but she remains a type of the sort of woman who has renounced all happiness for herself and who lives only for a principle. Nowhere more clearly than in *The Roaring Girl* can the hand of Middleton be distinguished from the hand of Dekker. Dekker is all sentiment; and, indeed, in the so admired passages of *A Fair Quarrel*, applauded by Lamb, the mood if not the hand of Dekker seems to the unexpert critic to be more present than Middleton's. *A Fair Quarrel* seems as much, if not more, Dekker's than Middleton's. Similarly with *The Spanish Gypsy*, which can with difficulty be attributed to Middleton. But the feeling about Moll Cut-Purse of *The Roaring Girl* is Middleton's rather than anybody's. In Middleton's tragedy there is a strain of realism underneath, which is one with the poetry; and in his comedy we find the same thing.

In her recent book on *The Social Mode of Restoration Comedy*, Miss Kathleen Lynch calls attention to the gradual transition from Elizabethan-Jacobean to Restoration comedy. She observes, what is certainly true, that Middleton is the greatest 'realist' in Jacobean comedy. Miss Lynch's extremely suggestive thesis is that the transition from Elizabethan-Jacobean to later Caroline comedy is primarily economic: that the interest changes from the citizen aping gentry to the citizen become gentry and accepting that code of manners. In the comedy of Middleton certainly there is as yet no code of manners; but the merchant of Cheapside is *aiming* at becoming a member of the county gentry. Miss Lynch remarks: 'Middleton's keen concentration on the spectacle of the interplay of different social classes marks an important development in realistic comedy'. She calls attention to this aspect of Middleton's comedy, that it marks, better than the romantic comedy of Shakespeare, or the comedy of Jonson, occupied with what Jonson thought to be permanent and not transient aspects of human nature, the transition between the aristocratic world which preceded the Tudors and the plutocratic modern world which the Tudors initiated and encouraged. By the time of the return of

Charles II, as Miss Lynch points out, society had been re-organized and formed, and social conventions had been created. In the Tudor times birth still counted (though nearly all the great families were extinct); by the time of Charles II only breeding counted. The comedy of Middleton, and the comedy of Brome, and the comedy of Shirley, is intermediate, as Miss Lynch remarks. Middleton, she observed, marks the transitional stage in which the London tradesman was anxious to cease to be a tradesman and to become a country gentleman. The words of his City Magnate in *Michaelmas Terme* had not yet lost their point:

A fine journey in the Whitsun holydays, i'faith, to ride with a number of citizens and their wives, some upon pillions, some upon side-saddles, I and little Thomasine i' the middle, our son and heir, Sim Quomodo, in a peach-colour taffeta jacket, some horse length, or a long yard before us – there will be a fine show on's I can tell you.

But Middleton's comedy is not, like the comedy of Congreve, the comedy of a set social behaviour; it is still, like the later comedy of Dickens, the comedy of individuals, in spite of the continual motions of city merchants towards county gentility. In the comedy of the Restoration a figure such as that of Moll Cut-Purse would have been impossible. As a social document the comedy of Middleton illustrates the transition from government by a landed aristocracy to government by a city aristocracy gradually engrossing the land. As such it is of the greatest interest. But as literature, as a dispassionate picture of human nature, Middleton's comedy deserves to be remembered chiefly by its real – perpetually real – and human figure of Moll the Roaring Girl. That Middleton's comedy was 'photographic', that it introduces us to the low life of the time far better than anything in the comedy of Shakespeare or the comedy of Jonson, better than anything except the pamphlets of Dekker and Greene and Nashe, there is little doubt. But it produced one great play – *The Roaring Girl* – a great play in spite of the tedious long speeches of some of the principal characters, in spite of the clumsy machinery of the plot: for the reason that Middleton was a great observer of human nature, without fear, without sentiment, without prejudice.

And Middleton in the end – after criticism has subtracted all that Rowley, all that Dekker, all that others contributed – is a great example of great English drama. He has no message; he is merely a great recorder. Incidentally, in flashes and when the dramatic need comes, he is a great poet, a great master of versification:

I that am of your blood was taken from you
For your better health; look no more upon't,
But cast it to the ground regardlessly,
Let the common sewer take it from distinction.
Beneath the stars, upon yon meteor
Ever hung my fate, 'mongst things corruptible;
I ne'er could pluck it from him; my loathing
Was prophet to the rest, but ne'er believed.

The man who wrote these lines remains inscrutable, solitary, unadmired; welcoming collaboration, indifferent to fame; dying no one knows when and no one knows how; attracting, in three hundred years, no personal admiration. Yet he wrote one tragedy which more than any play except those of Shakespeare has a profound and permanent moral value and horror; and one comedy which more than any Elizabethan comedy realizes a free and noble womanhood.

FRANCIS HERBERT BRADLEY

It is unusual that a book so famous and so influential should remain out of print so long as Bradley's *Ethical Studies*.[1] The one edition appeared in 1876: Bradley's refusal to reprint it never wavered. In 1893, in a footnote in *Appearance and Reality*, and in words characteristic of the man, he wrote: 'I feel that the appearance of other books, as well as the decay of those superstitions against which largely it was directed, has left me free to consult my own pleasure in the matter.' The dates of his three books, the *Ethical Studies* in 1876, the *Principles of Logic* in 1883, and *Appearance and Reality* in 1893, leave us in no doubt that his pleasure was the singular one of thinking rather than the common one of writing books. And Bradley always assumed, with what will remain for those who did not know him a curious blend of humility and irony, an attitude of extreme diffidence about his own work. His *Ethical Studies*, he told us (or told our fathers), did not aim at 'the construction of a system of Moral Philosophy'. The first words of the preface to his *Principles of Logic* are: 'The following work makes no claim to supply any systematic treatment of logic'. He begins the preface to *Appearance and Reality* with the words: 'I have described the following work as an essay in metaphysics. Neither in form nor extent does it carry out the idea of a system.' The phrase for each book is almost the same. And many readers, having in mind Bradley's polemical irony and his obvious zest in using it, his habit of discomfiting an opponent with a sudden profession of ignorance, of inability to understand, or of incapacity for abstruse thought, have concluded that this is all a mere pose – and even a somewhat unscrupulous one. But deeper study of Bradley's mind convinces us that the modesty is real, and his irony the weapon of a modest and highly sensitive man. Indeed, if this had been a pose it would never have worn so well as it has. We have to consider, then, what is the nature of Bradley's influence and why his writings and his personality fascinate those whom they do fascinate; and what are his claims to permanence.

[1] *Ethical Studies*, by F. H. Bradley, O.M., LL.D. Second Edition (Oxford: Clarendon Press. London: Milford).

Certainly one of the reasons for the power he still exerts, as well as an indubitable claim to permanence, is his great gift of style. It is for his purposes – and his purposes are more varied than is usually supposed – a perfect style. Its perfection has prevented it from cutting any great figure in prose anthologies and literature manuals, for it is perfectly welded with the matter. Ruskin's works are extremely readable in snippets even for many who take not a particle of interest in the things in which Ruskin was so passionately interested. Hence he survives in anthologies, while his books have fallen into undue neglect. Bradley's books can never fall into this neglect because they will never rise to this notoriety; they come to the hands only of those who are qualified to treat them with respect. But perhaps a profounder difference between a style like Bradley's and a style like Ruskin's is a greater purity and concentration of purpose. One feels that the emotional intensity of Ruskin is partly a deflection of something that was baffled in life, whereas Bradley, like Newman, is directly and wholly that which he is. For the secret of Bradley's style, like that of Bergson – whom he resembles in this if in nothing else – is the intense addiction to an intellectual passion.

The nearest resemblance in style, however, is not Ruskin but Matthew Arnold. It has not been sufficiently observed that Bradley makes use of the same means as Arnold, and for similar ends. To take first the most patent resemblance, we find in Bradley the same type of fun as that which Arnold has with his young friend Arminius. In *The Principles of Logic* there is a celebrated passage in which Bradley is attacking the theory of association of ideas according to Professor Bain, and explains how on this principle an infant comes to recognize a lump of sugar:

A young child, or one of the lower animals, is given on Monday a round piece of sugar, eats it and finds it sweet. On Tuesday it sees a square piece of sugar, and proceeds to eat it. . . . Tuesday's sensation and Monday's image are not only separate facts, which, because alike, are therefore *not* the same; but they differ perceptibly both in quality and environment. What is to lead the mind to take one for the other?

Sudden at this crisis, and in pity at distress, there leaves the heaven with rapid wing a goddess Primitive Credulity. Breathing in the ear of the bewildered infant she whispers, The thing which has happened once will happen once more. Sugar was sweet, and sugar will be sweet. And Primitive Credulity is accepted forthwith as the mistress of our life. She leads our steps on the path of experience, until her fallacies, which cannot always be pleasant, at length become suspect. We wake up indignant at the kindly fraud by which the goddess so long has deceived us. So she shakes her wings, and flying to the stars, where there are no philosophers, leaves us here to the guidance of – I cannot think what.

This sort of solemn banter is exactly what an admirer of Arnold is ready to enjoy. But it is not only in his fun, or in his middle style, that Bradley is like Arnold; they are alike in their purple passages. The two following may be compared. By Arnold:

And yet, steeped in sentiment as she lies, spreading her gardens to the moonlight, and whispering from her towers the last enchantments of the Middle Age, who will deny that Oxford, by her ineffable charm, keeps ever calling us nearer to the true goal of all of us, to the ideal, to perfection – to beauty, in a word, which is only truth seen from another side – nearer, perhaps, than all the science of Tübingen. Adorable dreamer, whose heart has been so romantic! who hast given thyself so prodigally, given thyself to sides and to heroes not mine, only never to the Philistines! home of lost causes, and forsaken beliefs, and unpopular names, and impossible loyalties! what example could ever so inspire us to keep down the Philistine in ourselves, what teacher could ever so save us from that bondage to which we are all prone, that bondage which Goethe, in his incomparable lines on the death of Schiller, makes it his friend's highest praise (and nobly did Schiller deserve the praise) to have left miles out of sight behind him – the bondage of 'was uns alle bändigt, *das Gemeine!*'.

The passage from *The Principles of Logic* is not so well known:

It may come from a failure in my metaphysics, or from a weakness of the flesh which continues to blind me, but the notion that existence could be the same as understanding strikes as cold and ghost-like as the dreariest materialism. That the glory of this world in the end is appearance leaves the world more glorious, if we feel it is a show of some fuller splendour; but the sensuous curtain is a deception and a cheat, if it hides some colourless movement of atoms, some spectral woof of impalpable abstractions, or unearthly ballet of bloodless categories. Though dragged to such conclusions, we cannot embrace them. Our principles may be true, but they are not reality. They no more *make* that Whole which commands our devotion than some shredded dissection of human tatters *is* that warm and breathing beauty of flesh which our hearts found delightful.

Any one who is at all sensitive to style will recognize the similarity of tone and tension and beat. It is not altogether certain that the passage from Bradley is not the better; at any rate such a phrase as Arnold's 'ineffable charm' has not worn at all well.

But if the two men fought with the same weapons – and fundamentally, in spite of Bradley's assualt upon Arnold, for the same causes – the weapons of Bradley had behind them a heavier force and a closer precision. Exactly what Bradley fought for and exactly what he fought against have not been quite understood; understanding has been obscured by the dust of Bradley's logical battles. People are inclined to believe that what Bradley did was to demolish the logic of Mill and the psychology of Bain. If he had done that, it would have been a lesser service than what he has done; and if he had done that it would have been less of a service than people think, for there is much that is good in the logic of Mill and the psychology of Bain. But Bradley did not attempt to destroy Mill's logic. Anyone who reads his own *Principles* will see that his force is directed not against Mill's logic as a whole but only against certain limitations, imperfections and abuses. He left the structure of Mill's logic standing, and never meant to do anything else. On the other hand, the *Ethical Studies* are not merely a demolition of the Utilitarian theory of conduct but an attack upon the whole Utilitarian mind. For Utilitarianism was, as every reader of Arnold knows, a great temple in Philistia. And of this temple Arnold hacked at the ornaments and cast down the images, and his best phrases remain for ever gibing and scolding in our memory. But Bradley, in his philosophical critique of Utilitarianism, undermined the foundations. The spiritual descendants of Bentham have built anew, as they always will; but at least, in building another temple for the same worship, they have had to apply a different style of architecture. And this is the social basis of Bradley's distinction, and the social basis is even more his claim to our gratitude than the logical basis: he replaced a philosophy which was crude and raw and provincial by one which was, in comparison, catholic, civilized, and universal. True, he was influenced by Kant and Hegel and Lotze. But Kant and Hegel and Lotze are not so despicable as some enthusiastic mediaevalists would have us believe, and they are, in comparison with the school of Bentham, catholic and civilized and universal. In fighting the battles that he fought in the 'seventies and 'eighties Bradley was fighting for a European and ripened and wise philosophy, against an insular and immature and cranky one; the same battle that Arnold was fighting against the *British Banner*, Judge Edmonds, Newman Weeks, Deborah Butler, Elderess Polly, Brother Noyes, Mr. Murphy, the Licensed Victuallers and the Commercial Travellers.

It is not to say that Arnold's work was vain if we say that it is to be done again; for we must know in advance, if we are prepared for that conflict, that the combat may have truces but never a peace. If we take the widest and wisest view of a Cause, there is no such thing as a Lost Cause because there is no such thing as a

Gained Cause. We fight for lost causes because we know that our defeat and dismay may be the preface to our successors' victory, though that victory itself will be temporary; we fight rather to keep something alive than in the expectation that anything will triumph. If Bradley's philosophy is today a little out of fashion, we must remark that what has superseded it, what is now in favour, is, for the most part, crude and raw and provincial (though infinitely more technical and scientific) and must perish in its turn. Arnold turned from mid-century Radicalism with the reflection 'A new power has suddenly appeared'. There is always a new power; but the new power destined to supersede the philosophy which has superseded Bradley will probably be something at the same time older, more patient, more supple and more wise. The chief characteristics of much contemporary philosophy are newness and crudeness, impatience, inflexibility in one respect and fluidity in another, and irresponsibility and lack of wisdom. Of wisdom Bradley had a large share; wisdom consists largely of scepticism and uncynical disillusion; and of these Bradley had a large share. And scepticism and disillusion are a useful equipment for religious understanding; and of that Bradley had a share too.

Those who have read the *Ethical Studies* will be ready with the remark that it was Bradley, in this book and in the year 1876, who knocked the bottom out of *Literature and Dogma*. But that does not mean that the two men were not on the same side; it means only that *Literature and Dogma* is irrelevant to Arnold's main position as given in the Essays and in *Culture and Anarchy*, that the greatest weakness of Arnold's culture was his weakness in philosophical training, and that in philosophical criticism Bradley exhibits the same type of culture that Arnold exhibited in political and social criticism. Arnold had made an excursion into a field for which he was not armed. Bradley's attack upon Arnold does not take up much space, but Bradley was economical of words; it is all in a few paragraphs and a few footnotes to the 'Concluding Remarks':

But here once more 'culture' has come to our aid, and has shown us how here, as everywhere, the study of polite literature, which makes for meekness, makes needless also all further education; and we felt already as if the clouds that metaphysic had wrapped about the matter were dissolving in the light of a fresh and sweet intelligence. And, as we turned towards the dawn, we sighed over poor Hegel, who had read neither Goethe nor Homer, nor the Old and New Testaments, nor any of the literature which has gone to form 'culture', but, knowing no facts, and reading no books, nor ever asking himself 'such a tyro's question as what being really was', sat spinning out of his head those foolish logomachies which impose on no person of refinement.

Here is the identical weapon of Arnold, sharpened to a razor edge and turned against Arnold.

But the 'stream' and the 'tendency' having served their turn, like last week's placards, now fall into the background, and we learn at last that 'the Eternal' is not eternal at all, unless we give that name to whatever a generation sees happen, and believes both has happened and will happen – just as the habit of washing ourselves might be termed 'the Eternal not ourselves that makes for cleanliness', or 'Early to bed and early to rise' the 'Eternal not ourselves that makes for longevity', and so on – that 'the Eternal', in short, is nothing in the world but a piece of literary clap-trap. The consequence is that all we are left with is the assertion that 'righteousness' is 'salvation' or welfare, and that there is a 'law' and a 'Power' which has something to do with this fact; and here again we must not be ashamed to say that we fail to understand what any one of these phrases means, and suspect ourselves once more to be on the scent of clap-trap.

A footnote continues the Arnold-baiting in a livelier style:

'Is there a God?' asks the reader. 'Oh yes,' replies Mr. Arnold, 'and I can verify him in experience.' 'And what is he then?' cries the reader. 'Be virtuous, and as a rule you will be happy,' is the answer. 'Well, and God?' 'That is God', says Mr. Arnold; 'there is no deception, and what more do you want?' I suppose we do want a good deal more. Most of us, certainly the public which Mr. Arnold addresses, want something they can worship; and they will not find that in an hypostasized copy-book heading, which is not much more adorable than 'Honesty is the best policy', or 'Handsome is that handsome does', or various other edifying maxims, which have not yet come to an apotheosis.

Such criticism is final. It is patently a great triumph of wit and a great delight to watch when a man's methods, almost his tricks of speech, are thus turned against himself. But if we look more closely into these words and into the whole chapter from which they are taken, we find Bradley to have been not only triumphant in polemic but right in reason. Arnold, with all his great virtues, was not always patient enough, or solicitious enough of any but immediate effect, to avoid inconsistency – as has been painstakingly shown by Mr. J. M. Robertson. In *Culture and Anarchy*, which is probably his greatest book, we hear something said about 'the will of God'; but the 'will of God' seems to become superseded in importance by 'our best self, or right reason, to which we want to give authority'; and this best self looks very much like Matthew Arnold slightly disguised. In our own time one of the most remarkable of our critics, one who is fundamentally on most questions in the right, and very often right quite alone, Professor Irving Babbitt, has said again and again that the old curbs of class, of authoritative government, and of religion must be supplied in our time by something he calls the 'inner check'. The inner check looks very much like the 'best self' of Matthew Arnold; and though supported by wider erudition and closer reasoning, is perhaps open to the same objections. There are words of Bradley's, and in the chapter from which we have already quoted, that might seem at first sight to support these two eminent doctrines:

How can the human-divine ideal ever be my will? The answer is, Your will it never can be as the will of your private self, so that your private self should become wholly good. To that self you must die, and by faith be made one with that ideal. You must resolve to give up your will, as the mere will of this or that man, and you must put your whole self, your entire will, into the will of the divine. That must be your one self, as it is your true self; that you must hold to both with thought and will, and all other you must renounce.

There is one direction in which these words – and, indeed, Bradley's philosophy as a whole – might be pushed, which would be dangerous; the direction of diminishing the value and dignity of the individual, of sacrificing him to a Church or a State. But, in any event, the words cannot be interpreted in the sense of Arnold. The distinction is not between a 'private self' and a 'public self' or a 'higher self', it is between the individual as himself and no more, a mere numbered atom, and the individual in communion with God. The distinction is clearly drawn between man's 'mere will' and 'the will of the Divine'. It may be noted also that Bradley is careful, in indicating the process, not to exaggerate either will or intellect at the expense of the other. And in all events it is a process which neither Arnold nor Professor Babbitt could accept. But *if* there is a 'will of God', as Arnold, in a hasty moment, admits, then some doctrine of Grace must be admitted too; or else the 'will of God' is just the same inoperative benevolence which we have all now and then received – and resented – from our fellow human beings. In the end it is a disappointment and a cheat.

Those who return to the reading of *Ethical Studies*, and those who now, after reading the other works of Bradley, read it for the first time, will be struck by the unity of Bradley's thought in the three books and in the collected Essays. But this unity is not the unity of mere fixity. In the *Ethical Studies*, for instance, he speaks of the awareness of the self, the knowledge of one's own existence as indubitable and identical. In *Appearance and Reality*, seventeen years later, he had seen much deeper into the matter; and had seen that no one 'fact' of experience in isolation is real or is evidence of anything. The unity of Bradley's thought is not the unity attained by a man who never changes his mind. If he had so little occasion to change it, that is because he usually saw his problems from the beginning in all their complexity and connections – saw them, in other words, with wisdom – and because he could never be deceived by his own metaphors – which, indeed, he used most sparingly – and was never tempted to make use of current nostrums.

If all of Bradley's writings are in some sense merely 'essays', that is not solely a matter of modesty, or caution, and certainly not of indifference, or even of ill health. It is that he perceived the contiguity and continuity of the various provinces of thought. 'Reflection on morality', he says, 'leads us beyond it. It leads us, in short, to see the necessity of a religious point of view.' Morality and religion are not the same thing, but they cannot beyond a certain point be treated separately. A system of ethics, if thorough, is explicitly or implicitly a system of theology; and to attempt to erect a complete theory of ethics without a religion is none the less to adopt some particular attitude towards religion. In this book, as in his others, Bradley is thoroughly empirical, much more empirical than the philosophies that he opposed. He wished only to determine how much of morality could be founded securely without entering into the religious questions at all. As in *Appearance and Reality* he assumes that our common everyday knowledge is on the whole true so far as it goes, but that we do not know how far it does go; so in the *Ethical Studies* he starts always with the assumption that our common attitude towards duty, pleasure, or self-sacrifice is correct so far as it goes – but we do not know how far it does go. And in this he is all in the Greek tradition. It is fundamentally a philosophy of common sense.

Philosophy without wisdom is vain; and in the greater philosophers we are usually aware of that wisdom which for the sake of emphasis and in the most accurate and profound sense could be called even worldly wisdom. Common sense does not mean, of course, either the opinion of the majority or the opinion of the moment; it is not a thing to be got at without maturity and study and thought. The lack of it produces those unbalanced philosophies, such as Behaviourism, of which we hear a great deal. A purely 'scientific' philosophy ends by denying what we know to be true; and, on the other hand, the great weakness of Pragmatism is that it ends by being of no *use* to anybody. Again, it is easy to underestimate Hegel, but it is easy to overestimate Bradley's debt to Hegel; in a philosophy like Bradley's the points at which he *stops* are always important points. In an unbalanced or uncultured philosophy words have a way of changing their meaning – as sometimes with Hegel; or else they are made, in a most ruthless and piratical manner, to walk the plank: such as the words which Professor J. B. Watson drops overboard, and which we know to have meaning and value. But Bradley, like Aristotle, is distinguished by his scrupulous respect for words, that their meaning should be neither vague nor exaggerated; and the tendency of his labours is to bring British philosophy closer to the Greek tradition.

DANTE

I
THE *INFERNO*

In my own experience of the appreciation of poetry I have always found that the less I knew about the poet and his work, before I began to read it, the better. A quotation, a critical remark, an enthusiastic essay, may well be the accident that sets one to reading a particular author; but an elaborate preparation of historical and biographical knowledge has always been to me a barrier. I am not defending poor scholarship; and I admit that such experience, solidified into a maxim, would be very difficult to apply in the study of Latin and Greek. But with authors of one's own speech, and even with some of those of other modern languages, the procedure is possible. At least, it is better to be spurred to acquire scholarship because you enjoy the poetry, than to suppose that you enjoy the poetry because you have acquired the scholarship. I was passionately fond of certain French poetry long before I could have translated two verses of it correctly. With Dante the discrepancy between enjoyment and understanding was still wider.

I do not counsel anyone to postpone the study of Italian grammar until he has read Dante, but certainly there is an immense amount of knowledge which, until one has read some of his poetry with intense pleasure – that is, with as keen pleasure as one is capable of getting from any poetry – is positively undesirable. In saying this I am avoiding two possible extremes of criticism. One might say that understanding of the scheme, the philosophy, the concealed meanings, of Dante's verse was *essential* to appreciation; and on the other hand one might say that these things were quite irrelevant, that the poetry in his poems was one thing, which could be enjoyed by itself without studying a framework which had served the author in producing the poetry but could not serve the reader in enjoying it. The latter error is the more prevalent, and is probably the reason why many people's knowledge of the *Comedy* is limited to the *Inferno*, or even to certain passages in it. The enjoyment of the *Divine Comedy* is a continuous process. If you get nothing out of it at first, you probably never will; but if from your first deciphering of it there comes now and then some direct shock of poetic intensity, nothing but laziness can deaden the desire for fuller and fuller knowledge.

What is surprising about the poetry of Dante is that it is, in one sense, extremely easy to read. It is a test (a positive test, I do not assert that it is always valid negatively), that genuine poetry can communicate before it is understood. The impression can be verified on fuller knowledge; I have found with Dante and with several other poets in languages in which I was unskilled, that about such impressions there was nothing fanciful. They were not due, that is, to *mis*understanding the passage, or to reading into it something not there, or to accidental sentimental evocations out of my own past. The impression was new, and of, I believe, the objective 'poetic emotion'. There are more detailed reasons for this experience on the first reading of Dante, and for my saying that he is easy to read. I do not mean that he writes very simple Italian, for he does not; or that his content is simple or always simply expressed. It is often expressed with such a force of compression that the elucidation of three lines needs a paragraph, and their allusions a page of commentary. What I have in mind is that Dante is, in a sense to be defined (for the word means little by itself), the most *universal* of poets in the modern languages. That does not mean that he is 'the greatest', or that he is the most comprehensive – there is greater variety and detail in Shakespeare. Dante's universality is not solely a personal matter. The Italian language, and especially the Italian language in Dante's age, gains much by being the product of universal Latin. There is something much more *local* about the languages in which Shakespeare and Racine had to express themselves. This is not to say, either, that English and French are inferior, as vehicles of poetry, to Italian. But the Italian vernacular of the late Middle Ages was still very close to Latin, as literary expression, for the reason that the men, like Dante, who used it, were trained, in philosophy and all abstract subjects, in mediaeval Latin. Now mediaeval Latin is a very fine language; fine prose and fine verse were written in it; and it had the quality of a highly developed and literary Esperanto. When you read modern philosophy, in English, French, German, and Italian, you must be struck by national or racial differences of thought: modern languages *tend* to separate abstract thought (mathematics is now the only universal language); but mediaeval Latin tended to concentrate on what men of various races and lands could think together. Some of the character of this universal language seems to me to inhere in Dante's Florentine speech; and the localization ('Florentine' speech) seems if anything to emphasize the universality, because it cuts across the modern division of nationality. To enjoy any French or German poetry, I think one needs to have some sympathy with the French or German mind; Dante, none the less an Italian and a patriot, is first a European.

This difference, which is one of the reasons why Dante is 'easy to read', may be discussed in more particular manifestations. The style of Dante has a peculiar lucidity – a *poetic* as distinguished from an *intellectual* lucidity. The thought may be obscure, but the word is lucid, or rather translucent. In English poetry words have a kind of opacity which is part of their beauty. I do not mean that the beauty of English poetry is what is called mere 'verbal beauty'. It is rather that words have associations, and the groups of words *in* association have associations, which is a kind of local self-consciousness, because they are the growth of a *particular* civilization; and the same thing is true of other modern languages. The Italian of Dante, though essentially the Italian of today, is not in this way a modern language. The culture of Dante was not of one European country but of Europe. I am aware, of course, of a directness of speech which Dante shares with other great poets of pre-Reformation and pre-Renaissance times, notably Chaucer and Villon. Undoubtedly there is something in common between the three, so much that I should expect an admirer of any one of them to be an admirer of the others; and undoubtedly there is an opacity, or inspissation of poetic style throughout Europe after the Renaissance. But the lucidity and universality of Dante are far beyond those qualities in Villon and Chaucer, though they are akin.

Dante is 'easier to read', for a foreigner who does not know Italian very well, for other reasons: but all related to this central reason, that in Dante's time Europe, with all its dissensions and dirtiness, was mentally more united than we can now conceive. It is not particularly the Treaty of Versailles that has separated nation from nation; nationalism was born long before; and the process of disintegration which for our generation culminates in that treaty began soon after Dante's time. One of the reasons for Dante's 'easiness' is the following – but first I must make a digression.

I must explain why I have said that Dante is 'easy to read', instead of talking about his 'universality'. The latter word would have been much easier to use. But I do not wish to be thought to claim a universality for Dante which I deny to Shakespeare or Molière or Sophocles. Dante is no more 'universal' than Shakespeare: though I feel that we can come nearer to understanding

Dante than a foreigner can come to understanding those others. Shakespeare, or even Sophocles, or even Racine and Molière, are dealing with what is as universally human as the material of Dante; but they had no choice but to deal with it in a more local way. As I have said, the Italian of Dante is very near in feeling to mediaeval Latin: and of the mediaeval philosophers whom Dante read, and who were read by learned men of his time, there were, for instance, St. Thomas who was an Italian, St. Thomas's predecessor Albertus, who was a German, Abelard who was French, and Hugh and Richard of St. Victor who were Scots. For the *medium* that Dante had to use compare the opening of the *Inferno*:

> *Nel mezzo del cammin di nostra vita*
> *mi ritrovai per una selva oscura,*
> *che la diritta via era smarrita.*

In the middle of the journey of our life I found myself in a dark wood, having lost the straight path.

with the lines with which Duncan is introduced to Macbeth's castle:

> *This castle hath a pleasant seat; the air*
> *Nimbly and sweetly recommends itself*
> *Unto our gentle senses.*
>   *This guest of summer*
> *The temple-haunting martlet, does approve*
> *By his loved masonry that the heaven's breath*
> *Smells wooingly here: no jutty, frieze,*
> *Buttress, nor coign of vantage, but this bird*
> *Hath made his pendant bed and procreant cradle:*
> *Where they most breed and haunt, I have observed*
> *The air is delicate.*

I do not at all pretend that we appreciate everything, even in one single line of Dante, that a cultivated Italian can appreciate. But I do maintain that more is lost in translating Shakespeare into Italian than in translating Dante into English. How can a foreigner find words to convey in his own language just that combination of intelligibility and remoteness that we get in many phrases of Shakespeare?

I am not considering whether the language of Dante or Shakespeare is superior, for I cannot admit the question: I merely affirm that the differences are such as make Dante easier for a foreigner. Dante's advantages are not due to greater genius, but to the fact that he wrote when Europe was still more or less one. And even had Chaucer or Villon been exact contemporaries of Dante, they would still have been farther, linguistically as well as geographically, from the centre of Europe than Dante.

But the simplicity of Dante has another detailed reason. He not only thought in a way in which every man of his culture in the whole of Europe then thought, but he employed a method which was common and commonly understood throughout Europe. I do not intend, in this essay, to go into questions of disputed interpretations of Dante's allegory. What is important for my purpose is the fact that the allegorical method was a definite method not confined to Italy; and the fact, apparently paradoxical, that the allegorical method makes for simplicity and intelligibility. We incline to think of allegory as a tiresome cross-word puzzle. We incline to associate it with dull poems (at best, *The Romance of the Rose*), and in a great poem to ignore it as irrelevant. What we ignore is, in a case like Dante's, its particular effect towards lucidity of style.

I do not recommend, in first reading the first canto of the *Inferno*, worrying about the identity of the Leopard, the Lion, or the She-Wolf. It is really better, at the start, not to know or care what they do mean. What we should consider is not so much the meaning of the images, but the reverse process, that which led a man having an idea to express it in images. We have to consider the type of mind which by nature and *practice* tended to express itself in allegory: and, for a competent poet, allegory means *clear visual images*. And clear visual images are given much more intensity by having a meaning – we do not need to know what that meaning is, but in our awareness of the image we must be aware that the meaning is there too. Allegory is only one poetic method, but it is a method which has very great advantages.

Dante's is a *visual* imagination. It is a visual imagination in a different sense from that of a modern painter of still life: it is visual in the sense that he lived in an age in which men still saw visions. It was a psychological habit, the trick of which we have forgotten, but as good as any of our own. We have nothing but dreams, and we have forgotten that seeing visions – a practice now relegated to the aberrant and uneducated – was once a more significant, interesting, and disciplined kind of dreaming. We take it for granted that our dreams spring from below: possibly the quality of our dreams suffers in consequence.

All that I ask of the reader, at this point, is to clear his mind, if he can, of every prejudice against allegory, and to admit at least that it was not a device to enable the uninspired to write verses, but really a mental habit, which when raised to the point of genius can make a great poet as well as a great mystic or saint. And it is the allegory which makes it possible for the reader who is not even a good Italian scholar to enjoy Dante. Speech varies, but our eyes are all the same. And allegory was not a local Italian custom, but a universal European method.

Dante's attempt is to make us see what he saw. He therefore employs very simple language, and very few metaphors, for allegory and metaphor do not get on well together. And there is a peculiarity about his *comparisons* which is worth noticing in passing.

There is a well-known comparison or simile in the great XVth canto of the *Inferno*, which Matthew Arnold singled out, rightly, for high praise; which is characteristic of the way in which Dante employs these figures. He is speaking of the crowd in Hell who peered at him and his guide under a dim light:

> *e sì ver noi aguzzevan le ciglia,*
> *come vecchio sartor fa nella cruna.*

and sharpened their vision (knitted their brows) at us, like an old tailor peering at the eye of his needle.

The purpose of this type of simile is solely to make us *see more definitely* the scene which Dante has put before us in the preceding lines.

> *she looks like sleep,*
> *As she would catch another Antony*
> *In her strong toil of grace.*

The image of Shakespeare's is much more complicated than Dante's, and more complicated than it looks. It has the grammatical form of a kind of simile (the 'as if' form), but of course 'catch in her toil' is a metaphor. But whereas the simile of Dante is merely to make you see more clearly how the people looked, and is explanatory, the figure of Shakespeare is expansive rather than intensive; its purpose is to *add* to what you see (either on the stage or in your imagination) a reminder of that fascination of Cleopatra which shaped her history and that of the world, and of that fascination being so strong that it prevails even in death. It is more elusive, and it is less possible to convey without close knowledge of the English language. Between men who could make such inventions as these there can be no question of greater or less. But as the whole poem of Dante is, if you like, one vast metaphor, there is hardly any place for metaphor in the detail of it.

There is all the more reason to acquaint oneself well with

Dante's poem first part by part, even dwelling specially on the parts that one likes most at first, because we cannot extract the full significance of any part without knowing the whole. We cannot understand the inscription at Hell Gate:

> *Giustizia mosse il mio alto Fattore;*
> *fecemi la divina Potestate,*
> *la somma Sapienza e il primo Amore.*

Justice moved my high Maker; what made me were the divine Power, the supreme Wisdom, and *the primal Love.*

until we have ascended to the highest Heaven and returned. But we can understand the first Episode that strikes most readers, that of Paolo and Francesca, enough to be moved by it as much as by any poetry, on the first reading. It is introduced by two similes of the same explanatory nature as that which I have just quoted:

> *E come gli stornei ne portan l'ali,*
> *nel freddo tempo, a schiera larga e piena,*
> *così quel fiato gli spiriti mali;*

And as their wings bear along the starlings, at the cold season, in large full troop.

> *E come i gru van cantando lor lai*
> *facendo in aer di sè lunga riga;*
> *così vid' io venir, traendo guai,*
> *ombre portate dalla detta briga;*

And as the cranes go chanting their lays, making themselves a long streak in the air, so I saw the wailing shadows come, wailing, carried on the striving wind.

We can see and feel the situation of the two lost lovers, though we do not yet understand the meaning which Dante gives it. Taking such an episode by itself, we can get as much out of it as we get from the reading of a whole single play of Shakespeare. We do not understand Shakespeare from a single reading, and certainly not from a single play. There is a relation between the various plays of Shakespeare, taken in order; and it is a work of years to venture even one individual interpretation of the pattern in Shakespeare's carpet. It is not certain that Shakespeare himself knew what it was. It is perhaps a larger pattern than Dante's, but the pattern is less distinct. We can read with full comprehension the lines:

Noi leggevamo un giorno per diletto
di Lancillotto, come amor lo strinse;
soli eravamo e senza alcun sospetto.
Per più fiate gli occhi ci sospinse
quella lettura, e scolorocci il viso;
ma solo un punto fu quel che ci vinse.
Quando leggemmo il disiato riso
esser baciato da cotanto amante,
questi, che mai da me non fia diviso,
La bocca me baciò tutto tremante:

One day, for pastime, we read of Lancelot, how love constrained him; we were alone, and without all suspicion. Several times that reading urged our eyes to meet, and changed the colour of our faces; but one moment alone it was that overcame us. When we read how the fond smile was kissed by such a lover, he, who shall never be divided from me, kissed my mouth all trembling.

When we come to fit the episode into its place in the whole *Comedy*, and see how this punishment is related to all other punishments and to purgations and rewards, we can appreciate better the subtle psychology of the simple line of Francesca:

se fosse amico il re dell' universo

if the King of the Universe were our friend. . . .

or of the line

Amor, che a nullo amato amar perdona

Love, which to no loved one permits excuse for loving. . . .

or indeed of the line already quoted:

questi, che mai da me non fia diviso

he, who shall never be divided from me. . . .

Proceeding through the *Inferno* on a first reading, we get a succession of phantasmagoric but clear images, of images which are coherent, in that each reinforces the last; of glimpses of individuals made memorable by a perfect phrase, like that of the proud Farinata degli Uberti:

ed ei s' ergea col petto e colla fronte,
come avesse lo inferno in gran dispitto.

He rose upright with breast and countenance, as though he entertained great scorn of Hell.

and of particular longer episodes, which remain separately in the memory. I think that among those which impress themselves most at the first reading are the episode of Brunctto Latini (Canto XV), Ulysses (Canto XXVI), Bertrand de Born (Canto XXVIII), Adamo di Brescia (Canto XXX), and Ugolino (Canto XXXIII).

Although I think it would be a mistake to skip, and find it much better to await these episodes until we come to them in due course, they certainly remain in my memory as the parts of the *Inferno* which first convinced me, and especially the Brunetto and the Ulysses episodes, for which I was unprepared by quotation or allusion. And the two may well be put together: for the first is Dante's testimony of a loved master of arts, the second his reconstruction of a legendary figure of ancient epic; yet both have the quality of *surprise* which Poe declared to be essential to poetry. This *surprise*, at its highest, could by nothing be better illustrated than by the final lines with which Dante dismisses the damned master whom he loves and respects:

> *Poi si rivolse, e parve di coloro*
> *che coronno a Verona il drappo verde*
> *per la campagna; e parve di costoro*
> *quegli che vince e non colui che perde.*

Then he turned back, and seemed like one of those who run for the green cloth at Verona through the open field; and of them he seemed like him who wins, and not like him who loses.

One does not need to know anything about the race for the roll of green cloth, to be *hit* by these lines; and in making Brunetto, so fallen, *run like the winner*, a quality is given to the punishment which belongs only to the greatest poetry. So Ulysses, unseen in the hornèd wave of flame,

> *Lo maggior corno della fiamma antica*
> *cominciò a crollarsi mormorando,*
> *pur come quella cui vento affatica.*
> *Indi la cima qua e là menando,*
> *come fosse la lingua che parlasse,*
> *gittò voce di fuori e disse: 'Quando*
> *mi diparti' da Circe, che sottrasse*
> *me più d'un anno la presso a Gaeta. . . .*

The greater horn of the ancient flame began to shake itself, murmuring, like a flame struggling against the wind. Then moving to and fro the peak, as though it were the tongue that spoke, threw forth a voice and said: 'When I left Circe, who kept me more than a year there near Gaeta. . . .'

is a creature of the pure poetic imagination, apprehensible apart from place and time and the scheme of the poem. The Ulysses episode may strike us first as a kind of excursion, an irrelevance, a self-indulgence on the part of Dante taking a holiday from his Christian scheme. But when we know the whole poem, we recognize how cunningly and convincingly Dante has made to fit in real men, his contemporaries, friends, and enemies, recent historical personages, legendary and Biblical figures, and figures of ancient fiction. He has been reproved or smiled at for satisfying personal grudges by putting in Hell men whom he knew and hated; but these, as well as Ulysses, are transformed in the whole; for the real and the unreal are all representative of types of sin, suffering, fault, and merit, and all become of the same reality and contemporary. The Ulysses episode is particularly 'readable', I think, because of its continuous straightforward narrative, and because to an English reader the comparison with Tennyson's poem – a perfect poem at that – is very instructive. It is worth while noticing the greatly superior degree of *simplification* of Dante's version. Tennyson, like most poets, like most even of those whom we can call great poets, has to get his effect with a certain amount of *forcing*. Thus the line about the sea which

moans round with many voices,

a true specimen of Tennyson-Virgilianism, is too *poetical* in comparison with Dante, to be the highest poetry. (Only Shakespeare can be so 'poetical' without giving any effect of overloading, or distracting us from the main issue:

Put up your bright swords or the dew will rust them.)

Ulysses and his shipmates pass through the pillars of Hercules, that 'narrow pass'

ov' Ercole segnò li suoi riguardi
acciocchè l'uom più oltre non si metta.

where Hercules set his marks, so that man should pass no farther.

'O frati', dissi, 'che per cento milia
perigli siete giunti all'occidente,
a questa tanto picciola vigilia
de' vostri sensi, ch'è del rimanente,
non vogliate negar l'esperienza
di retro al sol, del mondo senza gente.

Considerate la vostra semenza,
fatti non foste a viver come bruti
ma per seguir virtute e conoscenza.'

'O brothers!' Is said, 'who through a hundred thousand dangers have reached the West, deny not, to this so brief vigil of your senses that remains, experience of the world without men that lies behind the sun. Consider your nature, you were made not to live like beasts, but to pursue virtue and knowledge.'

They fare forth until suddenly

n'apparve una montagna bruna
per la distanza, e parvemi alta tanto
quanto veduta non n'aveva alcuna.
Noi ci allegrammo, e tosto tornò in pianto,
chè dalla nuova terra un turbo nacque,
e percosse del legno il primo canto.
Tre volte il fe' girar con tutte l'acque,
alla quarta levar la poppa in suso,
e la prora ire in giù, com' altrui piacque,
infin che il mar fu sopra noi richiuso.

there appeared a mountain brown in the distance; and it seemed to me the highest that I had ever seen. We rejoiced, but soon our joy was turned to lamentation: for a storm came up from the new land, and caught the stem of our ship. Three times it whirled her round with all the waters; the fourth time it heaved up the stern and drove her down at the head, as pleased Another; until the sea closed over us.

The story of Ulysses, as told by Dante, reads like a straightforward piece of romance, a well-told seaman's yarn; Tennyson's Ulysses is primarily a very self-conscious poet. But Tennyson's poem is flat, it has only two dimensions; there is nothing more in it than what the average Englishman, with a feeling for verbal beauty, can see. We do not need, at first, to know what mountain the mountain was, or what the words mean *as pleased Another*, to feel that Dante's sense has further depths.

It is worth pointing out again how very right was Dante to introduce among his historical characters at least one character who even to him could hardly have been more than a fiction. For the *Inferno* is relieved from any question of pettiness or arbitrariness in Dante's selection of damned. It reminds us that Hell is not a place but a *state*; that man is damned or blessed in the creatures of his imagination as well as in men who have actually lived; and that Hell, though a state, is a state which can only be thought of, and perhaps only experienced, by the projection of sensory images; and that the resurrection of the body has perhaps a deeper meaning than we understand. But these are such thoughts as come only after many readings; they are not necessary for the first poetic enjoyment..

The experience of a poem is the experience both of a moment and of a lifetime. It is very much like our intenser experiences of other human beings. There is a first, or an early moment which is unique, of shock and surprise, even of terror (*Ego dominus tuus*); a moment which can never be forgotten, but which is never repeated integrally; and yet which would become destitute of significance if it did not survive in a larger whole of experience; which survives inside a deeper and a calmer feeling. The majority of poems one outgrows and outlives, as one outgrows and outlives the majority of human passions: Dante's is one of those which one can only just hope to grow up to at the end of life.

The last canto (XXXIV) is probably the most difficult on first reading. The vision of Satan may seem grotesque, especially if we have fixed in our minds the curly-haired Byronic hero of Milton; it is too like a Satan in a fresco in Siena. Certainly no more than the Divine Spirit can the Essence of Evil be confined in one form and place; and I confess that I tend to get from Dante the impression of a Devil suffering like the human damned souls; whereas I feel that the *kind* of suffering experienced by the Spirit of Evil should be represented as utterly different. I can only say that Dante made the best of a bad job. In putting Brutus, the noble Brutus, and Cassius with Judas Iscariot he will also disturb at first the English reader, for whom Brutus and Cassius must always be the Brutus and Cassius of Shakespeare: but if my justification of Ulysses is valid, then the presence of Brutus and Cassius is also. If anyone is repelled by the last canto of the *Inferno*, I can only ask him to wait until he has read and lived for years with the last canto of the *Paradiso*, which is to my thinking the highest point that poetry has ever reached or ever can reach, and in which Dante amply repairs any failure of Canto XXXIV of the *Inferno*; but perhaps it is better, on our first reading of the *Inferno*, to omit the last canto and return to the beginning of Canto III:

> *Per me si va nella città dolente;*
> *per me si va nell' eterno dolore;*
> *per me si va tra la perduta gente.*
> *Giustizia mosse il mio alto Fattore;*
> *fecemi la divina Potestate,*
> *la somma Sapienza e il primo Amore.*

II

THE *PURGATORIO* AND THE *PARADISO*

For the science or art of writing verse, one has learned from the *Inferno* that the greatest poetry can be written with the greatest economy of words, and with the greatest austerity in the use of metaphor, simile, verbal beauty, and elegance. When I affirm that more can be learned about how to write poetry from Dante than from any English poet, I do not at all mean that Dante's way is the only right way, or that Dante is thereby *greater* than Shakespeare or, indeed, any other English poet. I put my meaning into other words by saying that Dante can do less *harm* to anyone trying to learn to write verse, than can Shakespeare. Most great English poets are *inimitable* in a way in which Dante was not. If you try to imitate Shakespeare you will certainly produce a series of stilted, forced, and violent distortions of language. The language of each great English poet is his own language; the language of Dante is the perfection of a common language. In a sense, it is more pedestrian than that of Dryden or Pope. If you follow Dante without talent, you will at worst be pedestrian and flat; if you follow Shakespeare or Pope without talent, you will make an utter fool of yourself.

But if one has learned this much from the *Inferno*, there are other things to be learnt from the two successive divisions of the poem. From the *Purgatorio* one learns that a straightforward philosophical statement can be great poetry; from the *Paradiso*, that more and more rarefied and remote *states of beatitude* can be the material for great poetry. And gradually we come to admit that Shakespeare understands a greater extent and variety of human life than Dante; but that Dante understands deeper degrees of degradation and higher degrees of exaltation. And a further wisdom is reached when we see clearly that this indicates the equality of the two men.

On the one hand, the *Purgatorio* and the *Paradiso* belong, in the way of understanding, together. It is apparently easier to accept damnation as poetic material than purgation or beatitude; less is involved that is strange to the modern mind. I insist that the full meaning of the *Inferno* can only be extracted after appreciation of the two later parts, yet it has sufficient meaning in and by itself for the first few readings. Indeed, the *Purgatorio* is, I think, the most difficult of the three parts. It cannot be enjoyed by itself like the *Inferno*, nor can it be enjoyed merely as a sequel to the *Inferno*; it requires appreciation of the *Paradiso* as well; which means that its first reading is arduous and apparently unre-munerative. Only when we have read straight though to the end of the *Paradiso*, and re-read the *Inferno*, does the *Purgatorio* begin to yield its beauty. Damnation and even blessedness are more exciting than purgation.

By compensation, the *Purgatorio* has a few episodes which, so to speak, 'let us up' (as the counterpart to letting down) more easily than the rest, from the *Inferno*. We must not stop to orient ourselves in the new astronomy of the Mount of Purgatory. We must linger first with the shades of Casella and Manfred slain, and especially Buonconte and La Pia, those whose souls were saved from Hell only at the last moment.

> *'Io fui di Montefeltro, io son Buonconte;*
> *Giovanna o altri non ha di me cura;*
> *per ch'io vo tra costor con bassa fronte'.*
> *Ed io a lui: 'Qual forza o qual ventura*
> *ti traviò sì fuor di Campaldino*
> *che non si seppe mai tua sepoltura?'*
> *'Oh', rispos' egli, 'a piè del Casentino*
> *traversa un' acqua che ha nome l'Archiano,*
> *che sopra l'Ermo nasce in Apennino.*
> *Dove il vocabol suo diventa vano*
> *arriva' io forato nella gola,*
> *fuggendo a piede e sanguinando il piano.*
> *Quivi perdei la vista, e la parola*
> *nel nome di Maria finii: e quivi*
> *caddi, e rimase la mia carne sola.'*

'I was of Montefeltro, I am Buonconte; neither Giovanna nor any other has care of me, wherefore I go with these, with lowered brow.' I said to him: 'What force or chance led you so far away from Cam-paldino that your place of sepulture has always been unknown?' 'Oh', said he, 'at the foot of Casentino a stream crosses, which is called Archiano, and rises in the Apennines above the Hermitage. There, where its name is lost, came I, jabbed in the throat, fleeing on foot, dripping blood over the plain. There my sight left me, and I ended speech with (crying on) the name of Mary. There I fell, and my flesh alone remained.'

When Buonconte ends his story, the third spirit speaks:

> *'Deh, quando tu sarai tornato al mondo,*
> *e riposato della lunga via,'*
> *seguitò il terzo spirito al secondo,*

'ricorditi di me, che son la Pia;
Siena mi fe', disfecemi Maremma:
salsi colui che innanellata, pria
disposando, m'avea con la suia gemma.'

'O pray, when you return to the world, and are rested from your long journey,' followed the third spirit after the second, 'remember me, who am La Pia. Siena made me, Maremma unmade me: this is known to him who after due engagement wedded me with his ring.'

The next episode that impresses the reader coming fresh from the *Inferno* is the meeting with Sordello the poet (Canto VI), the soul who appeared

altera e disdegnosa
e nel mover degli occhi onesta e tarda!

proud and disdainful, superb and slow in the movement of his eyes!

E il dolce duca incominciava:
'Mantova' . . . e l'ombra, tutta in sè romita,
surse ver lui del loco ove pria stava,
dicendo: 'O Mantovano, io son Sordello
della tua terra.' E l'un l'altro abbracciava.

The gentle guide (Virgil) began: 'Mantua' . . . and the shade, suddenly rapt, leapt towards him from the place where first it was, saying: 'O Mantuan, I am Sordello of thy very soil.' And the one embraced the other.

The meeting with Sordello *a guisa di leon quando si posa*, like a couchant lion, is no more affecting than that with the poet Statius, in Canto XXI. Statius, when he recognizes his master Virgil, stoops to clasp his feet, but Virgil answers – the lost soul speaking to the saved:

'Frate,
non far, chè tu se' ombra, ed ombra veda.'
Ed ei surgendo: 'Or puoi la quantitate
comprender dell' amor ch'a te mi scalda,
quando dismento nostra vanitate,
trattando l'ombre come cosa saldi.'

'Brother! refrain, for you are but a shadow, and a shadow is but what you see.' Then the other, rising: 'Now can you understand the quantity of love that warms me towards you, so that I forget our vanity, and treat the shadows like the solid thing.'

The last 'episode' at all comparable to those of the *Inferno* is the meeting with Dante's predecessors, Guido Guinicelli and Arnaut Daniel (Canto XXVI). In this canto the Lustful are purged in flame, yet we see clearly how the flame of purgatory differs from that of hell. In hell, the torment issues from the very nature of the damned themselves, expresses their essence; they writhe in the torment of their own perpetually perverted nature. In purgatory the torment of flame is deliberately and consciously accepted by the penitent. When Dante approaches with Virgil these souls in purgatory flame, they crowd towards him:

> *Poi verso me, quanto potevan farsi,*
> *certi si feron, sempre con riguardo*
> *di non uscir dove non fossero arsi.*

Then certain of them made towards me, so far as they could, but ever watchful not to come so far that they should *not be in the fire.*

The souls in purgatory suffer because they *wish to suffer,* for purgation. And observe that they suffer more actively and keenly, being souls preparing for blessedness, than Virgil suffers in eternal limbo. In their suffering is hope, in the anaesthesia of Virgil is hopelessness; that is the difference. The canto ends with the superb verses of Arnaut Daniel in his Provençal tongue:

> *'Ieu sui Arnaut, que plor e vau cantan;*
> *consiros vei la passada folor,*
> *e vei jausen lo jorn, qu' esper, denan.*
> *Ara vos prec, per aquella valor*
> *que vos guida al som de l'escalina,*
> *sovegna vos a temps de ma dolor.'*
> Poi s'ascose nel foco che gli affina.

'I am Arnold, who weeps and goes singing. I see in thought all the past folly. And I see with joy the day for which I hope, before me. And so I pray you, by that Virtue which leads you to the topmost of the stair — be mindful in due time of my pain.' Then dived he back into that fire which refines them.

These are the high episodes, to which the reader initiated by the *Inferno* must first cling, until he reaches the shore of Lethe, and Matilda, and the first sight of Beatrice. In the last cantos (XXIX-XXXIII) of the *Purgatorio* we are already in the world of the *Paradiso*.

But in between these episodes is the narrative of the ascent of the Mount, with meetings, visions, and philosophical expositions,

all important, and all difficult for the uninstructed reader who
finds it less exciting than the continuous phantasmagoria of the
Inferno. The allegory in the *Inferno* was easy to swallow or ignore,
because we could, so to speak, grasp the concrete end of it, its
solidification into imagery; but as we ascend from Hell to Heaven
we are more and more required to grasp the whole from idea to
image.

Here I must make a diversion, before tackling a specifically
philosophical passage of the *Purgatorio*, concerning the nature of
Belief. I wish merely to indicate certain tentative conclusions of
my own, which might affect one's reading of the *Purgatorio*.

Dante's debt to St. Thomas Aquinas, like his debt (a much
smaller one) to Virgil, can be easily exaggerated; for it must not
be forgotten that Dante read and made use of other great mediaeval philosophers as well. Nevertheless, the question of how much
Dante took from Aquinas and how much from elsewhere is one
which has been settled by others and is not relevant to my present
essay. But the question of what Dante 'believed' is always relevant.
It would not matter, if the world were divided between those
persons who are capable of taking poetry simply for what it is and
those who cannot take it at all; if so, there would be no need to
talk about this question to the former and no use in talking about
it to the latter. But most of us are somewhat impure and apt to
confuse issues: hence the justification of writing books about
books, in the hope of straightening things out.

My point is that you cannot afford to *ignore* Dante's philosophical and theological beliefs, or to skip the passages which
express them most clearly; but that on the other hand you are not
called upon to believe them yourself. It is wrong to think that
there are parts of the *Divine Comedy* which are of interest only to
Catholics or to mediaevalists. For there is a difference (which here
I hardly do more than assert) between philosophical *belief* and
poetic *assent*. I am not sure that there is not as great a difference
between philosophical belief and scientific belief; but that is a
difference only now beginning to appear, and certainly inapposite
to the thirteenth century. In reading Dante you must enter the
world of thirteenth-century Catholicism: which is not the world
of modern Catholicism, as his world of physics is not the world of
modern physics. You are not called upon to believe what Dante
believed, for your belief will not give you a groat's worth more of
understanding and appreciation; but you are called upon more
and more to understand it. If you can read poetry as poetry, you
will 'believe' in Dante's theology exactly as you believe in the
physical reality of his journey; that is, you suspend both belief
and disbelief. I will not deny that it may be in practice easier for

a Catholic to grasp the meaning, in many places, than for the ordinary agnostic; but that is not because the Catholic believes, but because he has been instructed. It is a matter of knowledge and ignorance, not of belief or scepticism. The vital matter is that Dante's poem is a whole; that you must in the end come to understand every part in order to understand any part.

Furthermore, we can make a distinction between what Dante believes as a poet and what he believed as a man. Practically, it is hardly likely that even so great a poet as Dante could have composed the *Comedy* merely with understanding and without belief; but his private belief becomes a differing thing in becoming poetry. It is interesting to hazard the suggestion that this is truer of Dante than of any other philosophical poet. With Goethe, for instance, I often feel too acutely 'this is what Goethe the man believed', instead of merely entering into a world which Goethe has created; with Lucretius also; less with the *Bhagavad-Gita*, which is the next greatest philosophical poem to the *Divine Comedy* within my experience. That is the advantage of a coherent traditional system of dogma and morals like the Catholic: it stands apart, for understanding and assent even without belief, from the single individual who propounds it. Goethe always arouses in me a strong sentiment of disbelief in what he believes: Dante does not. I believe that this is because Dante is the purer poet, not because I have more sympathy with Dante the man than Goethe the man.

We are not to take Dante for Aquinas or Aquinas for Dante. It would be a grievous error in psychology. The *belief attitude* of a man reading the *Summa* must be different from that of a man reading Dante, even when it is the same man, and that man a Catholic.

It is not necessary to have read the *Summa* (which usually means, in practice, reading some handbook) in order to understand Dante. But it is necessary to read the philosophical passages of Dante with the humility of a person visiting a new world, who admits that every part is essential to the whole. What is necessary to appreciate the poetry of the *Purgatorio* is not belief, but suspension of belief. Just as much effort is required of any modern person to accept Dante's allegorical method, as is required of the agnostic to accept his theology.

When I speak of understanding, I do not mean merely knowledge of books or words, any more than I mean belief: I mean a state of mind in which one sees certain beliefs, as the order of the deadly sins, in which treachery and pride are greater than lust, and despair the greatest, as *possible*, so that we suspend our judgment altogether.

In the XVIth Canto of the *Purgatorio* we meet Marco Lombardo, who discourses at some length on the Freedom of the Will, and on the Soul:

> *Esce di mano a lui, che la vagheggia*
> *prima che sia, a guisa di fanciulla*
> *che piangendo e ridendo pargoleggia,*
> *l'anima semplicetta, che sa nulla,*
> *salvo che, mossa da lieto fattore,*
> *volentier torna a ciò che la trastulla.*
> *Di picciol bene in pria sente sapore;*
> *quivi s'inganna, e retro ad esso corre,*
> *se guida o fren non torce suo amore.*
> *Onde convenne legge per fren porre;*
> *convenne rege aver, che discernesse*
> *della vera cittade almen la torre.*

From the hands of Him who loves her before she is, there issues like a little child that plays, with weeping and laughter, the simple soul, that knows nothing except that, come from the hands of a glad creator, she turns willingly to everything that delights her. First she tastes the flavour of a trifling good; then is beguiled, and pursues it, if neither guide nor check withhold her. Therefore laws were needed as a curb; a ruler was needed, who should at least see afar the tower of the true City.

Later (Canto XVII) it is Virgil himself who instructs Dante in the nature of Love:

> '*Nè creator nè creatura mai,*'
> *cominciò ei, 'figiuol, fu senza amore,*
> *o naturale o d'animo; e tu il sai.*
> *Lo natural è sempre senza errore,*
> *ma l'altro puote errar per malo obbietto,*
> *o per poco o per troppo di vigore.*
> *Mentre ch'egli è ne' primi ben diretto,*
> *e ne' secondi sè stesso misura,*
> *esser non può cagion di mal diletto;*
> *ma, quando al mal si torce, o con più cura*
> *o con men che non dee corre nel bene,*
> *contra il fattore adopra sua fattura.*
> *Quinci comprender puoi ch'esser conviene*
> *àmor sementa in voi d'ogni virtute,*
> *e d'ogni operazion che merta pene.*'

He began: 'Neither Creator, nor creature, my son, was ever without love, either natural or rational: and you know it. The natural is always without error; but the other may err through mistaking the object, or through excess or deficiency of force. While it is directed towards the primal goods, and in the secondary moderates itself, it cannot be the cause of delight of sin; but when it turns to evil, or hurries towards the good with more or less solicitude than is right, then the creature works against the Creator. Accordingly you may understand how Love must be the seed in you both of every virtue and of every act that merits punishment.'

I have quoted these two passages at some length, because they are of the sort that a reader might be inclined to skip, thinking that they are only for scholars, not for readers of poetry, or thinking that it is necessary to have studied the philosophy underlying them. It is not necessary to have traced the descent of this theory of the soul from Aristotle's *De Anima* in order to appreciate it as poetry. Indeed, if we worry too much about it at first as philosophy we are likely to prevent ourselves from receiving the poetic beauty. It is the philosophy of that world of poetry which we have entered.

But with the XXVIIth canto we have left behind the stage of punishment and the stage of dialectic, and approach the state of Paradise. The last cantos have the quality of the *Paradiso* and prepare us for it; they move straight forward, with no detour or delay. The three poets, Virgil, Statius, and Dante, pass through the wall of flame which separates Purgatory from the Earthly Paradise. Virgil dismisses Dante, who henceforth shall proceed with a higher guide, saying

> *Non aspettar mio dir più, nè mio cenno.*
> *Libero, dritto e sano è tuo arbitrio,*
> *e fallo fora non fare a suo senno:*
> *per ch'io te sopra te corono e mitrio.*

No more expect my word, or sign. Your Will is free, straight and whole, and not to follow its direction would be sin: wherefore I crown and mitre you (king and bishop) over yourself.

i.e. Dante has now arrived at a condition, for the purposes of the rest of his journey, which is that of the blessed: for political and ecclesiastical organization are only required because of the imperfections of the human will. In the Earthly Paradise Dante encounters a lady named Matilda, whose identity need not at first bother us,

una donna soletta, che si gia
cantando ed iscegliendo fior da fiore,
ond' era pinta tutta la sua via.

A lady alone, who went singing and plucking flower after flower, wherewith her path was pied.

After some conversation, and explanation by Matilda of the reason and nature of the place, there follows a 'Divine Pageant'. To those who dislike – not what are popularly called pageants – but the serious pageants of royalty, of the Church, of military funerals – the 'pageantry' which we find here and in the *Paradiso* will be tedious; and still more to those, if there be any, who are unmoved by the splendour of the Revelation of St. John. It belongs to the world of what I call the *high dream*, and the modern world seems capable only of the *low dream*. I arrived at accepting it, myself, only with some difficulty. There were at least two prejudices, one against Pre-Raphaelite imagery, which was natural to one of my generation, and perhaps affects generations younger than mine. The other prejudice – which affects this end of the *Purgatorio* and the whole of the *Paradiso* – is the prejudice that poetry not only must be found *through* suffering but can find its material only *in* suffering. Everything else was cheerfulness, optimism, and hopefulness; and these words stood for a great deal of what one hated in the nineteenth century. It took me many years to recognize that the states of improvement and beatitude which Dante describes are still further from what the modern world can conceive as cheerfulness, than are his states of damnation. And little things put one off: Rossetti's *Blessed Damozel*, first by my rapture and next by my revolt, held up my appreciation of Beatrice by many years.

We cannot understand fully Canto XXX of the *Purgatorio* until we know the *Vita Nuova*, which in my opinion should be read after the *Divine Comedy*. But at least we can begin to understand how skilfully Dante expresses the recrudescence of an ancient passion in a new emotion, in a new situation, which comprehends, enlarges, and gives a meaning to it.

sopra candido vel cinta d'oliva
donna m'apparve, sotto verde manto,
vestita di color di fiamma viva.
E lo spirito mio, che già cotanto
tempo era stato che alla sua presenza
non era di stupor, tremando, affranto,

senza degli occhi aver più conoscenza,
per occulta virtù che da lei mosse,
d'antico amor sentì la gran potenza.
Tosto che nella vista mi percosse
l'alta virtù, che già m'avea trafitto
primo ch'io fuor di puerizia fosse,
volsimi alla sinistra col rispitto
col quale il fantolin corre alla mamma,
quando ha paura o quando egli è afflitto,
per dicere a Virgilio: 'Men che dramma
di sangue m' è rimaso, che non tremi;
conosco i segni dell' antica fiamma.'

Olive-crowned over a white veil, a lady appeared to me, clad, under a green mantle, in colour of living flame. And my spirit, after so many years since trembling in her presence it had been broken with awe, without further knowledge by my eyes, felt, through hidden power which went out from her, the great strength of the old love. As soon as that lofty power struck my sense, which already had transfixed me before my adolescence, I turned leftwards with the trust of the little child who runs to his mama when he is frightened or distressed, to say to Virgil: 'Hardly a drop of blood in my body does not shudder: I know the tokens of the ancient flame.'

And in the dialogue that follows we see the passionate conflict of the old feelings with the new; the effort and triumph of a new renunciation, greater than renunciation at the grave, because a renunciation of feelings that persist beyond the grave. In a way, these cantos are those of the greatest *personal* intensity in the whole poem. In the *Paradiso* Dante himself, save for the Cacciaguida episode, becomes de- or super-personalized; and it is in these last cantos of the *Purgatorio*, rather than in the *Paradiso*, that Beatrice appears most clearly. But the Beatrice theme is essential to the understanding of the whole, *not* because we need to know Dante's biography – not, for instance, as the Wesendonck history is supposed to cast light upon *Tristan* – but because of Dante's *philosophy* of it. This, however, concerns more our examination of the *Vita Nuova*.

The *Purgatorio* is the most difficult because it is the *transitional* canto: the *Inferno* is one thing, comparatively easy; the *Paradiso* is another thing, more difficult as a whole than the *Purgatorio*, because more a whole. Once we have got the hang of the kind of feeling in it no one part is difficult. The *Purgatorio*, here and there might be called 'dry': the *Paradiso* is never dry, it is either incomprehensible or intensely exciting. With the exception of the episode of Cacciaguida – a pardonable exhibition of family and personal pride, because it provides splendid poetry – it is not episodic. All the other characters have the best credentials. At first, they seem less distinct than the earlier unblessed people; they seem ingeniously varied but fundamentally monotonous variations of insipid blessedness. It is a matter of gradual adjustment of our vision. We have (whether we know it or not) a prejudice against beatitude as material for poetry. The eighteenth and nineteenth centuries knew nothing of it; even Shelley, who knew Dante well and who towards the end of his life was beginning to profit by it, the one English poet of the nineteenth century who could even have begun to follow those footsteps, was able to enounce the proposition that our sweetest songs are those which tell of saddest thought. The early work of Dante might confirm Shelley; the *Paradiso* provides the counterpart, though a different counterpart from the philosophy of Browning.

The *Paradiso* is not monotonous. It is as various as any poem. And take the *Comedy* as a whole, you can compare it to nothing but the *entire* dramatic work of Shakespeare. The comparison of the *Vita Nuova* with the *Sonnets* is another, and interesting, occupation. Dante and Shakespeare divide the modern world between them; there is no third.

We should begin by thinking of Dante fixing his gaze on Beatrice:

> *Nel suo aspetto tal dentro mi fei,*
> *qual si fe' Glauco nel gustar dell' erba,*
> *che il fe' consorto in mar degli altri dei.*
> *Trasumanar significar per verba*
> *non si poria; pero l'esemplo basti*
> *a cui esperienza grazia serba.*

Gazing on her, so I became within, as did Glaucus, on tasting of the grass which made him sea-fellow of the other gods. To transcend humanity may not be told in words, wherefore let the instance suffice for him for whom that experience is reserved by Grace.

And as Beatrice says to Dante: '*You make yourself dull with false fancy*'; warns him, that here there are divers sorts of blessedness, as settled by Providence.

If this is not enough, Dante is informed by Piccarda (Canto III) in words which even those who know no Dante know:

> *la sua voluntate è nostra pace.*

His will is our peace.

It is the mystery of the inequality, and of the indifference of that inequality, in blessedness, of the blessed. It is all the same, and yet each degree differs.

Shakespeare gives the greatest *width* of human passion; Dante the greatest altitude and greatest depth. They complement each other. It is futile to ask which undertook the more difficult job. But certainly the 'difficult passages' in the *Paradiso* are Dante's difficulties rather than ours: his difficulty in making us apprehend sensuously the various states and stages of blessedness. Thus the long oration of Beatrice upon the Will (Canto IV) is really directed at making us *feel* the reality of the condition of Piccarda; Dante has to educate our senses as he goes along. The insistence throughout is upon states of feeling; the reasoning takes only its proper place as a means of reaching these states. We get constantly verses like

> *Beatrice mi guardò con gli occhi pieni*
> *di faville d'amor così divini,*
> *che, vinta, mia virtù diede le reni,*
> *e quasi mi perdei con gli occhi chini.*

Beatrice looked on me with eyes so divine filled with sparks of love, that my vanquished power turned away, and I became as lost, with downcast eyes.

The whole difficulty is in admitting that this is something that we are meant to feel, not merely decorative verbiage. Dante gives us every aid of images, as when

> *Come in peschiera, ch' è tranquilla e pura,*
> *traggonsi i pesci a ciò che vien di fuori*
> *per modo che lo stimin lor pastura;*
> *sì vid' io ben più di mille di splendori*
> *trarsi ver noi, ed in ciascun s'udia:*
> Ecco chi crescerà li nostri amori.

As in a fishpond still and clear, the fishes draw near to anything that falls from without in such a way as to make them think it something to eat, so I saw more than a thousand splendours draw towards us, and in each was heard: *Lo! here is one that shall increase our loves.*

About the persons whom Dante meets in the several spheres, we need only to enquire enough to consider why Dante placed them where he did.

When we have grasped the strict *utility* of the minor images, such as the one given above, or even the simple comparison admired by Landor:

Quale allodetta che in aere si spazia
prima cantando, e poi tace contenta
dell' ultima dolcezza che la sazia,

Like the lark which soars in the air, first singing, and then ceases, content with the last sweetness that sates her,

we may study with respect the more elaborate imagery, such as that of the figure of the Eagle composed by the spirits of the just, which extends from Canto XVIII onwards for some space. Such figures are not merely antiquated rhetorical devices, but serious and practical means of making the spiritual visible. An understanding of the rightness of such imagery is a preparation for apprehending the last and greatest canto, the most tenuous and most intense. Nowhere in poetry has experience so remote from ordinary experience been expressed so concretely, by a masterly use of that imagery of *light* which is the form of certain types of mystical experience.

Nel suo profondo vidi che s'interna,
  legato con amore in un volume,
  ciò che per l'universo si squaderna;
sustanzia ed accidenti, e lor costume,
  quasi conflati insieme per tal modo,
  che ciò ch' io dico è un semplice lume.
La forma universal di questo nodo
  credo ch' io vidi, perchè più di largo,
  dicendo questo, mi sento ch' io godo.
Un punto solo m'è maggior letargo,
  che venticinque secoli alla impresa,
  che fe' Nettuno ammirar l'ombra d'Argo.

Within its depths I saw ingathered, bound by love in one mass, the scattered leaves of the universe: substance and accidents and their relations, as though together fused, so that what I speak of is one simple flame. The universal form of this complex I think I saw, because, as I say this, more largely I feel myself rejoice. One single moment to me is more lethargy than twenty-five centuries upon the enterprise which made Neptune wonder at the shadow of the Argo (passing over him).

One can feel only awe at the power of the master who could thus at every moment realize the inapprehensible in visual images. And I do not know anywhere in poetry more authentic sign of greatness than the power of association which could in the last line, when the poet is speaking of the Divine vision, yet introduce the Argo passing over the head of wondering Neptune. Such association is utterly different from that of Marino speaking in one breath of the beauty of the Magdalen and the opulence of Cleopatra (so that you are not quite sure what adjectives apply to which). It is the real right thing, the power of establishing relations between beauty of the most diverse sorts; it is the utmost power of the poet.

> *O quanto è corto il dire, e come fioco*
> *al mio concetto!*

How scant the speech, and how faint, for my conception!

In writing of the *Divine Comedy* I have tried to keep to a few very simple points of which I am convinced. First that the poetry of Dante is the one universal school of style for the writing of poetry in any language. There is much, naturally, which can profit only those who write Dante's own Tuscan language; but there is no poet in any tongue – not even in Latin or Greek – who stands so firmly as a model for all poets. I tried to illustrate his universal mastery in the use of images. In the actual writing I went so far as to say that he is safer to follow, even for us, than any English poet, including Shakespeare. My second point is that Dante's 'allegorical' method has great advantages for the writing of *poetry*: it simplifies the diction, and makes clear and precise the images. That in good allegory, like Dante's, it is not necessary to understand the meaning first to enjoy the poetry, but that our enjoyment of the poetry makes us want to understand the meaning. And the third point is that the *Divine Comedy* is a complete scale of the *depths* and *heights* of human emotion; that the *Purgatorio* and *Paradiso* are to be read as extensions of the ordinarily very limited human range. Every degree of the feeling of humanity, from lowest to highest, has, moreover, an intimate relation to the next above and below, and all fit together according to the logic of sensibility. . . .

from BAUDELAIRE

. . . What is significant about Baudelaire is his theological innocence. He is discovering Christianity for himself; he is not assuming it as a fashion or weighing social or political reasons, or any other accidents. He is beginning, in a way, at the beginning; and, being a discoverer, is not altogether certain what he is exploring and to what it leads; he might almost be said to be making again, as one man, the effort of scores of generations. His Christianity is rudimentary or embryonic; at best, he has the excesses of a Tertullian (and even Tertullian is not considered wholly orthodox and well balanced). His business was not to practise Christianity, but – what was much more important for his time – to assert its *necessity*.

Baudelaire's morbidity of temperament cannot, of course, be ignored: and no one who has looked at the work of Crépet or the recent small biographical study of François Porché can forget it. We should be misguided if we treated it as an unfortunate ailment which can be discounted or attempted to detach the sound from the unsound in his work. Without the morbidity none of his work would be possible or significant; his weaknesses can be composed into a larger whole of strength, and this is implied in my assertion that neither the health of Goethe nor the malady of Baudelaire matters in itself: it is what both men made of their endowments that matters. To the eye of the world, and quite properly for all questions of private life, Baudelaire was thoroughly perverse and insufferable: a man with a talent for ingratitude and unsociability, intolerably irritable, and with a mulish determination to make the worst of everything; if he had money, to squander it; if he had friends, to alienate them; if he had any good fortune, to disdain it. He had the pride of the man who feels in himself great weakness and great strength. Having great genius, he had neither the patience nor the inclination, had he had the power to overcome

231

his weakness; on the contrary, he exploited it for theoretical purposes. The morality of such a course may be a matter for endless dispute; for Baudelaire, it was the way to liberate his mind and give us the legacy and lesson that he has left.

He was one of those who have great strength, but strength merely to *suffer*. He could not escape suffering and could not transcend it, so he *attracted* pain to himself. But what he could do, with that immense passive strength and sensibilities which no pain could impair, was to study his suffering. And in this limitation he is wholly unlike Dante, not even like any character in Dante's Hell. But, on the other hand, such suffering as Baudelaire's implies the possibility of a positive state of beatitude. Indeed, in his way of suffering is already a kind of presence of the supernatural and of the superhuman. He rejects always the purely natural and the purely human; in other words, he is neither 'naturalist' or 'humanist'. Either because he cannot adjust himself to the actual world he has to reject it in favour of Heaven and Hell, or because he has the perception of Heaven and Hell he rejects the present world: both ways of putting it are tenable. There is in his statements a good deal of romantic detritus; *ses ailes de géant l'empêchent de marcher*, he says of the Poet and of the Albatross, but not convincingly; but there is also truth about himself and about the world. His *ennui* may of course be explained, as everything can be explained in psychological or pathological terms; but it is also, from the opposite point of view, a true form of *acedia*, arising from the unsuccessful struggle towards the spiritual life.

From the poems alone, I venture to think, we are not likely to grasp what seems to me the true sense and significance of Baudelaire's mind. Their excellence of form, their perfection of phrasing, and their superficial coherence, may give them the appearance of presenting a definite and final state of mind. In reality, they seem to me to have the external but not the internal form of classic art. One might even hazard the conjecture that the care for perfection of form, among some of the romantic poets of the nineteenth century, was an effort to support, or to conceal from view, an inner disorder. Now the true claim of Baudelaire as an artist is not that he found a superficial form, but that he was searching for a form of life. In minor form he never indeed equalled Théophile Gautier, to whom he significantly dedicated his poems: in the best of the slight verse of Gautier there is a satisfaction, a balance of inwards and form, which we do not find in Baudelaire. He had a greater technical ability than Gautier, and yet the content of feeling is constantly bursting the receptacle. His apparatus, by which I do not mean his command of words and rhythms, but his stock of imagery (and every poet's stock of imagery is circumscribed somewhere), is not wholly perdurable or adequate. His prostitutes, mulattoes, Jewesses, serpents, cats, corpses form a machinery which has not worn very well; his Poet, or his Don Juan, has a romantic ancestry which is too clearly traceable. Compare with the costumery of Baudelaire the stock of imagery of the *Vita Nuova*, or of Cavalcanti, and you find Baudelaire's does not everywhere wear as well as that of several centuries earlier; compare him with Dante or Shakespeare, for what such a comparison is worth, and he is found not only a much smaller poet, but one in whose work much more that is perishable has entered.

To say this is only to say that Baudelaire belongs to a definite place in time. Inevitably the offspring of romanticism, and by his nature the first counter-romantic in poetry, he could, like anyone else, only work with the materials which were there. It must not be forgotten that a poet in a romantic age cannot be a 'classical' poet except in tendency. If he is sincere, he must express with individual differences the general state of mind – not as a *duty*, but simply because he cannot help participating in it. For such poets, we may expect often to get much help from reading their prose works and even notes and diaries; help in deciphering the discrepancies between head and heart, means and end, material and ideals.

What preserves Baudelaire's poetry from the fate of most French poetry of the nineteenth century up to his time, and has made him, as M. Valéry has said in a recent introduction to the *Fleurs du Mal*, the one modern French poet to be widely read abroad, is not quite easy to conclude. It is partly that technical mastery which can hardly be overpraised, and which has made his verse an inexhaustible study for later poets, not only in his own language. When we read

> *Maint joyau dort enseveli*
> *Dans les ténèbres et l'oubli,*
> *Bien loin des pioches et des sondes;*
> *Mainte fleur épanche à regret*
> *Son parfum doux comme un secret*
> *Dans les solitudes profondes,*

we might for a moment think it a more lucid bit of Mallarmé; and so original is the arrangement of words that we might easily overlook its borrowing from Gray's *Elegy*. When we read

> *Valse mélancolique et langoureux vertige!*

233

we are already in the Paris of Laforgue. Baudelaire gave to French poets as generously as he borrowed from English and American poets. The renovation of the versification of Racine has been mentioned often enough; quite genuine, but might be over-emphasized, as it sometimes comes near to being a trick. But even without this, Baudelaire's variety and resourcefulness would still be immense.

Furthermore, besides the stock of images which he used that seems already second-hand, he gave new possibilities to poetry in a new stock of imagery of contemporary life.

> . . . *Au cœur d'un vieux faubourg, labyrinthe fangeux*
> *Où l'humanité grouille en ferments orageux,*
> *On voit un vieux chiffonnier qui vient, hochant la tête,*
> *Buttant, et se cognant aux murs comme un poète.*

This introduces something new, and something universal in modern life. (The last line quoted, which in ironic terseness anticipates Corbière, might be contrasted with the whole poem *Bénédiction* which begins the volume.) It is not merely in the use of imagery of common life, not merely in the use of imagery of the sordid life of a great metropolis, but in the elevation of such imagery to the *first intensity* – presenting it as it is, and yet making it represent something much more than itself – that Baudelaire has created a mode of release and expression for other men.

This invention of language, at a moment when French poetry in particular was famishing for such invention, is enough to make of Baudelaire a great poet, a great landmark in poetry. Baudelaire is indeed the greatest exemplar in *modern* poetry in any language, for his verse and language is the nearest thing to a complete renovation that we have experienced. But his renovation of an attitude towards life is no less radical and no less important. In his verse, he is now less a model to be imitated or a source to be drained than a reminder of the duty, the consecrated task, of sincerity. From a fundamental sincerity he could not deviate. The superficies of sincerity (as I think has not always been remarked) is not always there. As I have suggested, many of his poems are insufficiently removed from their romantic origins, from Byronic paternity and Satanic fraternity. The 'satanism' of the Black Mass was very much in the air; in exhibiting it Baudelaire is the voice of his time; but I would observe that in Baudelaire, as in no one else, it is redeemed by *meaning something else*. He uses the same paraphernalia, but cannot limit its symbolism even to all that of which he is conscious. Compare him with Huysmans in *A rebours*, *En route*, and *Là-bas*. Huysmans, who is a first-rate realist of his time, only succeeds in making his diabolism interesting when he treats it externally, when he is merely describing a manifestation of his period (if such it was). His own interest in such matters is, like his interest in Christianity, a petty affair. Huysmans merely provides a document. Baudelaire would not even provide that, if he had been really absorbed in that ridiculous hocus-pocus. But actually Baudelaire is concerned, not with demons, black masses, and romantic blasphemy, but with the real problem of good and evil. It is hardly more than an accident of time that he uses the current imagery and vocabulary of blasphemy. In the middle nineteenth century, the age which (at its best) Goethe had prefigured, an age of bustle, programmes, platforms, scientific progress, humanitarianism and revolutions which improved nothing, an age of progressive degradation, Baudelaire perceived that what really matters is Sin and Redemption. It is a proof of his honesty that he went as far as he could honestly go and no further. To a mind observant of the post-Voltaire France (*Voltaire . . . le prédicateur des concierges*), a mind which saw the world of *Napoléon le petit* more lucidly than did that of Victor Hugo, a mind which at the same time had no affinity for the *Saint-Sulpicerie* of the day, the recognition of the reality of Sin is a New Life; and the possibility of damnation is so immense a relief in a world of electoral reform, plebiscites, sex reform and dress reform, that damnation itself is an immediate form of salvation – of salvation from the ennui of modern life, because it at last gives some significance to living. It is this, I believe, that Baudelaire is trying to express; and it is this which separates him from the modernist Protestantism of Byron and Shelley. It is apparently Sin in the Swinburnian sense, but really Sin in the permanent Christian sense, that occupies the mind of Baudelaire.

Yet, as I said, the sense of Evil implies the sense of good. Here too, as Baudelaire apparently confuses, and perhaps did confuse, Evil with its theatrical representations, Baudelaire is not always certain in his notion of the Good. The romantic idea of Love is never quite exorcized, but never quite surrendered to. In *Le Balcon*, which M. Valéry considers, and I think rightly, one of Baudelaire's most beautiful poems, there is all the romantic idea, but something more: the reaching out towards something which cannot be had *in*, but which may be had partly *through*, personal relations. Indeed, in much romantic poetry the sadness is due to the exploitation of the fact that no human relations are adequate to human desires, but also to the disbelief in any further object for human desires than that which, being human, fails to satisfy them. One of the unhappy necessities of human existence is that we have to 'find things out for ourselves'. If it were not so, the statement of Dante would, at least for poets, have done once for all. Baudelaire has all the romantic sorrow, but invents a new kind of romantic nostalgia – a derivative of his nostalgia being the *poésie des départs*, the *poésie des salles d'attente*. In a beautiful paragraph of the volume in question, *Mon cœur mis à nu*, he imagines the vessels lying in harbour as saying: *Quand partons-nous vers le bonheur?* and his minor successor Laforgue exclaims: *Comme ils sont beaux, les trains manqués*. The poetry of flight – which, in contemporary France, owes a great debt to the poems of the A. O. Barnabooth of Valery Larbaud – is, in its origin in this paragraph of Baudelaire, a dim recognition of the direction of beatitude.

But in the adjustment of the natural to the spiritual, of the bestial to the human and the human to the supernatural, Baudelaire is a bungler compared with Dante; the best that can be said, and that is a very great deal, is that what he knew he found out for himself. In his book, the *Journaux Intimes*, and especially in *Mon cœur mis à nu*, he has a great deal to say of the love of man and woman. One aphorism which has been especially noticed is the following: *la volupté unique et suprême de l'amour gît dans la certitude de faire le mal*. This means, I think, that Baudelaire has perceived that what distinguishes the relations of man and woman from the copulation of beasts is the knowledge of Good and Evil (of *moral* Good and Evil which are not natural Good and Bad or Puritan Right and Wrong). Having an imperfect, vague romantic conception of Good, he was at least able to understand that the sexual act as evil is more dignified, less boring, than as the natural, 'life-giving', cheery automatism of the modern world. For Baudelaire, sexual operation is at least something not analogous to Kruschen Salts.

So far as we are human, what we do must be either evil or good;[1] so far as we do evil or good, we are human; and it is better, in a paradoxical way, to do evil than to do nothing: at least, we exist. It is true to say that the glory of man is his capacity for salvation; it is also true to say that his glory is his capacity for damnation. The worst that can be said of most of our malefactors, from statesmen to thieves, is that they are not men enough to be damned. Baudelaire was man enough for damnation: whether he *is* damned is, of course, another question, and we are not prevented from praying for his repose. In all his humiliating traffic with other beings, he walked secure in this high vocation, that he was capable of a damnation denied to the politicians and the newspaper editors of Paris. . . .

[1] 'Know ye not, that to whom ye yield yourselves servants to obey, his servants ye are to whom ye obey; whether of sin unto death, or of obedience unto righteousness?' – Romans vi. 16.

from THE PENSÉES OF PASCAL

... Pascal's interest in society did not distract him from scientific research; nor did this period occupy much space in what is a very short and crowded life. Partly his natural dissatisfaction with such a life, once he had learned all it had to teach him, partly the influence of his saintly sister Jacqueline, partly increasing suffering as his health declined, directed him more and more out of the world and to thoughts of eternity. And in 1654 occurs what is called his 'second conversion', but which might be called his conversion simply.

He made a note of his mystical experience, which he kept always about him, and which was found, after his death, sewn into the coat which he was wearing. The experience occurred on 23 November 1654, and there is no reason to doubt its genuineness unless we choose to deny all mystical experience. Now, Pascal was not a mystic, and his works are not to be classified amongst mystical writings; but what can only be called mystical experience happens to many men who do not become mystics. The work which he undertook soon after, the *Lettres écrites à un provincial*, is a masterpiece of religious controversy at the opposite pole from mysticism. We know quite well that he was at the time when he received his illumination from God in extremely poor health; but it is a commonplace that some forms of illness are extremely favourable, not only to religious illumination, but to artistic and literary composition. A piece of writing meditated, apparently without progress, for months or years, may suddenly take shape and word; and in this state long passages may be produced which require little or no retouch. I have no good word to say for the cultivation of automatic writing as the model of literary composition; I doubt whether these moments *can* be cultivated by the writer; but he to whom this happens assuredly has the sensation of being a vehicle rather than a maker. No masterpiece can be produced whole by such means: but neither does even the higher form of religious inspiration suffice for the religious life; even the most exalted mystic must return to the world, and use his reason to employ the results of his experience in daily life. You may call it communion with the Divine, or you may call it a temporary crystallization of the mind. Until science can teach us to reproduce such phenomena at will, science cannot claim to have explained them; and they can be judged only by their fruits.

IN MEMORIAM

Tennyson is a great poet, for reasons that are perfectly clear. He has three qualities which are seldom found together except in the greatest poets: abundance, variety, and complete competence. We therefore cannot appreciate his work unless we read a good deal of it. We may not admire his aims: but whatever he sets out to do, he succeeds in doing, with a mastery which gives us the sense of confidence that is one of the major pleasures of poetry. His variety of metrical accomplishment is astonishing. Without making the mistake of trying to write Latin verse in English, he knew everything about Latin versification that an English poet could use; and he said of himself that he thought he knew the quantity of the sounds of every English word except perhaps *scissors*. He had the finest ear of any English poet since Milton. He was the master of Swinburne; and the versification of Swinburne, himself a classical scholar, is often crude and sometimes cheap in comparison with Tennyson's. Tennyson extended very widely the range of active metrical forms in English: in *Maud* alone the variety is prodigious. But innovation in metric is not to be measured solely by the width of the deviation from accepted practice. It is a matter of the historical situation: at some moments a more violent change may be necessary than at others. The problem differs at every period. At some times, a violent revolution may be neither possible nor desirable; at such times, a change which may appear very slight is the change which the important poet will make. The innovation of Pope, after Dryden, may not seem very great; but it is the mark of the master to be able to make small changes which will be highly significant, as at another time to make radical changes, through which poetry will curve back again to its norm.

There is an early poem, only published in the official biography, which already exhibits Tennyson as a master. According to a note, Tennyson later expressed regret that he had removed the poem from his Juvenilia; it is a fragmentary *Hesperides*, in which only the 'Song of the Three Sisters' is complete. The poem illustrates Tennyson's classical learning and his mastery of metre. The first stanza of the 'Song of the Three Sisters' is as follows:

The Golden Apple, the Golden Apple, the hallow'd fruit,
Guard it well, guard it warily,
Singing airily,
Standing about the charmèd root.
Round about all is mute,
As the snowfield on the mountain peaks,
As the sandfield at the mountain foot.
Crocodiles in briny creeks
Sleep and stir not; all is mute.
If ye sing not, if ye make false measure,
We shall lose eternal pleasure,
Worth eternal want of rest.
Laugh not loudly: watch the treasure
Of the wisdom of the West.
In a corner wisdom whispers. Five and three
(Let it not be preach'd abroad) make an awful mystery:
For the blossom unto threefold music bloweth;
Evermore it is born anew,
And the sap in threefold music floweth,
From the root,
Drawn in the dark,
Up to the fruit,
Creeping under the fragrant bark,
Liquid gold, honeysweet through and through.
Keen-eyed Sisters, singing airily,
Looking warily
Every way,
Guard the apple night and day,
Lest one from the East come and take it away.

A young man who can write like that has not much to learn about metric; and the young man who wrote these lines somewhere between 1828 and 1830 was doing something new. There is something not derived from any of his predecessors. In some of Tennyson's early verse the influence of Keats is visible – in songs and in blank verse; and less successfully, there is the influence of Wordsworth, as in *Dora*. But in the lines I have just quoted, and in the two Mariana poems, *The Sea Fairies, The Lotos-Eaters, The Lady of Shalott* and elsewhere, there is something wholly new.

> *All day within the dreamy house,*
> *The doors upon their hinges creak'd;*
> *The blue fly sung in the pane; the mouse*
> *Behind the mouldering wainscoat shriek'd,*
> *Or from the crevice peer'd about.*

The blue fly sung in the pane (the line would be ruined if you substituted *sang* for *sung*) is enough to tell us that something important has happened.

The reading of long poems is not nowadays much practised: in the age of Tennyson it appears to have been easier. For a good many long poems were not only written but widely circulated; and the level was high: even the second-rate long poems of that time, like *The Light of Asia*, are better worth reading than most long modern novels. But Tennyson's long poems are not long poems in quite the same sense as those of his contemporaries. They are very different in kind from *Sordello* or *The Ring and the Book*, to name the greatest by the greatest of his contemporary poets. *Maud* and *In Memoriam* are each a series of poems, given form by the greatest lyrical resourcefulness that a poet has ever shown. The *Idylls of the King* have merits and defects similar to those of *The Princess*. An idyll is a 'short poem descriptive of some picturesque scene or incident'; in choosing the name Tennyson perhaps showed an appreciation of his limitations. For his poems are always descriptive, and always picturesque; they are never really narrative. The *Idylls of the King* are no different in kind from some of his early poems; the *Morte d'Arthur* is in fact an early poem. *The Princess* is still an idyll, but an idyll that is too long. Tennyson's versification in this poem is as masterly as elsewhere: it is a poem which we must read, but which we excuse ourselves from reading twice. And it is worth while recognizing the reason why we return again and again, and are always stirred by the lyrics which intersperse it, and which are among the greatest of all poetry of their kind, and yet avoid the poem itself. It is not, as we may think while reading, the outmoded attitude towards the relations of the sexes, the exasperating views on the subjects of matrimony, celibacy and female education, that make us recoil from *The Princess*.[1] We can swallow the most antipathetic doctrines if we are given an exciting narrative. But for narrative Tennyson had no gift at all. For a static poem, and a moving poem, on the same subject, you have only to compare his *Ulysses* with the condensed and intensely exciting narrative of that hero in the XXVIth Canto of Dante's *Inferno*. Dante is telling a story. Tennyson is only stating an elegiac mood. The very greatest poets set before you real men talking, carry you on in real events moving. Tennyson could not tell a story at all. It is not that in

[1] For a revelation of the Victorian mind on these matters, and of opinions to which Tennyson would probably have subscribed, see the Introduction by Sir Edward Strachey, Bt., to his emasculated edition of the *Morte D'Arthur* of Malory, still current. Sir Edward admired the *Idylls of the King*.

The Princess he tries to tell a story and failed: it is rather that an idyll protracted to such length becomes unreadable. So *The Princess* is a dull poem; one of the poems of which we may say that they are beautiful but dull.

But in *Maud* and in *In Memoriam*, Tennyson is doing what every conscious artist does, turning his limitations to good purpose. *Maud* consists of a few very beautiful lyrics, such as *O let the solid ground*, *Birds in the high Hall-garden*, and *Go not, happy day*, around which the semblance of a dramatic situation has been constructed with the greatest metrical virtuosity. The whole situation is unreal; the ravings of the lover on the edge of insanity sound false, and fail, as do the bellicose bellowings, to make one's flesh creep with sincerity. It would be foolish to suggest that Tennyson ought to have gone through some experience similar to that described: for a poet with dramatic gifts, a situation quite remote from his personal experience may release the strongest emotion. And I do not believe for a moment that Tennyson was a man of mild feelings or weak passions. There is no evidence in his poetry that he knew the experience of violent passion for a woman; but there is plenty of evidence of emotional intensity and violence – but of emotion so deeply suppressed, even from himself, as to tend rather towards the blackest melancholia than towards dramatic action. And it is emotion which, so far as my reading of the poems can discover, attained no ultimate clear purgation. I should reproach Tennyson not for mildness, or tepidity, but rather for lack of serenity.

> *Of love that never found his earthly close,*
> *What sequel?*

The fury of *Maud* is shrill rather than deep, though one feels in every passage what exquisite adaptation of metre to the mood Tennyson is attempting to express. I think that the effect of feeble violence, which the poem as a whole produces, is the result of a fundamental error of form. A poet can express his feelings as fully through a dramatic, as through a lyrical form; but *Maud* is neither one thing nor the other: just as *The Princess* is more than an idyll, and less than a narrative. In *Maud*, Tennyson neither identifies himself with the lover, nor identifies the lover with himself: consequently, the real feelings of Tennyson, profound and tumultuous as they are, never arrive at expression.

It is, in my opinion, in *In Memoriam*, that Tennyson finds full expression. Its technical merit alone is enough to ensure its perpetuity. While Tennyson's technical competence is everywhere masterly and satisfying, *In Memoriam* is the most unapproachable of all his poems. Here are one hundred and thirty-two passages, each of several quatrains in the same form, and never monotony or repetition. And the poem has to be comprehended as a whole. We may not memorize a few passages, we cannot find a 'fair sample'; we have to comprehend the whole of a poem which is essentially the length that it is. We may choose to remember:

> Dark house, by which once more I stand
> Here in the long unlovely street,
> Doors, where my heart was used to beat
> So quickly, waiting for a hand,
>
> A hand that can be clasp'd no more –
> Behold me, for I cannot sleep,
> And like a guilty thing I creep
> At earliest morning to the door.
>
> He is not here; but far away
> The noise of life begins again,
> And ghastly thro' the drizzling rain
> On the bald street breaks the blank day.

This is great poetry, economical of words, a universal emotion related to a particular place; and it gives me the shudder that I fail to get from anything in *Maud*. But such a passage, by itself, is not *In Memoriam: In Memoriam* is the whole poem. It is unique: it is a long poem made by putting together lyrics, which have only the unity and continuity of a diary, the concentrated diary of a man confessing himself. It is a diary of which we have to read every word.

Apparently Tennyson's contemporaries, once they had accepted *In Memoriam*, regarded it as a message of hope and reassurance to their rather fading Christian faith. It happens now and then that a poet by some strange accident expresses the mood of his generation, at the same time that he is expressing a mood of his own which is quite remote from that of his generation. This is not a question of insincerity: there is an amalgam of yielding and opposition below the level of consciousness. Tennyson himself, on the conscious level of the man who talks to reporters and poses for photographers, to judge from remarks made in conversation and recorded in his son's Memoir, consistently asserted a convinced, if somewhat sketchy, Christian belief. And he was a friend of Frederick Denison Maurice – nothing seems odder about that age than the respect which its eminent people felt for each other. Nevertheless, I get a very different impression from *In Memoriam* from that which Tennyson's contemporaries seem to have got. It is of a very much more interesting and tragic Tennyson. His biographers have not failed to remark that he had a good deal of the temperament of the mystic – certainly not at all the mind of the theologian. He was desperately anxious to hold the faith of the believer, without being very clear about what he wanted to believe: he was capable of illumination which he was incapable of understanding. The 'Strong Son of God, immortal Love,' with an invocation of whom the poem opens, has only a hazy connection with the Logos, or the Incarnate God. Tennyson is distressed by the idea of a mechanical universe; he is naturally, in lamenting his friend, teased by the hope of immortality and reunion beyond death. Yet the renewal craved for seems at best but a continuance, or a substitute for the joys of friendship upon earth. His desire for immortality never is quite the desire for Eternal Life; his concern is for the loss of man rather than for the gain of God.

> *shall he,*
> *Man, her last work, who seem'd so fair,*
> *Such splendid purpose in his eyes,*
> *Who roll'd the psalm to wintry skies,*
> *Who built him fanes of fruitless prayer,*

> *Who trusted God was love indeed,*
> *And love Creation's final law –*
> *Tho' Nature, red in tooth and claw*
> *With ravine, shriek'd against his creed –*

> *Who loved, who suffer'd countless ills.*
> *Who battled for the True, the Just,*
> *Be blown about the desert dust,*
> *Or seal'd within the iron hills?*

That strange abstraction, 'Nature,' becomes a real god or goddess, perhaps more real, at moments, to Tennyson than God ('*Are God and Nature then at strife?*'). The hope of immortality is confused (typically of the period) with the hope of the gradual and steady improvement of this world. Much has been said of Tennyson's interest in contemporary science, and of the impression of Darwin. *In Memoriam*, in any case, antedates *The Origin of Species* by several years, and the belief in social progress by democracy antedates it by many more; and I suspect that the faith of Tennyson's age in human progress would have been quite as strong even had the discoveries of Darwin been postponed by fifty years. And after all, there is no logical connection: the belief in progress being current already, the discoveries of Darwin were harnessed to it:

> *No longer half-akin to brute,*
> *For all we thought, and loved and did*
> *And hoped, and suffer'd, is but seed*
> *Of what in them is flower and fruit;*

> *Whereof the man, that with me trod*
> *This planet, was a noble type*
> *Appearing ere the times were ripe,*
> *That friend of mine who lives in God,*

> *That God, which ever lives and loves,*
> *One God, one law, one element,*
> *And one far-off divine event,*
> *To which the whole creation moves.*

These lines show an interesting compromise between the religious attitude and, what is quite a different thing, the belief in human perfectibility; but the contrast was not so apparent to Tennyson's contemporaries. They may have been taken in by it, but I don't think that Tennyson himself was, quite: his feelings were more honest than his mind. There is evidence elsewhere – even in an early poem, *Locksley Hall*, for example – that Tennyson by no means regarded with complacency all the changes that were going on about him in the progress of industrialism and the rise of the mercantile and manufacturing and banking classes; and he may have contemplated the future of England, as his years drew out, with increasing gloom. Temperamentally, he was opposed to the doctrine that he was moved to accept and to praise.

Tennyson's feelings, I have said, were honest; but they were usually a good way below the surface. *In Memoriam* can, I think, justly be called a religious poem, but for another reason than that which made it seem religious to his contemporaries. It is not religious because of the quality of its faith, but because of the quality of its doubt. Its faith is a poor thing, but its doubt is a very intense experience. *In Memoriam* is a poem of despair, but of despair of a religious kind. And to qualify its despair with the adjective 'religious' is to elevate it above most of its derivatives. For *The City of Dreadful Night*, and *A Shropshire Lad*, and the poems of Thomas Hardy, are small works in comparison with *In Memoriam*: It is greater than they and comprehends them.[1]

In ending we must go back to the beginning and remember that *In Memoriam* would not be a great poem, or Tennyson a great poet, without the technical accomplishment. Tennyson is the great master of metric as well as of melancholia; I do not think any poet in English has ever had a finer ear for vowel sound, as well as a subtler feeling for some moods of anguish:

> *Dear as remember'd kisses after death,*
> *And sweet as those by hopeless fancy feign'd*
> *On lips that are for others; deep as love*
> *Deep as first love, and wild with all regret.*

And this technical gift of Tennyson's is no slight thing. Tennyson lived in a time which was already acutely time-conscious: a great many things seemed to be happening, railways were being built, discoveries were being made, the face of the world was changing. That was a time busy in keeping up to date. It had, for the most part, no hold on permanent things, on permanent truths about man and God and life and death. The surface of Tennyson stirred about with his time; and he had nothing to which to hold fast except his unique and unerring feeling for the sounds of words. But in this he had something that no one else had. Tennyson's surface, his technical accomplishment, is intimate with his depths: what we most quickly see about Tennyson is that which moves between the surface and the depths, that which is of slight importance. By looking innocently at the surface we are most likely to come to the depths, to the abyss of sorrow. Tennyson is not only a minor Virgil, he is also with Virgil as Dante saw him, a Virgil among the Shades, the saddest of all English poets, among the Great in Limbo, the most instinctive rebel against the society in which he was the most perfect conformist.

Tennyson seems to have reached the end of his spiritual development with *In Memoriam*; there followed no reconciliation, no resolution.

> *And now no sacred staff shall break in blossom,*
> *No choral salutation lure to light*
> *A spirit sick with perfume and sweet night,*

[1] There are other kinds of despair. Davidson's great poem, *Thirty Bob a Week*, is not derivative from Tennyson. On the other hand, there are other things derivative from Tennyson besides *Atalanta in Calydon*. Compare the poems of William Morris with *The Voyage of Maeldune*, and *Barrack Room Ballads* with several of Tennyson's later poems.

or rather with twilight, for Tennyson faced neither the darkness nor the light in his later years. The genius, the technical power, persisted to the end, but the spirit had surrendered. A gloomier end than that of Baudelaire: Tennyson had no *singulier avertissement*. And having turned aside from the journey through the dark night, to become the surface flatterer of his own time, he has been rewarded with the despite of an age that succeeds his own in shallowness.

YEATS[1]

The generations of poetry in our age seem to cover a span of about twenty years. I do not mean that the best work of any poet is limited to twenty years: I mean that it is about that length of time before a new school or style of poetry appears. By the time, that is to say, that a man is fifty, he has behind him a kind of poetry written by men of seventy, and before him another kind written by men of thirty. That is my position at present, and if I live another twenty years I shall expect to see still another younger school of poetry. One's relation to Yeats, however, does not fit into this scheme. When I was a young man at the university, in America, just beginning to write verse, Yeats was already a considerably figure in the world of poetry, and his early period was well defined. I cannot remember that his poetry at that stage made any deep impression upon me. A very young man, who is himself stirred to write, is not primarily critical or even widely appreciative. He is looking for masters who will elicit his consciousness of what he wants to say himself, of the kind of poetry that is in him to write. The taste of an adolescent writer is intense, but narrow: it is determined by personal needs. The kind of poetry that I needed, to teach me the use of my own voice, did not exist in English at all; it was only to be found in French. For this reason the poetry of the young Yeats hardly existed for me until after my enthusiasm had been won by the poetry of the older Yeats; and by that time – I mean, from 1919 on – my own course of evolution was already determined. Hence, I find myself regarding him, from one point of view, as a contemporary and not a predecessor; and from another point of view, I can share the feelings of younger men, who came to know and admire him by that work from 1919 on, which was produced while they were adolescent.

Certainly, for the younger poets of England and America, I am sure that their admiration for Yeats's poetry has been wholly good. His idiom was too different for there to be any danger of

[1] The first annual Yeats Lecture, delivered to the Friends of the Irish Academy at the Abbey Theatre, Dublin, in 1940. Subsequently published in *Purpose*.

imitation, his opinions too different to flatter and confirm their prejudices. It was good for them to have the spectacle of an unquestionably great living poet, whose style they were not tempted to echo and whose ideas opposed those in vogue among them. You will not see, in their writing, more than passing evidences of the impression he made, but the work, and the man himself as poet, have been of the greatest significance to them for all that. This may seem to contradict what I have been saying about the kind of poetry that a young poet chooses to admire. But I am really talking about something different. Yeats would not have this influence had he not become a great poet; but the influence of which I speak is due to the figure of the poet himself, to the integrity of his passion for his art and his craft which provided such an impulse for his extraordinary development. When he visited London he liked to meet and talk to younger poets. People have sometimes spoken of him as arrogant and overbearing. I never found him so; in his conversations with a younger writer I always felt that he offered terms of equality, as to a fellow worker, a practitioner of the same mistery. It was, I think, that, unlike many writers, he cared more for poetry than for his own reputation as a poet or his picture of himself as a poet. Art was greater than the artist: and this feeling he communicated to others; which was why younger men were never ill at ease in his company.

This, I am sure, was part of the secret of his ability, after becoming unquestionably the master, to remain always a contemporary. Another is the continual development of which I have spoken. This has become almost a commonplace of criticism of his work. But while it is often mentioned, its causes and its nature have not been often analysed. One reason, of course, was simply concentration and hard work. And behind that is character: I mean the special character of the artist as artist – that is, the force of character by which Dickens, having exhausted his first inspiration, was able in middle age to proceed to such a masterpiece, so different from his early work, as *Bleak House*. It is difficult and unwise to generalize about ways of composition – so many men, so many ways – but it is my experience that towards middle age a man has three choices: to stop writing altogether, to repeat himself with perhaps an increasing skill of virtuosity, or by taking thought to adapt himself to middle age and find a different way of working. Why are the later long poems of Browning and Swinburne mostly unread? It is, I think, because one gets the essential Browning or Swinburne entire in earlier poems; and in the later, one is reminded of the early freshness which they lack, without being made aware of any compensating new qualities. When a man is engaged in work of abstract thought – if there is such a thing as wholly abstract thought outside of the mathematical and the physical sciences – his mind can mature, while his emotions either remain the same or only atrophy, and it will not matter. But maturing as a poet means maturing as the whole man, experiencing new emotions appropriate to one's age, and with the same intensity as the emotions of youth.

One form, a perfect form, of development is that of Shakespeare, one of the few poets whose work of maturity is just as exciting as that of their early manhood. There is, I think, a difference between the development of Shakespeare and Yeats, which makes the latter case still more curious. With Shakespeare, one sees a slow, continuous development of mastery of his craft of verse, and the poetry of middle age seems implicit in that of early maturity. After the first few verbal exercises you say of each piece of work: 'This is the perfect expression of the sensibility of that stage of his development.' That a poet should develop at all, that he should find something new to say, and say it equally well, in middle age, has always something miraculous about it. But in the case of Yeats the kind of development seems to me different. I do not want to give the impression that I regard his earlier and his later work almost as if they had been written by two different men. Returning to his earlier poems after making a close acquaintance with the later, one sees, to begin with, that in technique there was a slow and continuous development of what is always the same medium and idiom. And when I say development, I do not mean that many of the early poems, for what they are, are not as beautifully written as they could be. There are some, such as *Who Goes with Fergus?*, which are as perfect of their kind as anything in the language. But the best, and the best known of them, have this limitation: that they are as satisfactory in isolation, as 'anthology pieces', as they are in the context of his other poems of the same period.

I am obviously using the term 'anthology piece' in a rather special sense. In any anthology, you find some poems which give you complete satisfaction and delight in themselves, such that you are hardly curious who wrote them, hardly want to look further into the work of that poet. There are others, not necessarily so perfect or complete, which make you irresistibly curious to know more of that poet through his other work. Naturally, this distinction applies only to short poems, those in which a man has been able to put only a part of his mind, if it is a mind of any size. With some such you feel at once that the man who wrote them must have had a great deal more to say, in different contexts, of equal interest. Now among all the poems in Yeats's earlier volumes I find only in a line here or there, that sense of a unique personality which makes one sit up in excitement and eagerness to learn more about the author's mind and feelings. The intensity of Yeats's own emotional experience hardly appears. We have sufficient evidence of the intensity of experience of his youth, but it is from the retrospections in some of his later work that we have our evidence.

I have, in early essays, extolled what I called impersonality in art, and it may seem that, in giving as a reason for the superiority of Yeats's later work the greater expression of personality in it, I am contradicting myself. It may be that I expressed myself badly, or that I had only an adolescent grasp of that idea – as I can never bear to re-read my own prose writings, I am willing to leave the point unsettled – but I think now, at least, that the truth of the matter is as follows. There are two forms of impersonality: that which is natural to the mere skilful craftsman, and that which is more and more achieved by the maturing artist. The first is that of what I have called the 'anthology piece', of a lyric by Lovelace or Suckling, or of Campion, a finer poet than either. The second impersonality is that of the poet who, out of intense and personal experience, is able to express a general truth; retaining all the particularity of his experience, to make of it a general symbol. And the strange thing is that Yeats, having been a great craftsman in the first kind, became a great poet in the second. It is not that he became a different man, for, as I have hinted, one feels sure that the intense experience of youth had been lived through – and indeed, without this early experience he could never have attained anything of the wisdom which appears in his later writing. But he had to wait for a later maturity to find expression of early experience; and this makes him, I think, a unique and especially interesting poet.

Consider the early poem which is in every anthology, *When you are old and grey and full of sleep*, or *A Dream of Death* in the same volume of 1893. They are beautiful poems, but only craftsman's work, because one does not feel present in them the particularity which must provide the material for the general truth. By the time of the volume of 1904 there is a development visible in a very lovely poem, *The Folly of Being Comforted*, and in *Adam's Curse*; something is coming through, and in beginning to speak as a particular man he is beginning to speak for man. This is clearer still in the poem *Peace*, in the 1910 volume. But it is not fully evinced until the volume of 1914, in the violent and terrible epistle dedicatory of *Responsibilities*, with the great lines

Pardon that for a barren passion's sake,
Although I have come close on forty-nine. . . .

And the naming of his age in the poem is significant. More than half a lifetime to arrive at this freedom of speech. It is a triumph. There was much also for Yeats to work out of himself, even in technique. To be a younger member of a group of poets, none of them certainly of anything like his stature, but further developed in their limited path, may arrest for a time a man's development of idiom. Then again, the weight of the pre-Raphaelite prestige must have been tremendous. The Yeats of the Celtic twilight – who seems to me to have been more the Yeats of the pre-Raphaelite twilight – uses Celtic folklore almost as William Morris uses Scandinavian folklore. His longer narrative poems bear the mark of Morris. Indeed, in the pre-Raphaelite phase, Yeats is by no means the least of the pre-Raphaelites. I may be mistaken, but the play, *The Shadowy Waters*, seems to me one of the most perfect expressions of the vague enchanted beauty of that school: yet it strikes me – this may be an impertinence on my part – as the western seas descried through the back window of a house in Kensington, an Irish myth for the Kelmscott Press; and when I try to visualize the speakers in the play, they have the great dim, dreamy eyes of the knights and ladies of Burne-Jones. I think that the phase in which he treated Irish legend in the manner of Rossetti or Morris is a phase of confusion. He did not master this legend until he made it a vehicle for his own creation of character – not, really, until he began to write the *Plays for Dancers*. The point is, that in becoming more Irish, not in subject-matter but in expression, he became at the same time universal.

The points that I particularly wish to make about Yeats's development are two. The first, on which I have already touched, is that to have accomplished what Yeats did in the middle and later years is a great and permanent example – which poets-to-come should study with reverence – of what I have called Character of the Artist: a kind of moral, as well as intellectual, excellence. The second point, which follows naturally after what I have said in criticism of the lack of complete emotional expression in his early work, is that Yeats is pre-eminently the poet of middle age. By this I am far from meaning that he is a poet only for middle-aged readers: the attitude towards him of younger poets who write in English, the world over, is enough evidence to the contrary. Now, in theory, there is no reason why a poet's inspiration or material should fail, in middle age or at any time before senility. For a man who is capable of experience finds himself in a different world in every decade of his life; as he sees it with different eyes, the material of his art is continually renewed. But in fact, very few poets have shown this capacity of adaptation to the years. It requires, indeed, an exceptional honesty and courage to face the

252

change. Most men either cling to the experiences of youth, so that their writing becomes an insincere mimicry of their earlier work, or they leave their passion behind, and write only from the head, with a hollow and wasted virtuosity. There is another and even worse temptation: that of becoming dignified, of becoming public figures with only a public existence – coat-racks hung with decorations and distinctions, doing, saying, and even thinking and feeling only what they believe the public expects of them. Yeats was not that kind of poet: and it is, perhaps, a reason why young men should find his later poetry more acceptable than older men easily can. For the young can see him as a poet who in his work remained in the best sense always young, who even in one sense became young as he aged. But the old, unless they are stirred to something of the honesty with oneself expressed in the poetry, will be shocked by such a revelation of what a man really is and remains. They will refuse to believe that *they* are like that.

> *You think it horrible that lust and rage*
> *Should dance attendance upon my old age;*
> *They were not such a plague when I was young:*
> *What else have I to spur me into song?*

These lines are very impressive and not very pleasant, and the sentiment has recently been criticized by an English critic whom I generally respect. But I think he misread them. I do not read them as a personal confession of a man who differed from other men, but of a man who was essentially the same as most other men; the only difference is in the greater clarity, honesty and vigour. To what honest man, old enough, can these sentiments be entirely alien? They can be subdued and disciplined by religion, but who can say that they are dead? Only those to whom the maxim of La Rochefoucauld applies: 'Quand les vices nous quittent, nous nous flattons de la créance que c'est nous qui les quittons.' The tragedy of Yeats's epigram is all in the last line.

Similarly, the play *Purgatory* is not very pleasant either. There are aspects of it which I do not like myself. I wish he had not given it this title, because I cannot accept a purgatory in which there is no hint, or at least no emphasis upon Purgation. But, apart from the extraordinary theatrical skill with which he has put so much action within the compass of a very short scene of but little movement, the play gives a masterly exposition of the emotions of an old man. I think that the epigram I have just quoted seems to me just as much to be taken in a dramatic sense as the play *Purgatory*. The lyric poet – and Yeats was always lyric, even when dramatic – can speak for every man, or for men very different from himself; but to do this he must for the moment be able to identify himself with every man or other men; and it is only his imaginative power of becoming this that deceives some readers into thinking that he is speaking for and of himself alone – especially when they prefer not to be implicated.

I do not wish to emphasize this aspect only of Yeats's poetry of age. I would call attention to the beautiful poem in *The Winding Stair*, in memory of Eva Gore-Booth and Con Markiewicz, in which the picture at the beginning, of:

> *Two girls in silk kimonos, both*
> *Beautiful, one a gazelle,*

gets great intensity from the shock of the later line;

> *When withered, old and skeleton gaunt,*

and also to *Coole Park*, beginning

> *I meditate upon a swallow's flight,*
> *Upon an aged woman and her house.*

In such poems one feels that the most lively and desirable emotions of youth have been preserved to receive their full and due expression in retrospect. For the interesting feelings of age are not just different feelings; they are feelings into which the feelings of youth are integrated.

Yeats's development in his dramatic poetry is as interesting as that in his lyrical poetry. I have spoken of him as having been a lyric poet – in a sense in which I should not think of myself, for instance, as lyric; and by this I mean rather a certain kind of selection of emotion rather than particular metrical forms. But there is no reason why a lyric poet should not also be a dramatic poet; and to me Yeats is the type of lyrical dramatist. It took him many years to evolve the dramatic form suited to his genius. When he first began to write plays, poetic drama meant plays written in blank verse. Now, blank verse has been a dead metre for a long time. It would be outside of my frame to go into all the reasons for that now: but it is obvious that a form which was handled so supremely well by Shakespeare has its disadvantages. If you are writing a play of the same type as Shakespeare's, the reminiscence is oppressive; if you are writing a play of a different type, it is distracting. Furthermore, as Shakespeare is so much greater than any dramatist who has followed him, blank verse can hardly be dissociated from the life of the sixteenth and seventeenth centuries:

it can hardly catch the rhythms with which English is spoken nowadays. I think that if anything like regular blank verse is ever to be re-established, it can [only] be after a long departure from it, during the course of which it will have liberated itself from period associations. At the time of Yeats's early plays it was not possible to use anything else for a poetry play: that is not a criticism of Yeats himself, but an assertion that changes in verse forms come at one moment and not at another. His early verse-plays, including the *Green Helmet*, which is written in a kind of irregular rhymed fourteener, have a good deal of beauty in them, and, at least, they are the best verse-plays written in their time. And even in these one notices some development of irregularity in the metric. Yeats did not quite invent a new metre, but the blank verse of his later plays shows a great advance towards one; and what is most astonishing is the virtual abandonment of blank verse metre in *Purgatory*. One device used with great success in some of the later plays is the lyrical choral interlude. But another, and important, cause of improvement is the gradual purging out of poetical ornament. This, perhaps, is the most painful part of the labour, so far as the versification goes, of the modern poet who tries to write a play in verse. The course of improvement is towards a greater and greater starkness. The beautiful line for its own sake is a luxury dangerous even for the poet who has made himself a virtuoso of the technique of the theatre. What is necessary is a beauty which shall not be in the line or the isolable passage, but woven into the dramatic texture itself; so that you can hardly say whether the lines give grandeur to the drama, or whether it is the drama which turns the words into poetry. (One of the most thrilling lines in *King Lear* is the simple:

Never, never, never, never, never

but, apart from a knowledge of the context, how can you say that it is poetry, or even competent verse?) Yeats's purification of his verse becomes much more evident in the four *Plays for Dancers* and in the two in the posthumous volume: those, in fact, in which he had found his right and final dramatic form.

It is in the first three of the *Plays for Dancers*, also, that he shows the internal, as contrasted with the external, way of handling Irish myth of which I have spoken earlier. In the earlier plays, as in the earlier poems, about legendary heroes and heroines, I feel that the characters are treated, with the respect that we pay to legend, as creatures of a different world from ours. In the later plays they are universal men and women. I should, perhaps, not include *The Dreaming of the Bones* quite in this category, because

Dermot and Devorgilla are characters from modern history, not figures of pre-history; but I would remark in support of what I have been saying that in this play these two lovers have something of the universality of Dante's Paolo and Francesca, and this the younger Yeats could not have given them. So with the Cuchulain of *The Hawk's Well*, the Cuchulain, Emer and Eithne of *The Only Jealousy of Emer*; the myth is not presented for its own sake, but as a vehicle for a situation of universal meaning.

I see at this point that I may have given the impression, contrary to my desire and my belief, that the poetry and the plays of Yeats's earlier period can be ignored in favour of his later work. You cannot divide the work of a great poet so sharply as that. Where there is the continuity of such a positive personality and such a single purpose, the later work cannot be understood, or properly enjoyed, without a study and appreciation of the earlier; and the later work again reflects light upon the earlier, and shows us beauty and significance not before perceived. We have also to take account of the historical conditions. As I have said above, Yeats was born into the end of a literary movement, and an English movement at that: only those who have toiled with language know the labour and constancy required to free oneself from such influences – yet, on the other hand, once we are familiar with the older voice, we can hear its individual tones even in his earliest published verse. In my own time of youth there seemed to be no immediate great powers of poetry either to help or to hinder, either to learn from or to rebel against, yet I can understand the difficulty of the other situation, and the magnitude of the task. With the verse-play, on the other hand, the situation is reversed, because Yeats had nothing, and we have had Yeats. He started writing plays at a time when the prose-play of contemporary life seemed triumphant, with an indefinite future stretching before it; when the comedy of light farce dealt only with certain privileged strata of metropolitan life; and when the serious play tended to be an ephemeral tract on some transient social problem. We can begin to see now that even the imperfect early attempts he made are probably more permanent literature than the plays of Shaw; and that his dramatic work as a whole may prove a stronger defence against the successful urban Shaftesbury Avenue vulgarity which he opposed as stoutly as they. Just as, from the beginning, he made and thought his poetry in terms of speech and not in terms of print, so in the drama he always meant to write plays to be played and not merely to be read. He cared, I think, more for the theatre as an organ for the expression of the consciousness of a people, than as a means to his own fame or achievement; and I am convinced that it is only if you serve it in this spirit that you can hope to accomplish anything worth doing with it. Of course, he had some great advantages, the recital of which does not rob him of any of his glory: his colleagues, a people with a natural and unspoilt gift for speech and for acting. It is impossible to disentangle what he did for the Irish theatre from what the Irish theatre did for him. From this point of advantage, the idea of the poetic drama was kept alive when everywhere else it had been driven underground. I do not know where our debt to him as a dramatist ends – and in time, it will not end until that drama itself ends. In his occasional writings on dramatic topics he has asserted certain principles to which we must hold fast: such as the primacy of the poet over the actor, and of the actor over the scene-painter; and the principle that the theatre, while it need not be concerned only with 'the people' in the narrow Russian sense, must be for the people; that to be permanent it must concern itself with fundamental situations. Born into a world in which the doctrine of 'Art for Art's sake' was generally accepted, and living on into one in which art has been asked to be instrumental to social purposes, he held firmly to the right view which is between these, though not in any way a compromise between them, and showed that an artist, by serving his art with entire integrity, is at the same time rendering the greatest service he can to his own nation and to the whole world.

To be able to praise, it is not necessary to feel complete agreement; and I do not dissimulate the fact that there are aspects of Yeats's thought and feeling which to myself are unsympathetic. I say this only to indicate the limits which I have set to my criticism. The questions of difference, objection and protest arise in the field of doctrine, and these are vital questions. I have been concerned only with the poet and dramatist, so far as these can be isolated. In the long run they cannot be wholly isolated. A full and elaborate examination of the total work of Yeats must some day be undertaken; perhaps it will need a longer perspective. There are some poets whose poetry can be considered more or less in isolation, for experience and delight. There are others whose poetry, though giving equally experience and delight, has a larger historical importance. Yeats was one of the latter: he was one of those few whose history is the history of their own time, who are a part of the consciousness of an age which cannot be understood without them. This is a very high position to assign to him: but I believe that it is one which is secure.

MILTON I[1]

While it must be admitted that Milton is a very great poet indeed, it is something of a puzzle to decide in what his greatness consists. On analysis, the marks against him appear both more numerous and more significant than the marks to his credit. As a man, he is antipathetic. Either from the moralists' point of view, or from the theologian's point of view, or from the psychologist's point of view, or from that of the political philosopher, or judging by the ordinary standards of likeableness in human beings, Milton is unsatisfactory. The doubts which I have to express about him are more serious than these. His greatness as a poet has been sufficiently celebrated, though I think largely for the wrong reasons, and without the proper reservations. His misdeeds as a poet have been called attention to, as by Mr. Ezra Pound, but usually in passing. What seems to me necessary is to assert at the same time his greatness – in that what he could do well he did better than any one else has ever done – and the serious charges to be made against him, in respect of the deterioration – the peculiar kind of deterioration – to which he subjected the language.

Many people will agree that a man may be a great artist, and yet have a bad influence. There is more of Milton's influence in the badness of the bad verse of the eighteenth century than of anybody's else: he certainly did more harm than Dryden and Pope, and perhaps a good deal of the obloquy which has fallen on these two poets, especially the latter, because of their influence, ought to be transferred to Milton. But to put the matter simply in terms of 'bad influence' is not necessarily to bring a serious charge: because a good deal of the responsibility, when we state the problem in these terms, may devolve on the eighteenth-century poets themselves for being such bad poets that they were incapable of being influenced except for ill. There is a good deal more to the charge against Milton than this; and it appears a good deal more serious if we affirm that Milton's poetry could *only* be an influence

Contributed to *Essays and Studies* of The English Association, Oxford University Press, 1936.

for the worse, upon any poet whatever. It is more serious, also, if we affirm that Milton's bad influence may be traced much farther than the eighteenth century, and much farther than upon bad poets: if we say that it was an influence against which we still have to struggle.

There is a large class of persons, including some who appear in print as critics, who regard any censure upon a 'great' poet as a breach of the peace, as an act of wanton iconoclasm, or even hoodlumism. The kind of derogatory criticism that I have to make upon Milton is not intended for such persons, who cannot understand that it is more important, in some vital respects, to be a *good* poet than to be a *great* poet; and of what I have to say I consider that the only jury of judgment is that of the ablest poetical practitioners of my own time.

The most important fact about Milton, for my purpose, is his blindness. I do not mean that to go blind in middle life is itself enough to determine the whole nature of a man's poetry. Blindness must be considered in conjunction with Milton's personality and character, and the peculiar education which he received. It must also be considered in connection with his devotion to, and expertness in, the art of music. Had Milton been a man of very keen senses – I mean of *all* the five senses – his blindness would not have mattered so much. But for a man whose sensuousness, such as it was, had been withered early by book-learning, and whose gifts were naturally aural, it mattered a great deal. It would seem, indeed, to have helped him to concentrate on what he could do best.

At no period is the visual imagination conspicuous in Milton's poetry. It would be as well to have a few illustrations of what I mean by visual imagination. From *Macbeth*:

> *This guest of summer,*
> *The temple-haunting martlet, does approve*
> *By his loved mansionry that the heaven's breath*
> *Smells wooingly here: no jutty, frieze,*
> *Buttress, nor coign of vantage, but this bird*
> *Hath made his pendent bed and procreant cradle:*
> *Where they most breed and haunt, I have observed*
> *The air is delicate.*

It may be observed that such an image, as well as another familiar quotation from a little later in the same play,

> *Light thickens, and the crow*
> *Makes wing to the rooky wood.*

259

not only offer something to the eye, but, so to speak, to the common sense. I mean that they convey the feeling of being in a particular place at a particular time. The comparison with Shakespeare offers another indication of the peculiarity of Milton. With Shakespeare, far more than with any other poet in English, the combinations of words offer perpetual novelty; they enlarge the meaning of the individual words joined: thus 'procreant cradle', 'rooky wood'. In comparison, Milton's images do not give this sense of particularity, nor are the separate words developed in significance. His language is, if one may use the term without disparagement, *artificial* and *conventional*.

> *O'er the smooth enamel'd green . . .*

> *. . . paths of this drear wood*
> *The nodding horror of whose shady brows*
> *Threats the forlorn and wandering passenger.*

('Shady brow' here is a diminution of the value of the two words from their use in the line from *Dr. Faustus*

> *Shadowing more beauty in their airy brows.*)

The imagery in *L'Allegro* and *Il Penseroso* is all general:

> *While the ploughman near at hand,*
> *Whistles o'er the furrowed land,*
> *And the milkmaid singeth blithe,*
> *And the mower whets his scythe,*
> *And every shepherd tells his tale,*
> *Under the hawthorn in the dale.*

It is not a particular ploughman, milkmaid, and shepherd that Milton sees (as Wordsworth might see them); the sensuous effect of these verses is entirely on the ear, and is joined to the concepts of ploughman, milkmaid, and shepherd. Even in his most mature work, Milton does not infuse new life into the word, as Shakespeare does.

> *The sun to me is dark*
> *And silent as the moon,*
> *When she deserts the night*
> *Hid in her vacant interlunar cave.*

Here *interlunar* is certainly a stroke of genius, but is merely combined with 'vacant' and 'cave', rather than giving and receiving life from them. Thus it is not so unfair, as it might at first appear, to say that Milton writes English like a dead language. The criticism has been made with regard to his involved syntax. But a tortuous style, when its peculiarity is aimed at precision (as with Henry James), is not necessarily a dead one; only when the complication is dictated by a demand of verbal music, instead of by any demand of sense.

> *Thrones, dominations, princedoms, virtues, powers,*
> *If these magnific titles yet remain*
> *Not merely titular, since by decree*
> *Another now hath to himself engrossed*
> *All power, and us eclipsed under the name*
> *Of King anointed, for whom all this haste*
> *Of midnight march, and hurried meeting here,*
> *This only to consult how we may best*
> *With what may be devised of honours new*
> *Receive him coming to receive from us*
> *Knee-tribute yet unpaid, prostration vile,*
> *Too much to one, but double how endured,*
> *To one and to his image now proclaimed?*

With which compare:

However, he didn't mind thinking that if Cissy should prove all that was likely enough their having a subject in common couldn't but practically conduce; though the moral of it all amounted rather to a portent, the one that Haughty, by the same token, had done least to reassure him against, of the extent to which the native jungle harboured the female specimen and to which its ostensible cover, the vast level of mixed growths stirred wavingly in whatever breeze, was apt to be identifiable but as an agitation of the last redundant thing in ladies' hats.

This quotation, taken almost at random from *The Ivory Tower*, is not intended to represent Henry James at any hypothetical 'best', any more than the noble passage from *Paradise Lost* is meant to be Milton's hypothetical worst. The question is the difference of intention, in the elaboration of styles both of which depart so far from lucid simplicity. The sound, of course, is never irrelevant, and the style of James certainly depends for its effect a good deal on the sound of a voice, James's own, painfully explaining. But the complication, with James, is due to a determination not to simplify, and in that simplification lose any of the real intricacies and by-paths of mental movement; whereas the complication of a Miltonic sentence is an active complication, a

261

complication deliberately introduced into what was a previously simplified and abstract thought. The dark angel here is not *thinking* or conversing, but making a speech carefully prepared for him; and the arrangement is for the sake of musical value, not for significance. A straightforward utterance, as of a Homeric or Dantesque character, would make the speaker very much more real to us; but reality is no part of the intention. We have in fact to read such a passage not analytically, to get the poetic impression. I am not suggesting that Milton has no idea to convey which he regards as important: only that the syntax is determined by the musical significance, by the auditory imagination, rather than by the attempt to follow actual speech or thought. It is at least more nearly possible to distinguish the pleasure which arises from the *noise*, from the pleasure due to other elements, than with the verse of Shakespeare, in which the auditory imagination and the imagination of the other senses are more nearly fused, and fused together with the thought. The result with Milton is, in one sense of the word, *rhetoric*. That term is not intended to be derogatory. This kind of 'rhetoric' is not necessarily bad in its influence; but it may be considered bad in relation to the historical life of a language as a whole. I have said elsewhere that the living English which was Shakespeare's became split up into two components one of which was exploited by Milton and the other by Dryden. Of the two, I still think Dryden's development the healthier, because it was Dryden who preserved, so far as it was preserved at all, the tradition of conversational language in poetry: and I might add that it seems to me easier to get back to healthy language from Dryden than it is to get back to it from Milton. For what such a generalization is worth, Milton's influence on the eighteenth century was much more deplorable than Dryden's.

If several very important reservations and exceptions are made, I think that it is not unprofitable to compare Milton's development with that of James Joyce. The initial similarities are musical taste and abilities, followed by musical training, wide and curious knowledge, gift for acquiring languages, and remarkable powers of memory perhaps fortified by defective vision. The important difference is that Joyce's imagination is not naturally of so purely auditory a type as Milton's. In his early work, and at least in part of *Ulysses*, there is visual and other imagination of the highest kind; and I may be mistaken in thinking that the later part of *Ulysses* shows a turning from the visible world to draw rather on the resources of phantasmagoria. In any case, one may suppose that the replenishment of visual imagery during later years has been insufficient; so that what I find in *Work in Progress* is an auditory imagination abnormally sharpened at the expense of the visual. There is still a little to be seen, and what there is to see is worth looking at. And I would repeat that with Joyce this development seems to me largely due to circumstances: whereas Milton may be said never to have seen anything. For Milton, therefore, the concentration on sound was wholly a benefit. Indeed, I find, in reading *Paradise Lost*, that I am happiest where there is least to visualize. The eye is not shocked in his twilit Hell as it is in the Garden of Eden, where I for one can get pleasure from the verse only by the deliberate effort not to visualize Adam and Eve and their surroundings.

I am not suggesting any close parallel between the 'rhetoric' of Milton and the later style of Joyce. It is a different music; and Joyce always maintains some contact with the conversational tone. But it may prove to be equally a blind alley for the future development of the language.

A disadvantage of the rhetorical style appears to be, that a dislocation takes place, through the hypertrophy of the auditory imagination at the expense of the visual and tactile, so that the inner meaning is separated from the surface, and tends to become something occult, or at least without effect upon the reader until fully understood. To extract everything possible from *Paradise Lost*, it would seem necessary to read it in two different ways, first solely for the sound, and second for the sense. The full beauty of his long periods can hardly be enjoyed while we are wrestling with the meaning as well; and for the pleasure of the ear the meaning is hardly necessary, except in so far as certain key-words indicate the emotional tone of the passage. Now Shakespeare, or Dante, will bear innumerable readings, but at each reading all the elements of appreciation can be present. There is no interruption between the surface that these poets present to you and the core. While therefore, I cannot pretend to have penetrated to any 'secret' of these poets, I feel that such appreciation of their work as I am capable of points in the right direction; whereas I cannot feel that my appreciation of Milton leads anywhere outside of the mazes of sound. That, I feel, would be the matter for a separate study, like that of Blake's prophetic books; it might be well worth the trouble, but would have little to do with my interest in the poetry. So far as I perceive anything, it is a glimpse of a theology that I find in large part repellent, expressed through a mythology which would have better been left in the Book of *Genesis*, upon which Milton has not improved. There seems to me to be a division, in Milton, between the philosopher or theologian and the poet; and, for the latter, I suspect also that this concentration upon the auditory imagination leads to at least an occasional levity. I can enjoy the roll of

> *. . . Cambula, seat of Cathaian Can*
> *And Samarchand by Oxus, Temir's throne,*
> *To Paquin of Sinaean kings, and thence*
> *To Agra and Lahor of great Mogul*
> *Down to the golden Chersonese, or where*
> *The Persian in Ecbatan sate, or since*
> *In Hispahan, or where the Russian Ksar*
> *On Mosco, or the Sultan in Bizance,*
> *Turchestan-born . . .,*

and the rest of it, but I feel that this is not serious poetry, not poetry fully occupied about its business, but rather a solemn game. More often, admittedly, Milton uses proper names in moderation, to obtain the same effect of magnificence with them as does Marlowe – nowhere perhaps better than in the passage from *Lycidas*:

> *Whether beyond the stormy Hebrides,*
> *Where thou perhaps under the whelming tide*
> *Visit'st the bottom of the monstrous world;*
> *Or whether thou to our moist vows deny'd*
> *Sleep'st by the fable of Bellerus old,*
> *Where the great vision of the guarded Mount*
> *Looks toward Namancos and Bayona's hold . . .*

than which for the single effect of grandeur of sound, there is nothing finer in poetry.

I make no attempt to appraise the 'greatness' of Milton in relation to poets who seem to me more comprehensive and better balanced; it has seemed to me more fruitful for the present to press the parallel between *Paradise Lost* and *Work in Progress*; and both Milton and Joyce are so exalted in their own kinds, in the whole of literature, that the only writers with whom to compare them are writers who have attempted something very different. Our views about Joyce, in any case, must remain at the present time tentative. But there are two attitudes both of which are necessary and right to adopt in considering the work of any poet. One is when we isolate him, when we try to understand the rules of his own game, adopt his own point of view: the other, perhaps less usual, is when we measure him by outside standards, most pertinently by the standards of language and of something called Poetry, in our own language and in the whole history of European literature. It is from the second point of view that my objections to Milton are made: it is from this point of view that we can go so far as to say that, although his work realizes superbly one important element in poetry, he may still be considered as having done damage to the English language from which it has not wholly recovered.

264

from MILTON II

...The reproach against Milton, that his technical influence has been bad, appears to have been made by no one more positively than by myself. I find myself saying, as recently as 1936, that this charge against Milton

appears a good deal more serious if we affirm that Milton's poetry could *only* be an influence for the worse, upon any poet whatever. It is more serious, also, if we affirm that Milton's bad influence may be traced much farther than the eighteenth century, and much farther than upon bad poets: if we say that it was an influence against which we still have to struggle.

In writing these sentences I failed to draw a threefold distinction, which now seems to me of some importance. There are three separate assertions implied. The first is, that an influence has been bad in the past: this is to assert that good poets, in the eighteenth or nineteenth century, would have written better if they had not submitted themselves to the influence of Milton. The second assertion is, that the contemporary situation is such that Milton is a master whom we should avoid. The third is, that the influence of Milton, or of any particular poet, can be *always* bad, and that we can predict that wherever it is found at any time in the future, however remote, it will be a bad influence. Now, the first and third of these assertions I am no longer prepared to make, because, detached from the second, they do not appear to me to have any meaning.

For the first, when we consider one great poet of the past, and one or more other poets, upon whom we say he has exerted a bad influence, we must admit that the responsibility, if there be any, is rather with the poets who were influenced than with the poet whose work exerted the influence. We can, of course, show that certain tricks or mannerisms which the imitators display are due to conscious or unconscious imitation and emulation, but that is a reproach against their injudicious choice of a model and not against their model itself. And we can never prove that any particular poet would have written better poetry if he had escaped

265

that influence. Even if we assert, what can only be a matter of faith, that Keats would have written a very great epic poem if Milton had not preceded him, is it sensible to pine for an unwritten masterpiece, in exchange for one which we possess and acknowledge? And as for the remote future, what can we affirm about the poetry that will be written then, except that we should probably be unable to understand or to enjoy it, and that therefore we can hold no opinion as to what 'good' and 'bad' influences will *mean* in that future? The only relation in which the question of influence, good and bad, is significant, is the relation to the immediate future. With that question I shall engage at the end. I wish first to mention another reproach against Milton, that represented by the phrase 'dissociation of sensibility'.

I remarked many years ago, in an essay on Dryden, that:

In the seventeenth century a dissociation of sensibility set in, from which we have never recovered; and this dissociation, as is natural, was due to the influence of the two most powerful poets of the century, Milton and Dryden.

The longer passage from which this sentence is taken is quoted by Dr. Tillyard in his *Milton*. Dr. Tillyard makes the following comment:

Speaking only of what in this passage concerns Milton, I would say that there is here a mixture of truth and falsehood. Some sort of dissociation of sensibility in Milton, not necessarily undesirable, has to be admitted; but that he was responsible for any such dissociation in others (at least till this general dissociation had inevitably set in) is untrue.

I believe that the general affirmation represented by the phrase 'dissociation of sensibility' (one of the two or three phrases of my coinage – like 'objective correlative' – which have had a success in the world astonishing to their author) retains some validity; but I now incline to agree with Dr. Tillyard that to lay the burden on the shoulders of Milton and Dryden was a mistake. If such a dissociation did take place, I suspect that the causes are too complex and too profound to justify our accounting for the change in terms of literary criticism. All we can say is, that something like this did happen; that it had something to do with the Civil War; that it would even be unwise to say it was caused by the Civil War, but that it is a consequence of the same causes which brought about the Civil War; that we must seek the causes in Europe, not in England alone; and for what these causes were, we may dig and dig until we get to a depth at which words and concepts fail us.

Before proceeding to take up the case against Milton, as it

stood for poets twenty-five years ago – the second, and only significant meaning of 'bad influence' – I think it would be best to consider what permanent strictures of reproof may be drawn: those censures which, when we make them, we must assume to be made by enduring laws of taste. The essence of the permanent censure of Milton is, I believe, to be found in Johnson's essay. This is not the place in which to examine certain particular and erroneous judgments of Johnson; to explain his condemnation of *Comus* and *Samson* as the application of dramatic canons which to us seem inapplicable; or to condone his dismissal of the versification of *Lycidas* by the specialization, rather than the absence, of his sense of rhythm. Johnson's most important censure of Milton is contained in three paragraphs, which I must ask leave to quote in full.

Throughout all his greater works [*says Johnson*] there prevails an uniform peculiarity of *diction*, a mode and cast of expression which bears little resemblance to that of any former writer; and which is so far removed from common use, that an unlearned reader, when he first opens the book, finds himself surprised by a new language.

This novelty has been, by those who can find nothing wrong with Milton, imputed to his laborious endeavours after words suited to the grandeur of his ideas. *Our language*, says Addison, *sunk under him*. But the truth is, that both in prose and in verse, he had formed his style by a perverse and pedantic principle. He was desirous to use English words with a foreign idiom. This in all his prose is discovered and condemned; for there judgment operates freely, neither softened by the beauty, nor awed by the dignity of his thoughts; but such is the power of his poetry, that his call is obeyed without resistance, the reader feels himself in captivity to a higher and nobler mind, and criticism sinks in admiration.

Milton's style was not modified by his subject; what is shown with greater extent in *Paradise Lost* may be found in *Comus*. One source of his peculiarity was his familiarity with the Tuscan poets; the disposition of his words is, I think, frequently Italian; perhaps sometimes combined with other tongues. Of him at last, may be said what Jonson said of Spenser, that he *wrote no language*, but has formed what Butler called a *Babylonish dialect*, in itself harsh and barbarous, but made by exalted genius and extensive learning the vehicle of so much instruction and so much pleasure, that, like other lovers, we find grace in its deformity.

This criticism seems to me substantially true: indeed, unless we accept it, I do not think we are in the way to appreciate the peculiar greatness of Milton. His style is not a *classic* style, in that it is not the elevation of a *common* style, by the final touch of genius, to greatness. It is, from the foundation, and in every particular, a personal style, not based upon common speech, or common prose, or direct communication of meaning. Of some great poetry one has difficulty in pronouncing just what it is, what infinitesimal touch, that has made all the difference from a plain statement which anyone could make; the slight transformation which, while it leaves a plain statement a plain statement, has always the maximal, never the minimal, alteration of ordinary language. Every distortion of construction, the foreign idiom, the use of a word in a foreign way or with the meaning of the foreign word from which it is derived rather than the accepted meaning in English, every idiosyncrasy is a particular act of violence which Milton has been the first to commit. There is no cliché, no poetic diction in the derogatory sense, but a perpetual sequence of original acts of lawlessness. Of all modern writers of verse, the nearest analogy seems to me to be Mallarmé, a much smaller poet, though still a great one. The personalities, the poetic theories of the two men could not have been more different; but in respect of the violence which they could do to language, and justify, there is a remote similarity. Milton's poetry is poetry at the farthest possible remove from prose; his prose seems to me too near to half-formed poetry to be a good prose.

To say that the work of a poet is at the farthest possible remove from prose would once have struck me as condemnatory: it now seems to me simply, when we have to do with a Milton, the precision of its peculiar greatness. As a poet, Milton seems to me probably the greatest of all eccentrics. His work illustrates no general principles of good writing; the only principles of writing that it illustrates are such as are valid only for Milton himself to observe. There are two kinds of poet who can ordinarily be of use to other poets. There are those who suggest, to one or another of their successors, something which they have not done themselves, or who provoke a different way of doing the same thing: these are likely to be not the greatest, but smaller, imperfect poets with whom later poets discover an affinity. And there are the great poets from whom we can learn negative rules: no poet can teach another to write well, but some great poets can teach others some of the things to avoid. They teach us what to avoid, by showing us what great poetry can do without – how *bare* it can be. Of these are Dante and Racine. But if we are ever to make use of Milton we must do so in quite a different way. Even a small poet can learn something from the study of Dante, or from the study of Chaucer: we must perhaps wait for a great poet before we find one who can profit from the study of Milton.

I repeat that the remoteness of Milton's verse from ordinary
268

speech, his invention of his own poetic language, seems to me one of the marks of his greatness. Other marks are his sense of structure, both in the general design of *Paradise Lost* and *Samson*, and in his syntax; and finally, and not least, his inerrancy, conscious or unconscious, in writing so as to make the best display of his talents, and the best concealment of his weaknesses.

The appropriateness of the subject of *Samson* is too obvious to expatiate upon: it was probably the one dramatic story out of which Milton could have made a masterpiece. But the complete suitability of *Paradise Lost* has not, I think, been so often remarked. It was surely an intuitive perception of what he could not do, that arrested Milton's project of an epic on King Arthur. For one thing, he had little interest in, or understanding of, individual human beings. In *Paradise Lost* he was not called upon for any of that understanding which comes from an affectionate observation of men and women. But such an interest in human beings was not required – indeed its *absence* was a necessary condition – for the creation of his figures of Adam and Eve. These are not a man and woman such as any we know: if they were, they would not be Adam and Eve. They are the original *Man* and *Woman*, not types, but prototypes. They have the general characteristics of men and women, such that we can recognize, in the temptation and the fall, the first motions of the faults and virtues, the abjection and the nobility, of all their descendants. They have ordinary humanity to the right degree, and yet are not, and should not be, ordinary mortals. Were they more particularized they would be false, and if Milton had been more interested in humanity, he could not have created them. Other critics have remarked upon the exactness, without defect or exaggeration, with which Moloch, Belial, and Mammon, in the second book, speak according to the particular sin which each represents. It would not be suitable that the infernal powers should have, in the human sense, characters, for a character is always mixed; but in the hands of an inferior manipulator, they might easily have been reduced to *humours*.

The appropriateness of the material of *Paradise Lost* to the genius and the limitations of Milton, is still more evident when we consider the visual imagery. I have already remarked, in a paper written some years ago, on Milton's weakness of visual observation, a weakness which I think was always present – the effect of his blindness may have been rather to strengthen the compensatory qualities than to increase a fault which was already present. Mr. Wilson Knight, who has devoted close study to recurrent imagery in poetry, has called attention to Milton's propensity towards images of engineering and mechanics; to me it seems that Milton is at his best in imagery suggestive of vast size, limitless space, abysmal depth, and light and darkness. No theme and no setting, other than that which he chose in *Paradise Lost*, could have given him such scope for the kind of imagery in which he excelled, or made less demand upon those powers of visual imagination which were in him defective.

Most of the absurdities and inconsistencies to which Johnson calls attention, and which, so far as they can justly be isolated in this way, he properly condemns, will I think appear in a more correct proportion if we consider them in relation to this general judgment. I do not think that we should attempt to *see* very clearly any scene that Milton depicts: it should be accepted as a shifting phantasmagory. To complain, because we first find the arch-fiend 'chain'd on the burning lake', and in a minute or two see him making his way to the shore, is to expect a kind of consistency which the world to which Milton has introduced us does not require.

This limitation of visual power, like Milton's limited interest in human beings, turns out to be not merely a negligible defect, but a positive virtue, when we visit Adam and Eve in Eden. Just as a higher degree of characterization of Adam and Eve would have been unsuitable, so a more vivid picture of the earthly Paradise would have been less paradisiacal. For a greater definiteness, a more detailed account of flora and fauna, could only have assimilated Eden to the landscapes of earth with which we are familiar. As it is, the impression of Eden which we retain, is the most suitable, and is that which Milton was most qualified to give: the impression of *light* – a daylight and a starlight, a light of dawn and of dusk, the light which, remembered by a man in his blindness, has a supernatural glory unexperienced by men of normal vision.

We must, then, in reading *Paradise Lost*, not expect to see clearly; our sense of sight must be blurred, so that our *hearing* may become more acute. *Paradise Lost*, like *Finnegans Wake* (for I can think of no work which provides a more interesting parallel: two books by great blind musicians, each writing a language of his own based upon English) makes this peculiar demand for a readjustment of the reader's mode of apprehension. The emphasis is on the sound, not the vision, upon the word, not the idea; and in the end it is the unique versification that is the most certain sign of Milton's intellectual mastership.

On the subject of Milton's versification, so far as I am aware, little enough has been written. We have Johnson's essay in the *Rambler*, which deserves more study than it has received, and we have a short treatise by Robert Bridges on *Milton's Prosody*. I speak of Bridges with respect, for no poet of our time has given such close attention to prosody as he. Bridges catalogues the systematic irregularites which give perpetual variety to Milton's verse, and I can find no fault with his analysis. But however interesting these analyses are, I do not think that it is by such means that we gain an appreciation of the peculiar rhythm of a poet. It seems to me also that Milton's verse is especially refractory to yielding up its secrets to examination of the single line. For his verse is not formed in this way. It is the period, the sentence and still more the paragraph, that is the unit of Milton's verse; and emphasis on the line structure is the minimum necessary to provide a counter-pattern to the period structure. It is only in the period that the wave-length of Milton's verse is to be found: it is his ability to give a perfect and unique pattern to every paragraph, such that the full beauty of the line is found in its context, and his ability to work in larger musical units than any other poet – that is to me the most conclusive evidence of Milton's supreme mastery. The peculiar feeling, almost a physical sensation of a breathless leap, communicated by Milton's long periods, and by his alone, is impossible to procure from rhymed verse. Indeed, this mastery is more conclusive evidence of his intellectual power, than is his grasp of any *ideas* that he borrowed or invented. To be able to control so many words at once is the token of a mind of most exceptional energy.

It is interesting at this point to recall the general observations upon blank verse, which a consideration of *Paradise Lost* prompted Johnson to make towards the end of his essay.

The music of the English heroic lines strikes the ear so faintly, that it is easily lost, unless all the syllables of every line co-operate together; this co-operation can only be obtained by the preservation of every verse unmingled with another as a distinct system of sounds; and this distinctness is obtained and preserved by the artifice of rhyme. The variety of pauses, so much boasted by the lovers of blank verse, changes the measures of an English poet to the periods of a declaimer; and there are only a few skilful and happy readers of Milton, who enable their audience to perceive where the lines end or begin. *Blank verse*, said an ingenious critic, *seems to be verse only to the eye.*

Some of my audience may recall that this last remark, in almost the same words, was often made, a literary generation ago, about the 'free verse' of the period: and even without this encouragement from Johnson it would have occurred to my mind to declare Milton to be the greatest master of free verse in our language. What is interesting about Johnson's paragraph, however, is that it represents the judgment of a man who had by no means a deaf ear, but simply a *specialized* ear, for verbal music. Within the limits of the poetry of his own period, Johnson is a very good judge of the relative merits of several poets as writers of blank verse. But on the whole, the blank verse of his age might more properly be called unrhymed verse; and nowhere is this difference more evident than in the verse of his own tragedy *Irene*: the phrasing is admirable, the style elevated and correct, but each line cries out for a companion to rhyme with it. Indeed, it is only with labour, or by occasional inspiration, or by submission to the influence of the older dramatists, that the blank verse of the nineteenth century succeeds in making the absence of rhyme inevitable and right, with the rightness of Milton. Even Johnson admitted that he could not wish that Milton had been a rhymer. Nor did the nineteenth century succeed in giving to blank verse the flexibility which it needs if the tone of common speech, talking of the topics of common intercourse, is to be employed; so that when our more modern practitioners of blank verse do not touch the sublime, they frequently sink to the ridiculous. Milton perfected non-dramatic blank verse and at the same time imposed limitations, very hard to break, upon the use to which it may be put if its greatest musical possibilities are to be exploited.

I come at last to compare my own attitude, as that of a poetical practitioner perhaps typical of a generation twenty-five years ago, with my attitude today. I have thought it well to take matters in the order in which I have taken them to discuss first the censures and detractions which I believe to have permanent validity, and which were best made by Johnson, in order to make clearer the causes, and the justification, for hostility to Milton on the part of poets at a particular juncture. And I wished to make clear those excellences of Milton which particularly impress me, before explaining why I think that the study of his verse might at last be of benefit to poets.

I have on several occasions suggested, that the important changes in the idiom of English verse which are represented by the names of Dryden and Wordsworth, may be characterized as successful attempts to escape from a poetic idiom which had ceased to have a relation to contemporary speech. This is the sense of Wordsworth's Prefaces. By the beginning of the present century another revolution in idiom – and such revolutions bring with them an alteration of metric, a new appeal to the ear – was due. It inevitably happens that the young poets engaged in such a revolution will exalt the merits of those poets of the past who offer them example and stimulation, and cry down the merits of poets who do not stand for the qualities which they are zealous to realize. This is not only inevitable, it is right. It is even right, and certainly inevitable, that their practice, still more influential than

their critical pronouncements, should attract their own readers to
the poets by whose work they have been influenced. Such influence has certainly contributed to the taste (if we can distinguish
the *taste* from the *fashion*) for Donne. I do not think that any
modern poet, unless in a fit of irresponsible peevishness, has ever
denied Milton's consummate powers. And it must be said that
Milton's diction is not a poetic diction in the sense of being a
debased currency: when he violates the English language he is
imitating nobody, and he is inimitable. But Milton does, as I have
said, represent poetry at the extreme limit from prose; and it was
one of our tenets that verse should have the virtues of prose, that
diction should become assimilated to cultivated contemporary
speech, before aspiring to the elevation of poetry. Another tenet
was that the subject-matter and the imagery of poetry should be
extended to topics and objects related to the life of a modern man
or woman; that we were to seek the non-poetic, to seek even
material refractory to transmutation into poetry, and words and
phrases which had not been used in poetry before. And the study
of Milton could be of no help here: it was only a hindrance.

We cannot, in literature, any more than in the rest of life, live
in a perpetual state of revolution. If every generation of poets
made it their task to bring poetic diction up to date with the
spoken language, poetry would fail in one of its most important
obligations. For poetry should help, not only to refine the language of the time, but to prevent it from changing too rapidly: a
development of language at too great a speed would be a development in the sense of a progressive deterioration, and that is our
danger today. If the poetry of the rest of this century takes the
line of development which seems to me, reviewing the progress of
poetry though the last three centuries, the right course, it will
discover new and more elaborate patterns of a diction now established. In this search it might have much to learn from Milton's
extended verse structure; it might also avoid the danger of a
servitude to colloquial speech and to current jargon. It might also
learn that the music of verse is strongest in poetry which has a
definite meaning expressed in the properest words. Poets might be
led to admit that a knowledge of the literature of their own language, with a knowledge of the literature and the grammatical
construction of other languages, is a very valuable part of the
poet's equipment. And they might, as I have already hinted,
devote some study to Milton as, outside the theatre, the greatest
master in our language of freedom within form. A study of *Samson*
should sharpen anyone's appreciation of the justified irregularity,
and put him on guard against the pointless irregularity. In
studying *Paradise Lost* we come to perceive that the verse is

continuously animated by the departure from, and return to, the regular measure; and that, in comparison with Milton, hardly any subsequent writer of blank verse appears to exercise any freedom at all. We can also be led to the reflection that a monotony of unscannable verse fatigues the attention even more quickly than a monotony of exact feet. In short, it now seems to me that poets are sufficiently liberated from Milton's reputation, to approach the study of his work without danger, and with profit to their poetry and to the English language.

PART TWO

SOCIAL AND RELIGIOUS CRITICISM

THE HUMANISM OF
IRVING BABBITT

It is proverbially easier to destroy than to construct; and, as a corollary of this proverb, it is easier for readers to apprehend the destructive than the constructive side of an author's thought. More than this: when a writer is skilful in destructive criticism, the public is satisfied with that. If he has no constructive philosophy, it is not demanded; if he has, it is overlooked. This is especially true when we are concerned with critics of society, from Arnold to the present day. All such critics are criticized from one common standard, and that the lowest: the standard of brilliant attack upon aspects of contemporary society which we know and dislike. It is the easiest standard to take. For the criticism deals with concrete things in our world which we know, and the writer may be merely echoing, in neater phrasing, our own thoughts; whereas construction deals with things hard and unfamiliar. Hence the popularity of Mr. Mencken.

But there are more serious critics than Mr. Mencken, and of these we must ask in the end what they have to offer in place of what they denounce. M. Julien Benda, for instance, makes it a part of his deliberate programme to offer nothing; he has a romantic view of critical detachment which limits his interest. Mr. Wyndham Lewis is obviously striving courageously toward a positive theory, but in his published work has not yet reached that point. But in Professor Babbitt's latest book, *Democracy and Leadership*, the criticism is related to a positive theory and dependent upon it. This theory is not altogether expounded, but is partly assumed. What I wish to do in the present essay is to ask a few questions about Mr. Babbitt's constructive theory.

The centre of Mr. Babbitt's philosophy is the doctrine of humanism. In his earlier books we were able to accept this idea without analysis; but in *Democracy and Leadership* – which I take to be at this point the summary of his theory – we are tempted to question it. The problem of humanism is undoubtedly related to the problem of religion. Mr. Babbitt makes it very clear, here and there throughout the book, that he is unable to take the religious

277

view – that is to say that he cannot accept any dogma or revelation; and that humanism is the *alternative* to religion. And this brings up the question: is this alternative any more than a *substitute*? and, if a substitute, does it not bear the same relation to religion that 'humanitarianism' bears to humanism? Is it, in the end, a view of life that will work by itself, or is it a derivative of religion which will work only for a short time in history, and only for a few highly cultivated persons like Mr. Babbitt – whose ancestral traditions, furthermore, are Christian, and who is, like many people, at the distance of a generation or so from definite Christian belief? Is it, in other words, durable beyond one or two generations?

Mr. Babbitt says, of the 'representatives of the humanitarian movement', that

they wish to live on the naturalistic level, and at the same time to enjoy the benefits that the past had hoped to achieve as a result of some humanistic or religious discipline.

The definition is admirable, but provokes us to ask whether, by altering a few words, we cannot arrive at the following statement about humanists:

they wish to live on the humanistic level, and at the same time to enjoy the benefits that the past had hoped to achieve as a result of some religious discipline.

If this transposition is justified, it means that the difference is only of one step: the humanitarian has suppressed the properly human, and is left with the animal; the humanist has suppressed the divine, and is left with a human element which may quickly descend again to the animal from which he has sought to raise it.

Mr. Babbitt is a stout upholder of tradition and continuity, and he knows, with his immense and encyclopaedic information, that the Christian religion is an essential part of the history of our race. Humanism and religion are thus, as historical facts, by no means parellel; humanism has been sporadic, but Christianity continuous. It is quite irrelevant to conjecture the possible development of the European races without Christianity – to imagine, that is, a tradition of humanism equivalent to the actual tradition of Christianity. For all we can say is that we should have been very different creatures, whether better or worse. Our problem being to form the future, we can only form it on the materials of the past; we must *use* our heredity, instead of denying it. The religious habits of the race are still very strong, in all places, at all times, and for all people. There is no humanistic habit: humanism is, I think, merely the state of mind of a few persons in a few places at a few times. To exist at all, it is dependent upon some other attitude, for it is essentially critical – I would even say parasitical. It has been, and can still be, of great value; but it will never provide showers of partridges or abundance of manna for the chosen peoples.

It is a little difficult to define humanism in Mr. Babbitt's terms, for he is very apt to line it up in battle order *with* religion *against* humanitarianism and naturalism; and what I am trying to do is to *contrast* it with religion. Mr. Babbitt is very apt to use phrases like 'tradition humanistic and religious' which suggest that you could say also 'tradition humanistic *or* religious'. So I must make shift to define humanism as I can from a few of the examples that Mr. Babbitt seems to hold up to us.

I should say that he regarded Confucius, Buddha, Socrates, and Erasmus as humanists (I do not know whether he would include Montaigne). It may surprise some to see Confucius and Buddha, who are popularly regarded as founders of religions, in this list. But it is always the human reason, not the revelation of the supernatural, upon which Mr. Babbitt insists. Confucius and Buddha are not in the same boat, to begin with. Mr. Babbitt of course knows infinitely more about both of these men than I do; but even people who know even less about them than I do, know that Confucianism endured by fitting in with popular religion, and that Buddhism endured by becoming[1] as distinctly a *religion* as Christianity – recognizing a dependence of the human upon the divine.

And finally, the attitude of Socrates and that of Erasmus toward the religion of their place and time were very different from what I take to be the attitude of Professor Babbitt. How much Socrates believed, and whether his legendary request of the sacrifice of a cock was merely gentlemanly behaviour or even irony, we cannot tell; but the equivalent would be Professor Babbitt receiving Extreme Unction, and that I cannot at present conceive. But both Socrates and Erasmus were content to remain critics, and to leave the religious fabric untouched. So that I find Mr. Babbitt's humanism to be very different from that of any of the humanists above mentioned.

This is no small point, but the question is a difficult one. It is not at all that Mr. Babbitt has *misunderstood* any of these persons, or that he is not fully acquainted with the civilizations out of which they sprang. On the contrary, he knows all about them. It is rather, I think, that in his interest in the messages of individuals –

---

[1] I wrote *becoming*, but to me it seems that Buddhism is as truly a religion from the beginning as is Christianity.

messages conveyed in books – he has tended merely to neglect the conditions. The great men whom he holds up for our admiration and example are torn from their contexts of race, place, and time. And in consequence, Mr. Babbitt seems to me to tear himself from his own context. His humanism is really something quite different from that of his exemplars, but (to my mind) alarmingly like very liberal Protestant theology of the nineteenth century: it is, in fact, a product – a by-product – of Protestant theology in its last agonies.

I admit that all humanists – as humanists – have been individualists. As humanists, they have had nothing to offer to the mob. But they have usually left a place, not only for the mob, but (what is more important) for the mob part of the mind in themselves. Mr. Babbitt is too rigorous and conscientious a Protestant to do that: hence there seems to be a gap between his own individualism (and indeed intellectualism, beyond a certain point, must be individualistic) and his genuine desire to offer something which will be useful to the American nation primarily and to civilization itself. But the historical humanist, as I understand him, halts at a certain point and admits that the reason will go no further, and that it cannot feed on honey and locusts.

Humanism is either an alternative to religion, or is ancillary to it. To my mind, it always flourishes most when religion has been strong; and if you find examples of humanism which are antireligious, or at least in opposition to the religious faith of the place and time, then such humanism is purely destructive, for it has never found anything to replace what it destroyed. Any religion, of course, is for ever in danger of petrifaction into mere ritual and habit, though ritual and habit be essential to religion. It is only renewed and refreshed by an awakening of feeling and fresh devotion, or by the critical reason. The latter may be the part of the humanist. But if so, then the function of humanism, though necessary, is secondary. You cannot make humanism itself into a religion.

What Mr. Babbitt, on one side, seems to me to be trying to do is to make humanism – his own form of humanism – work without religion. For otherwise, I cannot see the significance of his doctrine of self-control. This doctrine runs throughout his work, and sometimes appears as the 'inner check'. It appears as an alternative to both political and religious anarchy. In the political form it is more easily acceptable. As forms of government become more democratic, as the outer restraints of kingship, aristocracy, and class disappear, so it becomes more and more necessary that the individual no longer controlled by authority or habitual respect should control himself. So far, the doctrine is obviously true and impregnable. But Mr. Babbitt seems to think also that the 'outer' restraints of an orthodox religion, as they weaken, can be supplied by the inner restraint of the individual over himself. If I have interpreted him correctly, he is thus trying to build a Catholic platform out of Protestant planks. By tradition an individualist, and jealous of the independence of individual thought, he is struggling to make something that will be valid for the nation, the race, the world.

The sum of a population of individuals, all ideally and efficiently checking and controlling themselves, will never make a whole. And if you distinguish so sharply between 'outer' and 'inner' checks as Mr. Babbitt does, then there is nothing left for the individual to check himself by but his own private notions and his judgment, which is pretty precarious. As a matter of fact, when you leave the political field for the theological, the distinction between outer and inner becomes far from clear. Given the most highly organized and temporally powerful hierarchy, with all the powers of inquisition and punishment imaginable, still the idea of the religion is the *inner* control – the appeal not to a man's behaviour but to his soul. If a religion cannot touch a man's self, so that in the end he is controlling himself instead of being merely controlled by priests as he might be by policemen, then it has failed in its professed task. I suspect Mr. Babbitt at times of an instinctive dread of organized religion, a dread that it should cramp and deform the free operations of his own mind. If so, he is surely under a misapprehension.

And what, one asks, are all these millions, even these thousands, or the remnant of a few intelligent hundreds, going to control themselves *for*? Mr. Babbitt's critical judgment is exceptionally sound, and there is hardly one of his several remarks that is not, by itself, acceptable. It is the joints of his edifice, not the materials, that sometimes seem a bit weak. He says truly:

It has been a constant experience of man in all ages that mere rationalism leaves him unsatisfied. Man craves in some sense or other of the word an enthusiasm that will lift him out of his merely rational self.

But it is not clear that Mr. Babbitt has any other enthusiasm to offer except the enthusiasm for being lifted out of one's merely rational self by some enthusiasm. Indeed, if he can infect people with enthusiasm for getting even up to the level of their rational selves, he will accomplish a good deal.

But this seems to me just the point at which 'humanistic control' ends, if it gets that far. He speaks of the basis 'of religion and humanistic control' in Burke, but what we should like to know is the respective parts played by religion and humanism in this basis. And with all the references that Mr. Babbitt makes to the rôle of religion in the past, and all the connections that he perceives between the decline of theology and the growth of the modern errors that he detests, he reveals himself as uncompromisingly detached from any religious belief, even the most purely 'personal':

To be modern has meant practically to be increasingly positive and critical, to refuse to receive anything on an authority 'anterior, exterior, and superior' to the individual. With those who still cling to the principle of outer authority I have no quarrel. I am not primarily concerned with them. I am myself a thoroughgoing individualist, writing for those who are, like myself, irrevocably committed to the modern experiment. In fact, so far as I object to the moderns at all, it is because they have not been sufficiently modern, or, what amounts to the same thing, have not been sufficiently experimental.

Those of us who lay no claim to being modern may not be involved in the objection, but, as bystanders, we may be allowed to inquire whither all this modernity and experimenting is going to lead. Is everybody to spend his time experimenting? And on what, and to what end? And if the experimenting merely leads to the conclusion that self-control is good, that seems a very frosty termination to our hunt for 'enthusiasm'. What is the higher will to *will*, if there is nothing either 'anterior, exterior, or superior' to the individual? If this will is to have anything on which to operate, it must be in relation to external objects and to objective values. Mr. Babbitt says:

To give the first place to the higher will is only another way of declaring that life is an act of faith. One may discover on positive grounds a deep meaning in the old Christian tenet that we do not know in order that we may believe, but we believe in order that we may know.

This is quite true; but if life is an act of faith, in what is it an act of faith? The Life-Forcers, with Mr. Bernard Shaw at their head, would say I suppose 'in Life itself'; but I should not accuse Mr. Babbitt of anything so silly as that. However, a few pages farther on he gives something more definite to will: it is civilization.

The next idea, accordingly, to be examined is that of civilization. It seems, on the face of it, to mean something definite; it is, in fact, merely a frame to be filled with definite objects, not a definite object itself. I do not believe that I can sit down for three minutes to will civilization without my mind's wandering to something else. I do not mean that civilization is a mere word; the word means something quite real. But the minds of the individuals who can be said to 'have willed civilization' are minds filled with a great variety of objects of will, according to place, time, and individual constitution; what they have in common is rather a habit in the same direction than a will to civilization. And unless by civilization you mean material progress, cleanliness, etc. – which is not what Mr. Babbitt means; if you mean a spiritual and intellectual coordination on a high level, then it is doubtful whether civilization can endure without religion, and religion without a church.

I am not here concerned with the question whether such a 'humanistic' civilization as that aimed at by Professor Babbitt is or is not *desirable*; only with the question whether it is *feasible*. From this point of view the danger of such theories is, I think, the danger of collapse. For those who had not followed Mr. Babbitt very far, or who had felt his influence more remotely, the collapse would be back again into humanitarianism thinly disguised. For others who had followed him hungrily to the end and had found no hay in the stable, the collapse might well be into a Catholicism *without* the element of humanism and criticism, which would be a Catholicism of despair. There is a hint of this in Mr. Babbitt's own words:

The choice to which the modern man will finally be reduced, it has been said, is that of being a Bolshevist or a Jesuit. In that case (assuming that by Jesuit is meant the ultramontane Catholic) there does not seem to be much room for hesitation. Ultramontane Catholicism does not like Bolshevism, strike at the very root of civilization. In fact, under certain conditions that are already partly in sight, the Catholic Church may perhaps be the only institution left in the Occident that can be counted upon to uphold civilized standards. It may also be possible, however, to be a thoroughgoing modern and at the same time civilized. . . .

The last sentence somehow seems to me to die away a little faintly. But the point is that Mr. Babbitt seems to be giving away to the Church in anticipation more than would many who are more concerned with it in the present than he. Mr. Babbitt is much more ultramontane than I am. One may feel a very deep respect and even love for the Catholic Church (by which I understand Mr. Babbitt means the hierarchy in communion with the Holy See); but if one studies its history and vicissitudes, its difficulties and problems past and present, one is struck with admiration and awe certainly, but is not the more tempted to place all the hopes of humanity on one institution.

But my purpose has been, not to predict a bad end for Mr. Babbitt's philosophy, but to point out the direction which I think it should follow if the obscurities of 'humanism' were cleared up. It should lead, I think, to the conclusion that the humanistic point of view is auxiliary to and dependent upon the religious point of view. For us, religion is Christianity; and Christianity implies, I think, the conception of the Church. It would be not only interesting but invaluable if Professor Babbitt, with his learning, his great ability, his influence, and his interest in the most important questions of the time, could reach this point. His influence might thus join with that of another philosopher – Charles Maurras – and might, indeed, correct some of the extravagances of that writer.

Such a consummation is impossible. Professor Babbitt knows too much; and by that I do not mean merely erudition or information or information or scholarship. I mean that he knows too many religions and philosophies, has assimilated their spirit too thoroughly (there is probably no one in England or America who understands early Buddhism better than he) to be able to give himself to any. The result is humanism. I believe that it is better to recognize the weaknesses of humanism at once, and allow for them, so that the structure may not crash beneath an excessive weight; and so that we may arrive at an enduring recognition of its value for us, and of our obligation to its author.

from THE IDEA OF A
CHRISTIAN SOCIETY

[*i*

...The attitudes and beliefs of Liberalism are destined to disappear, are already disappearing. They belong to an age of free exploitation which has passed; and our danger now is, that the term may come to signify for us only the disorder the fruits of which we inherit, and not the permanent value of the negative element. Out of Liberalism itself come philosophies which deny it. We do not proceed, from Liberalism to its apparent end of authoritarian democracy, at a uniform pace in every respect. There are so many centres of it – Britain, France, America and the Dominions – that the development of western society must proceed more slowly than that of a compact body like Germany, and its tendencies are less apparent. Furthermore, those who are the most convinced of the necessity of *étatisme* as a control of some activities of life, can be the loudest professors of libertarianism in others, and insist upon the preserves of 'private life' in which each man may obey his own convictions or follow his own whim: while imperceptibly this domain of 'private life' becomes smaller and smaller, and may eventually disappear altogether. It is possible that a wave of terror of the consequences of depopulation might lead to legislation having the effect of compulsory breeding.

If, then, Liberalism disappears from the philosophy of life of a people, what positive is left? We are left only with the term 'democracy', a term which, for the present generation, still has a Liberal connotation of 'freedom'. But totalitarianism can retain the terms 'freedom' and 'democracy' and give them its own meaning: and its right to them is not so easily disproved as minds inflamed by passion suppose. We are in danger of finding ourselves with nothing to stand for except a *dislike* of everything maintained by Germany and/or Russia: a dislike which, being a compost of newspaper sensations and prejudice, can have two results, at the same time, which appear at first incompatible. It may lead us to reject possible improvements, because we should owe them to the example of one or both of these countries; and it may equally well lead us to be mere imitators *à rebours*, in making us adopt uncritically almost any attitude which a foreign nation rejects.

We are living at present in a kind of doldrums between opposing winds of doctrine, in a period in which one political philosophy has lost its cogency for behaviour, though it is still the only one in which public speech can be framed. This is very bad for the English language; it is this disorder (for which we are all to blame) and not individual insincerity, which is responsible for the hollowness of many political and ecclesiastical utterances. You have only to examine the mass of newspaper leading articles, the mass of political exhortation, to appreciate the fact that good prose cannot be written by a people without convictions. The fundamental objection to fascist doctrine, the one which we conceal from ourselves because it might condemn ourselves as well, is that it is pagan. There are other objections too, in the political and economic sphere, but they are not objections that we can make with dignity until we set our own affairs in order. There are still other objections, to oppression and violence and cruelty, but however strongly we feel, these are objections to means and not to ends. It is true that we sometimes use the word 'pagan', and in the same context refer to ourselves as 'Christian'. But we always dodge the real issue. Our newspapers have done all they could with the red herring of the 'German national religion', an eccentricity which is after all no odder than some cults held in Anglo-Saxon countries: this 'German national religion' is comforting in that it persuades us that *we* have a Christian civilization; it helps to disguise the fact that our aims, like Germany's, are materialistic. And the last thing we should like to do would be to examine the 'Christianity' which, in such contexts as this, we say we keep.

If we have got so far as accepting the belief that the only alternative to a progressive and insidious adaptation to totalitarian worldliness for which the pace is already set, is to aim at a Christian society, we need to consider both what kind of a society we have at this time, and what a Christian society would be like. We should also be quite sure of what we want: if your real ideals are those of materialistic efficiency, then the sooner you know your own mind, and face the consequences, the better. Those who, either complacently or despairingly, suppose that the aim of Christianization is chimerical, I am not here attempting to convert. To those who realize what a well organized pagan society would mean for us, there is nothing to say. But it is as well to remember that the imposition of a pagan theory of the State does not necessarily mean a wholly pagan society. A compromise between the theory of the State and the tradition of society exists in Italy, a country which is still mainly agricultural and Catholic. The more highly industrialized the country, the more easily a materialistic philosophy will flourish in it, and the more deadly that philosophy will be. Britain has been highly industrialized longer than any other country. And the tendency of unlimited industrialism is to create bodies of men and women – of all classes – detached from tradition, alienated from religion, and susceptible to mass suggestion: in other words, a mob. And a mob will be no less a mob if it is well fed, well clothed, well housed, and well disciplined.

The Liberal notion that religion was a matter of private belief and of conduct in private life, and that there is no reason why Christians should not be able to accommodate themselves to any world which treats them good-naturedly, is becoming less and less tenable. This notion would seem to have become accepted gradually, as a false inference from the subdivision of English Christianity into sects, and the happy results of universal toleration. The reason why members of different communions have been able to rub along together, is that in the greater part of the ordinary business of life they have shared the same assumptions about behaviour. When they have been wrong, they have been wrong together. We have less excuse than our ancestors for un-Christian conduct, because the growth of an un-Christian society about us, its more obvious intrusion upon our lives, has been breaking down the comfortable distinction between public and private morality. The problem of leading a Christian life in a non-Christian society is now very present to us, and it is a very different problem from that of the accommodation between an Established Church and dissenters. It is not merely the problem of a minority in a society of *individuals* holding an alien belief. It is the problem constituted by our implication in a network of institutions from which we cannot dissociate ourselves: institutions the operation of which appears no longer neutral, but non-Christian. And as for the Christian who is not conscious of his dilemma – and he is in the majority – he is becoming more and more de-Christianized by all sorts of unconscious pressure: paganism holds all the most valuable advertising space. Anything like Christian traditions transmitted from generation to generation within the family must disappear, and the small body of Christians will consist entirely of adult recruits. I am saying nothing at this point that has not been said before by others, but it is relevant. I am not concerned with the problem of Christians as a persecuted minority. When the Christian is treated as an enemy of the State, his course is very much harder, but it is simpler. I am concerned with the dangers to the tolerated minority; and in the modern world, it may turn out that the most intolerable thing for Christians is to be tolerated.

To attempt to make the prospect of a Christian society immediately attractive to those who see no prospect of deriving direct personal benefit from it, would be idle; even the majority of professing Christians may shrink from it. No scheme for a change of society can be made to appear immediately palatable, except by falsehood, until society has become so desperate that it will accept any change. A Christian society only becomes acceptable after you have fairly examined the alternatives. We might, of course, merely sink into an apathetic decline: without faith, and therefore without faith in ourselves; without a philosophy of life, either Christian or pagan; and without art. Or we might get a 'totalitarian democracy', different but having much in common with other pagan societies, because we shall have changed step by step in order to keep pace with them: a state of affairs in which we shall have regimentation and conformity, without respect for the needs of the individual soul; the puritanism of a hygienic morality in the interest of efficiency; uniformity of opinion through propaganda, and art only encouraged when it flatters the official doctrines of the time. To those who can imagine, and are therefore repelled by, such a prospect, one can assert that the only possibility of control and balance is a religious control and balance; that the only hopeful course for a society which would thrive and continue its creative activity in the arts of civilization, is to become Christian. That prospect involves, at least, discipline, inconvenience and discomfort: but here as hereafter the alternative to hell is purgatory.

[*ii*

. . . It may be that the conditions unfavourable to the arts today lie too deep and are too extensive to depend upon the differences between one form of government and another; so that the prospect before us is either of slow continuous decay or of sudden extinction. You cannot, in any scheme for the reformation of society, aim directly at a condition in which the arts will flourish: these activities are probably by-products for which we cannot deliberately arrange the conditions. On the other hand, their decay may always be taken as a symptom of some social ailment to be investigated. The future of art and thought in a democratic society does not appear any brighter than any other, unless democracy is to mean something very different from anything actual. It is not that I would defend a moral censorship: I have always expressed strong objections to the suppression of books possessing, or even laying claim to literary merit. But what is more insidious than any censorship, is the steady influence which operates silently in any mass society organized for profit, for the depression of standards of art and culture. The increasing organization of advertisement and propaganda – or the influencing of masses of men by any means except through their intelligence – is all against them. The economic system is against them; the chaos of ideals and confusion of thought in our large scale mass education is against them; and against them also is the disappearance of any class of people who recognize public and private responsibility of patronage of the best that is made and written. At a period in which each nation has less and less 'culture' for its own consumption, all are making furious efforts to export their culture, to impress upon each other their achievements in arts which they are ceasing to cultivate or understand. And just as those who should be the intellectuals regard theology as a special study, like numismatics or heraldry, with which they need not concern themselves, and theologians observe the same indifference to literature and art, as special studies which do not concern *them*, so our political classes regard both fields as territories of which they have no reason to be ashamed of remaining in complete ignorance. Accordingly the more serious authors have a limited, and even provincial audience, and the more popular write for an illiterate and uncritical mob.

You cannot expect continuity and coherence in politics, you cannot expect reliable behaviour on fixed principles persisting through changed situations, unless there is an underlying political philosophy: not of a party, but of the nation. You cannot expect continuity and coherence in literature and the arts, unless you have a certain uniformity of culture, expressed in education by a settled, though not rigid agreement as to what everyone should know to some degree, and a positive distinction – however undemocratic it may sound – between the educated and the uneducated. I observed in America, that with a very high level of intelligence among undergraduates, progress was impeded by the fact that one could never assume that any two, unless they had been at the same school under the influence of the same masters at the same moment, had studied the same subjects or read the same books, though the number of subjects in which they had been instructed was surprising. Even with a smaller amount of total information, it might have been better if they had read fewer, but the same books. In a negative liberal society you have no agreement as to there being any body of knowledge which any educated persons should have acquired at any particular stage: the idea of wisdom disappears, and you get sporadic and unrelated experimentation. A nation's system of education is much more important than its system of government; only a proper system of education can unify the active and the contemplative life, action and speculation, politics and the arts. But 'education', said Coleridge, 'is to be reformed, and defined as synonymous with instruction'. This revolution has been effected: to the populace education *means* instruction. The next step to be taken by the clericalism of secularism, is the inculcation of the political principles approved by the party in power. . . .

[*iii*

We may say that religion, as distinguished from modern paganism, implies a life in conformity with nature. It may be observed that the natural life and the supernatural life have a conformity to each other which neither has with the mechanistic life: but so far has our notion of what is natural become distorted, that people who consider it 'unnatural' and therefore repugnant, that a person of either sex should elect a life of celibacy, consider it perfectly 'natural' that families should be limited to one or two children. It would perhaps be more natural, as well as in better conformity with the Will of God, if there were more celibates and if those who were married had larger families. But I am thinking of 'conformity to nature' in a wider sense than this. We are being made aware that the organization of society on the principle of private profit, as well as public destruction, is leading both to the deformation of humanity by unregulated industrialism, and to the exhaustion of natural resources, and that a good deal of our material progress is a progress for which succeeding generations may have to pay dearly. I need only mention, as an instance now very much before the public eye, the results of 'soil-erosion' – the exploitation of the earth, on a vast scale for two generations, for commercial profit: immediate benefits leading to dearth and desert. I would not have it thought that I condemn a society because of its material ruin, for that would be to make its material success a sufficient test of its excellence; I mean only that a wrong attitude towards nature implies, somewhere, a wrong attitude towards God, and that the consequence is an inevitable doom. For a long enough time we have believed in nothing but the values arising in a mechanized, commercialized, urbanized way of life: it would be as well for us to face the permanent conditions upon which God allows us to live upon this planet. And without sentimentalizing the life of the savage, we might practise the humility to observe, in some of the societies upon which we look down as primitive or backward, the operation of a social-religious-artistic complex which we should emulate upon a higher plane. We have been accustomed to regard 'progress' as always integral; and have yet to learn that it is only by an effort and a discipline, greater than society has yet seen the need of imposing upon itself, that material knowledge and power is gained without loss of spiritual knowledge and power. The struggle to recover the sense of relation to nature and to God, the recognition that even the most primitive feelings should be part of our heritage, seems to me to be the explanation and justification of the life of D. H. Lawrence, and the excuse for his aberrations. But we need not only to learn how to look at the world with the eyes of a Mexican Indian – and I hardly think that Lawrence succeeded – and we certainly cannot afford to stop there. We need to know how to see the world as the Christian Fathers saw it; and the purpose of reascending to origins is that we should be able to return, with greater spiritual knowledge, to our own situation. We need to recover the sense of religious fear, so that it may be overcome by religious hope.

from NOTES TOWARDS THE
DEFINITION OF CULTURE

[*i*

. . .It is obvious that among the more primitive communities the
several activities of culture are inextricably interwoven. The
Dyak who spends the better part of a season in shaping, carving
and painting his barque of the peculiar design required for the
annual ritual of head-hunting, is exercising several cultural
activities at once – of art and religion, as well as of amphibious
warfare. As civilization becomes more complex, greater occupa-
tional specialization evinces itself: in the 'stone age' New Heb-
rides, Mr. John Layard says, certain islands specialize in particular arts and crafts, exchanging their wares and displaying
their accomplishments to the reciprocal satisfaction of the
members of the archipelago. But while the individuals of a tribe,
or of a group of islands or villages, may have separate functions –
of which the most peculiar are those of the king and the witch-
doctor – it is only at a much further stage that religion, science,
politics and art become abstractly conceived apart from each
other. And just as the functions of individuals become hereditary,
and hereditary function hardens into class or caste distinction,
and class distinction leads to conflict, so do religion, politics,
science and art reach a point at which there is conscious struggle
between them for autonomy or dominance. This friction is, at
some stages and in some situations, highly creative: how far it is
the result, and how far the cause, of increased consciousness need
not here be considered. The tension within the society may
become also a tension within the mind of the more conscious
individual: the clash of duties in *Antigone*, which is not simply a
clash between piety and civil obedience, or between religion and
politics, but between conflicting laws within what is still a
religious-political complex, represents a very advanced stage of
civilization: for the conflict must have meaning in the audience's
experience before it can be made articulate by the dramatist and
receive from the audience the response which the dramatist's art
requires.

As a society develops towards functional complexity and differentiation, we may expect the emergence of several cultural levels: in short, the culture of the class or group will present itself. It will not, I think, be disputed that in any future society, as in every civilized society of the past, there must be these different levels. I do not think that the most ardent champions of social equality dispute this: the difference of opinion turns on whether the transmission of group culture must be by inheritance – whether each cultural level must propagate itself – or whether it can be hoped that some mechanism of selection will be found, so that every individual shall in due course take his place at the highest cultural level for which his natural aptitudes qualify him. What is pertinent at this point is that the emergence of more highly cultured groups does not leave the rest of society unaffected: it is itself part of a process in which the whole society changes. And it is certain – and especially obvious when we turn our attention to the arts – that as new values appear, and as thought, sensibility and expression become more elaborate, some earlier values vanish. That is only to say that you cannot expect to have all stages of development at once; that a civilization cannot simultaneously produce great folk poetry at one cultural level and *Paradise Lost* at another. Indeed, the one thing that time is ever sure to bring about is the loss: gain or compensation is almost always conceivable but never certain.

While it appears that progress in civilization will bring into being more specialized culture groups, we must not expect this development to be unattended by perils. Cultural disintegration may ensue upon cultural specialization: and it is the most radical disintegration that a society can suffer. It is not the only kind, or it is not the only aspect under which disintegration can be studied; but, whatever be cause or effect, the disintegration of culture is the most serious and the most difficult to repair. (Here, of course, we are emphasizing the culture of the whole society.) It must not be confused with another malady, ossification into caste, as in Hindu India, of what may have been originally only a hierarchy of functions: even though it is possible that both maladies have some hold upon British society today. Cultural disintegration is present when two or more strata so separate that these become in effect distinct cultures; and also when culture at the upper group level breaks into fragments each of which represents one cultural activity alone. If I am not mistaken, some disintegration of the classes in which culture is, or should be, most highly developed, has already taken place in western society – as well as some cultural separation between one level of society and another. Religious thought and practice, philosophy and art, all tend to become

293

isolated areas cultivated by groups in no communication with each other. The artistic sensibility is impoverished by its divorce from the religious sensibility, the religious by its separation from the artistic; and the vestige of *manners* may be left to a few survivors of a vanishing class who, their sensibility untrained by either religion or art and their minds unfurnished with the material for witty conversation, will have no context in their lives to give value to their behaviour. And deterioration on the higher levels is a matter of concern, not only to the group which is visibly affected, but to the whole people.

The causes of a total decline of culture are as complex as the evidence of it is various. Some may be found in the accounts given, by various specialists, of the causes of more readily apprehended social ailments for which we must continue to seek specific remedies. Yet we become more and more aware of the extent to which the baffling problem of 'culture' underlies the problems of the relation of every part of the world to every other. When we concern ourselves with the relation of the great nations to each other; the relation of the great to the small nations;[1] the relation of intermixed 'communities', as in India, to each other; the relation of parent nations to those which have originated as colonies; the relation of the colonist to the native; the relation between peoples of such areas as the West Indies, where compulsion or economic inducement has brought together large numbers of different races: behind all these perplexing questions, involving decisions to be made by many men every day, there is the question of what culture is, and the question whether it is anything that we can control or deliberately influence. These questions confront us whenever we devise a theory, or frame a policy, of education. If we take culture seriously, we see that a people does not need merely enough to eat (though even that is more than we seem able to ensure) but a proper and particular *cuisine*: one symptom of the decline of culture in Britain is indifference to the art of preparing food. Culture may even be

---

[1] This point is touched upon, though without any discussion of the meaning of 'culture', by E. H. Carr: *Conditions of Peace*, Part I, ch. iii. He says: 'in a clumsy but convenient terminology which originated in Central Europe, we must distinguish between "cultural nation" and "state nation". The existence of a more or less homogeneous racial or linguistic group bound together by a common tradition and the cultivation of a common culture must cease to provide a *prima facie* case for the setting up or the maintenance of an independent political unit.' But Mr. Carr is here concerned with the problem of political unity, rather than with that of the preservation of cultures, or the question whether they are worth preserving, in the political unit.

described simply as that which makes life worth living. And it is what justifies other peoples and other generations in saying, when they contemplate the remains and the influence of an extinct civilization, that it was *worth while* for that civilization to have existed.

I have already asserted, in my introduction, that no culture can appear or develop except in relation to a religion. But the use of the term *relation* here may easily lead us into error. The facile assumption of a relationship between culture and religion is perhaps the most fundamental weakness of Arnold's *Culture and Anarchy*. Arnold gives the impression that Culture (as he uses the term) is something more comprehensive than religion; that the latter is no more than a necessary element, supplying ethical formation and some emotional colour, to Culture which is the ultimate value.

It may have struck the reader that what I have said about the development of culture, and about the dangers of disintegration when a culture has reached a highly developed stage, may apply also in the history of religion. The development of culture and the development of religion, in a society uninfluenced from without, cannot be clearly isolated from each other: and it will depend upon the bias of the particular observer, whether a refinement of culture is held to be the cause of progress in religion, or whether a progress in religion is held to be the cause of a refinement of the culture. What perhaps influences us towards treating religion and culture as two different things is the history of the penetration of Graeco-Roman culture by the Christian Faith – a penetration which had profound effects both upon that culture and upon the course of development taken by Christian thought and practice. But the culture with which primitive Christianity came into contact (as well as that of the environment in which Christianity took its origins) was itself a religious culture in decline. So, while we believe that the same religion may inform a variety of cultures, we may ask whether any culture could come into being, or maintain itself, without a religious basis. We may go further and ask whether what we call the culture, and what we call the religion, of a people are not different aspects of the same thing: the culture being, essentially, the incarnation (so to speak) of the religion of a people. To put the matter in this way may throw light on my reservations concerning the word *relation*.

As a society develops, a greater number of degrees and kinds of religious capacity and function – as well as of other capacities and functions – will make their appearance. It is to be noticed that in some religions the differentiation has been so wide that there have resulted in effect two religions – one for the populace and one for the adepts. The evils of 'two nations' in religion are obvious. Christianity has resisted this malady better than Hinduism. The schisms of the sixteenth century, and the subsequent multiplication of sects, can be studied either as the history of division of religious thought, or as a struggle between opposing social groups – as the variation of doctrine, or as the disintegration of European culture. Yet, while these wide divergences of belief on the same level are lamentable, the Faith can, and must, find room for many degrees of intellectual, imaginative and emotional receptivity to the same doctrines, just as it can embrace many variations of order and ritual. The Christian Faith also, psychologically considered – as systems of beliefs and attitudes in particular embodied minds – will have a history: though it would be a gross error to suppose that the sense in which it can be spoken of as developing and changing, implies the possibility of greater sanctity or divine illumination becoming available to human beings through collective progress. (We do not assume that there is, over a long period, progress even in art, or that 'primitive' art is, as art, necessarily inferior to the more sophisticated.) But one of the features of development, whether we are taking the religious or the cultural point of view, is the appearance of *scepticism* – by which, of course, I do not mean infidelity or destructiveness (still less the unbelief which is due to mental sloth) but the habit of examining evidence and the capacity for delayed decision. Scepticism is a highly civilized trait, though, when it declines into pyrrhonism, it is one of which civilization can die. Where scepticism is strength, pyrrhonism is weakness: for we need not only the strength to defer a decision, but the strength to make one.

The conception of culture and religion as being, when each term is taken in the right context, different aspects of the same thing, is one which requires a good deal of explanation. But I should like to suggest first, that it provides us with the means of combating two complementary errors. The one more widely held is that culture can be preserved, extended and developed in the absence of religion. This error may be held by the Christian in common with the infidel, and its proper refutation would require an historical analysis of considerable refinement, because the truth is not immediately apparent, and may seem even to be contradicted by appearances: a culture may linger on, and indeed produce some of its most brilliant artistic and other successes after the religious faith has fallen into decay. The other error is the belief that the preservation and maintenance of religion need not reckon with the preservation and maintenance of culture: a belief which may even lead to the rejection of the products of culture as frivolous obstructions to the spiritual life. To be in a position to reject this error, as with the other, requires us to take a distant view; to refuse to accept the conclusion, when the culture that we see is a culture in decline, that culture is something to which we can afford to remain indifferent. And I must add that to see the unity of culture and religion in this way neither implies that all the products of art can be accepted uncritically, nor provides a criterion by which everybody can immediately distinguish between them. Aesthetic sensibility must be extended into spiritual perception, and spiritual perception must be extended into aesthetic sensibility and disciplined taste before we are qualified to pass judgment upon decadence or diabolism or nihilism in art. To judge a work of art by artistic or by religious standards, to judge a religion by religious or artistic standards should come in the end to the same thing: though it is an end at which no individual can arrive.

The way of looking at culture and religion which I have been trying to adumbrate is so difficult that I am not sure I grasp it myself except in flashes, or that I comprehend all its implications. It is also one which involves the risk of error at every moment, by some unperceived alteration of the meaning which either term has when the two are coupled in this way, into some meaning which either may have when taken alone. It holds good only in the sense in which people are unconscious of both their culture and their religion. Anyone with even the slightest religious consciousness must be afflicted from time to time by the contrast between his religious faith and his behaviour; anyone with the taste that *individual* or *group* culture confers must be aware of values which he cannot call religious. And both 'religion' and 'culture', besides meaning different things from each other, should mean for the individual and for the group something towards which they strive, not merely something which they possess. Yet there is an aspect in which we can see a religion as the *whole way of life* of a people, from birth to the grave, from morning to night and even in sleep, and that way of life is also its culture. And at the same time we must recognize that when this identification is complete, it means in actual societies both an inferior culture and an inferior religion. A universal religion is at least potentially higher than one which any race or nation claims exclusively for itself; and a culture realizing a religion also realized in other cultures is at least potentially a higher culture than one which has a religion exclusively to itself. From one point of view we may identify: from another, we must separate.

Taking now the point of view of identification, the reader must remind himself as the author has constantly to do, of how much is here embraced by the term *culture*. It includes all the characteristic activities and interests of a people: Derby Day, Henley Regatta, Cowes, the twelfth of August, a cup final, the dog races, the pin table, the dart board, Wensleydale cheese, boiled cabbage cut into sections, beetroot in vinegar, nineteenth-century Gothic churches and the music of Elgar. The reader can make his own list. And then we have to face the strange idea that what is part of our culture is also a part of our *lived* religion.

We must not think of our culture as completely unified – my list above was designed to avoid that suggestion. And the actual religion of no European people has ever been purely Christian, or purely anything else. There are always bits and traces of more primitive faiths, more or less absorbed; there is always the tendency towards parasitic beliefs; there are always perversions, as when patriotism, which pertains to natural religion and is therefore licit and even encouraged by the Church, becomes exaggerated into a caricature of itself. And it is only too easy for a people to maintain contradictory beliefs and to propitiate mutually antagonistic powers.

The reflection that what we believe is not merely what we formulate and subscribe to, but that behaviour is also belief, and that even the most conscious and developed of us live also at the level on which belief and behaviour cannot be distinguished, is one that may, once we allow our imagination to play upon it, be very disconcerting. It gives an importance to our most trivial pursuits, to the occupation of our every minute, which we cannot contemplate long without the horror of nightmare. When we consider the quality of the integration required for the full cultivation of the spiritual life, we must keep in mind the possibility of grace and the exemplars of sanctity in order not to sink into despair. And when we consider the problem of evangelization, of the development of a Christian society, we have reason to quail. To believe that *we* are religious people and that other people are without religion is a simplification which approaches distortion. To reflect that from one point of view religion is culture, and from another point of view culture is religion, can be very disturbing. To ask whether the people have not a religion already, in which Derby Day and the dog track play their parts, is embarrassing; so is the suggestion that part of the religion of the higher ecclesiastic is gaiters and the Athenaeum. It is inconvenient for Christians to find that as Christians they do not believe enough, and that on the other hand they, with everybody else, believe in too many things: yet this is a consequence of reflecting, that bishops are a part of English culture, and horses and dogs are a part of English religion.

It is commonly assumed that there is culture, but that it is the property of a small section of society; and from this assumption it is usual to proceed to one of two conclusions: either that culture can only be the concern of a small minority, and that therefore there is no place for it in the society of the future; or that in the society of the future the culture which has been the possession of the few must be put at the disposal of everybody. This assumption and its consequences remind us of the Puritan antipathy to monasticism and the ascetic life: for just as a culture which is only accessible to the few is now deprecated, so was the enclosed and contemplative life condemned by extreme Protestantism, and celibacy regarded with almost as much abhorrence as perversion.

In order to apprehend the theory of religion and culture which I have endeavoured to set forth in this chapter, we have to try to avoid the two alternative errors: that of regarding religion and culture as two separate things between which there is a *relation*, and that of *identifying* religion and culture. I spoke at one point of the culture of a people as an *incarnation* of its religion; and while I am aware of the temerity of employing such an exalted term, I cannot think of any other which would convey so well the intention to avoid *relation* on the one hand and *identification* on the other. The truth, partial truth, or falsity of a religion neither consists in the cultural achievements of the peoples professing that religion, nor submits to being exactly tested by them. For what a people may be said to believe, as shown by its behaviour, is, as I have said, always a great deal more and a great deal less than its professed faith in its purity. Furthermore, a people whose culture has been formed together with a religion of partial truth, may live that religion (at some period in its history, at least) with greater fidelity than another people which has a truer light. It is only when we imagine our culture as it ought to be, if our society were a really Christian society, that we can dare to speak of Christian culture as the highest culture; it is only by referring to all the phases of this culture, which has been the culture of Europe, that we can affirm that it is the highest culture that the world has ever known. In comparing our culture as it is today, with that of non-Christian peoples, we must be prepared to find that ours is in one respect or another inferior. I do not overlook the possibility that Britain, if it consummated its apostasy by reforming itself according to the prescriptions of some inferior or materialistic religion, might blossom into a culture more brilliant than that we can show today. That would not be evidence that the new religion was true, and that Christianity was false. It would merely prove that any religion, while it lasts, and on its own level, gives an apparent meaning to life, provides the frame-work for a culture, and protects the mass of humanity from boredom and despair.

[*ii*

In an élite composed of individuals who find their way into it solely for their individual pre-eminence, the differences of background will be so great, that they will be united only by their common interests, and separated by everything else. An élite must therefore be attached to *some* class, whether higher or lower: but so long as there are classes at all it is likely to be the dominant class that attracts this élite to itself. What would happen in a classless society – which is much more difficult to envisage than people think – brings us into the area of conjecture. There are, however, some guesses which seem to me worth venturing.

The primary channel of transmission of culture is the family: no man wholly escapes from the kind, or wholly surpasses the degree of culture which he acquired from his early environment. It would not do to suggest that this can be the *only* channel of transmission: in a society of any complexity it is supplemented and continued by other conduits of tradition. Even in relatively primitive societies this is so. In more civilized communities of specialized activities, in which not all the sons would follow the occupation of their father, the apprentice (ideally, at least) did not merely serve his master, and did not merely learn from him as one would learn at a technical school – he became assimilated into a way of life which went with that particular trade or craft; and perhaps the lost secret of the craft is this, that not merely a skill but an entire way of life was transmitted. Culture – distinguishable from knowledge about culture – was transmitted by the older universities: young men have profited there who have been profitless students, and who have acquired no taste for learning, or for Gothic architecture, or for college ritual and form. I suppose that something of the same sort is transmitted also by societies of the masonic type: for initiation is an introduction into a way of life, of however restricted viability, received from the past and to be perpetuated in the future. But by far the most important channel of transmission of culture remains the family: and when family life fails to play its part, we must expect our culture to deteriorate. Now the family is an institution of which nearly everybody speaks well: but it is advisable to remember that this is a term that may vary in extension. In the present age it means little more than the living members. Even if living members, it is a rare exception when an advertisement depicts a large family of three generations: the usual family on the hoardings consists of two parents and one or two young children. What is held up for admiration is not devotion to a family, but personal affection between the members of it: and the smaller the family, the more easily can this personal affection be sentimentalized. But when I speak of the family, I have in mind a bond which embraces a longer period of time than this: a piety towards the dead, however obscure, and a solicitude for the unborn, however remote. Unless this reverence for past and future is cultivated in the home, it can never be more than a verbal convention in the community. Such an interest in the past is different from the vanities and pretensions of genealogy; such a responsibility for the future is different from that of the builder of social programmes.

I should say then that in a vigorous society there will be visible both class and élite, with some overlapping and constant interaction between them. An élite, if it is a governing élite, and so far as the natural impulse to pass on to one's offspring both power and prestige is not artificially checked, will tend to establish itself as a class – it is this metamorphosis, I think, which leads to what appears to me an oversight on the part of Dr. Mannheim. But an élite which thus transforms itself tends to lose its function as élite, for the qualities by which the original members won their position, will not all be transmitted equally to their descendants. On the other hand, we have to consider what would be the consequence when the converse took place, and we had a society in which the functions of class were assumed by élites. Dr. Mannheim seems to have believed that this will happen; he showed himself, as a passage which I have quoted shows, aware of the dangers; and he docs not appear to have been ready to propose definite safeguards against them.

The situation of a society without classes, and dominated exclusively by élites is, I submit, one about which we have no reliable evidence. By such a society, I suppose we must mean one in which every individual starts without advantage or handicap; and in which, by some mechanism set up by the best designers of such machinery, everybody will find his way, or be directed, to that station of life which he is best fitted to fill, and every position will be occupied by the man or woman best fitted for it. Of course, not even the most sanguine would expect the system to work as well as that: if, by and large, it seemed to come nearer to putting the right people in the right places than any previous system, we should all be satisfied. When I say 'dominated', rather than 'governed' by élites, I mean that such a society must not be content to be *governed* by the right people: it must see that the ablest artists and architects rise to the top, influence taste, and execute the important public commissions; it must do the same by the other arts and by science; and above all, perhaps, it must be such that the ablest minds will find expression in speculative thought. The system must not only do all this for society in a particular situation – it must *go on* doing it, generation after generation. It would be folly to deny that in a particular phase of a country's development, and *for a limited purpose*, an élite can do a very good job. It may, by expelling a previous governing group, which in contrast to itself may be a *class*, save or reform or re-vitalize the national life. Such things have happened. But we have very little evidence about the perpetuation of government by élite, and such as we have is unsatisfactory. . . .

[*iii*

I said at the end of my second talk that I should want to make a little clearer what I mean when I use the term culture. Like 'democracy', this is a term which needs to be, not only defined, but illustrated, almost every time we use it. And it is necessary to be clear about what we mean by 'culture', so that we may be clear about the distinction between the material organization of Europe, and the spiritual organism of Europe. If the latter dies, then what you organize will not be Europe, but merely a mass of human beings speaking several different languages. And there will be no longer any justification for their continuing to speak different languages, for they will no longer have anything to say which can-not be said equally well in any language: they will, in short, have no longer anything to say in poetry. I have already affirmed that there can be no 'European' culture if the several countries are isolated from each other: I add now that there can be no European culture if these countries are reduced to identity. We need variety in unity: not the unity of organization, but the unity of nature.

By 'culture', then, I mean first of all what the anthropologists mean: the way of life of a particular people living together in one place. That culture is made visible in their arts, in their social system, in their habits and customs, in their religion. But these things added together do not constitute the culture, though we often speak for convenience as if they did. These things are simply the parts into which a culture can be anatomized, as a human body can. But just as a man is something more than an assemblage of the various constituent parts of his body, so a culture is more than the assemblage of its arts, customs, and religious beliefs. These things all act upon each other, and fully to understand one you have to understand all. Now there are of course higher cul-tures and lower cultures, and the higher cultures in general are distinguished by differentiation of function, so that you can speak of the less cultured and the more cultured strata of society, and finally, you can speak of individuals as being exceptionally cultured. The culture of an artist or a philosopher is distinct from that of a mine worker or field labourer; the culture of a poet will be somewhat different from that of a politician; but in a healthy society these are all parts of the same culture; and the artist, the poet, the philosopher, the politician and the labourer will have a culture in common, which they do not share with other people of the same occupations in other countries.

Now it is obvious that one unity of culture is that of the people who live together and speak the same language: because speaking the same language means thinking, and feeling, and having emotions, rather differently from people who use a different language. But the cultures of different peoples do affect each other: in the world of the future it looks as if every part of the world would affect every other part. I have suggested earlier, that the cultures of the different countries of Europe have in the past derived very great benefit from their influence upon each other. I have suggested that the national culture which isolates itself voluntarily, or the national culture which is cut off from others by circumstances which it cannot control, suffers from this isolation. Also, that the country which receives culture from abroad, without having anything to give in return, and the country which aims to impose its culture on another, without accepting anything in return, will both suffer from this lack of reciprocity.

There is something more than a general exchange of culture influences, however. You cannot even attempt to trade equally with every other nation: there will be some who need the kind of goods that you produce, more than others do, and there will be some who produce the goods you need yourselves, and others who do not. So cultures of people speaking different languages can be more or less closely related: and sometimes so closely related that we can speak of their having a common culture. Now when we speak of 'European culture', we mean the identities which we can discover in the various national cultures; and of course even within Europe, some cultures are more closely related than others. Also, one culture within a group of cultures can be closely related, on different sides, to two cultures which are not closely related to each other. Your cousins are not all cousins of each other, for some are on the father's side and some on the mother's. Now, just as I have refused to consider the culture of Europe simply as the sum of a number of unrelated cultures in the same area, so I refused to separate the world into quite unrelated cultural groups; I refused to draw any absolute line between East and West, between Europe and Asia. There are, however, certain common features in Europe, which make it possible to speak of a European culture. What are they?

The dominant force in creating a common culture between peoples each of which has its distinct culture, is religion. Please do not, at this point, make a mistake in anticipating my meaning. This is not a religious talk, and I am not setting out to convert anybody. I am simply stating a fact. I am not so much concerned with the communion of Christian believers today; I am talking about the common tradition of Christianity which has made Europe what it is, and about the common cultural elements which this common Christianity has brought with it. If Asia were converted to Christianity tomorrow, it would not thereby become a part of Europe. It is in Christianity that our arts have developed; it is in Christianity that the laws of Europe have – until recently – been rooted. It is against a background of Christianity that all our thought has significance. An individual European may not believe that the Christian Faith is true, and yet what he says, and makes, and does, will all spring out of his heritage of Christian culture and depend upon that culture for its meaning. Only a Christian culture could have produced a Voltaire or a Nietzsche. I do not believe that the culture of Europe could survive the complete disappearance of the Christian Faith. And I am convinced of that, not merely because I am a Christian myself, but as a student of social biology. If Christianity goes, the whole of our culture goes. Then you must start painfully again, and you cannot put on a new culture ready made. You must wait for the grass to grow to feed the sheep to give the wool out of which your new coat will be made. You must pass through many centuries of barbarism. We should not live to see the new culture, nor would our great-great-great-grandchildren: and if we did, not one of us would be happy in it.

To our Christian heritage we owe many things beside religious faith. Through it we trace the evolution of our arts, through it we have our conception of Roman Law which has done so much to shape the Western World, through it we have our conceptions of private and public morality. And through it we have our common standards of literature, in the literatures of Greece and Rome. The Western world has its unity in this heritage, in Christianity and in the ancient civilizations of Greece, Rome and Israel, from which, owing to two thousand years of Christianity, we trace our descent. I shall not elaborate this point. What I wish to say is, that this unity in the common elements of culture, throughout many centuries, is the true bond between us. No political and economic organization, however much goodwill it commands, can supply what this culture unity gives. If we dissipate or throw away our common patrimony of culture, then all the organization and planning of the most ingenious minds will not help us, or bring us closer together.

The unity of culture, in contrast to the unity of political organization, does not require us all to have only one loyalty: it means that there will be a variety of loyalties. It is wrong that the only duty of the individual should be held to be towards the State; it is fantastic to hold that the supreme duty of every individual should be towards a Super-State. I will give one instance of what I mean by a variety of loyalties. No university ought to be merely a national institution, even if it is supported by the nation. The universities of Europe should have their common ideals, they should have their obligations towards each other. They should be independent of the governments of the countries in which they are situated. They should not be institutions for the training of an efficient bureaucracy, or for equipping scientists to get the better of foreign scientists; they should stand for the preservation of learning, for the pursuit of truth, and in so far as men are capable of it, the attainment of wisdom. . . .

Appendix A

NOTES

These notes serve two very limited purposes. They provide a bare indication as to the first publication of each piece; and they give the sources of Eliot's verse quotations whenever they are not apparent from the context. Nothing else is attempted, except that I draw attention to a few misquotations, not, I hope, from pedantry, but from a conviction that in the poet Eliot misquotation is sometimes creative; and I have also added one or two notes for readers seeking help with unfamiliar languages, or wondering who wrote a particular book or poem when its author goes unmentioned. I am indebted to Valerie Eliot, John Sutherland, Christopher Ricks, Ian Fletcher and especially Keith Walker, whom I consulted when baffled.

p. 31 'Reflections on *Vers Libre*' (first published *New Statesman*, 3 March 1917).
Once, in finesse of fiddles... T. E. Hulme, 'The Embankment', *The Complete Poetical Works of T. E. Hulme*, published at the end of Pound's *Ripostes*, 1912.
There shut up in his castle... Ezra Pound, 'Near Perigord,' III; *Personae*, 169.
I recover, like a spent taper... Webster, *The White Devil*, 5.6.
Cover her face... Webster, *The Duchess of Malfi*, 4.2.
You have cause... *The Duchess of Malfi*, 3.2.
This is a vain poetry... *The Duchess of Malfi*, 3.2.
I loved this woman... Middleton, *The Changeling*, 5.3 (should read: 'in spite of her heart'; Eliot quotes it correctly in 'Thomas Middleton,' *Selected Essays*, 164).
I would have these herbs... *The White Devil*, 5.4.
Whether the spirit... *The Duchess of Malfi*, 1.1.
The boughs of the trees... H. D. 'Hermes of the Ways', ii.

307

When the white dawn first. . . Matthew Arnold, *The Strayed Reveller*, 24ff.

p. 37 'Tradition and the Individual Talent' (first published *Egoist* September and December 1919).

And now methinks. . . 'Tourneur', *The Revenger's Tragedy*, 3.5.

ὁ δὲ νοῦς ἴσως. . . 'The mind is doubtless more divine and less subject to passion' (Aristotle, *De Anima*, 1.4).

p. 45 '*Hamlet*' (first published, as 'Hamlet and his problems', in *Athenaeum*, 26 September 1919).

p. 50 'The Perfect Critic' (first published *Athenaeum*, 23 July 1920).

Lettres à l'Amazone: by Remy de Gourmont (1914).

Le Problème du style: By Remy de Gourmont (1902).

p. 59 'The Metaphysical Poets' (first published *Times Literary Supplement*, 20 October 1921).

On a round ball. . . Donne, 'A Valediction: Of Weeping', 10ff.

A bracelet. . . Donne, 'The Relique', 6.

Notre âme. . . Baudelaire, 'Le Voyage', II.

His fate was. . . Vanity of Human Wishes, 219ff. (misquoted; first line begins 'His fall was. . .', third line 'He left the name. . .').

So when from hence. . . Lord Herbert of Cherbury, 'Ode upon a Question Moved, Whether Love should Continue for ever?' st. 33–5.

in this one thing. . . The Revenge of Bussy D'Ambois, 4.1.

No, when the fight. . . 'Bishop Blougram's Apology', 693ff.

One walked between. . . 'The Two Voices', 412ff.

O géraniums. . . Jules Laforgue, *Derniers Vers* (1890), X.

Elle est bien loin. . . Laforgue, 'Sur une defunte', *Derniers Vers*.

Pour l'enfant. . . Baudelaire, 'Le Voyage', I.

p. 68 'The Function of Criticism' (first published *Criterion*, October 1923).

p. 77 Preface to *Anabasis* (first published 1930; *Anabasis* is Eliot's translation of the *Anabase* of St.-Jean Perse (Alexis Léger) published in French 1924).

p. 79 *The Use of Poetry and the Use of Criticism* (lectures delivered at Harvard University 1932–3; first published 1933. The titles here given to the extracts have been provided by the editor).

Some have accused me. . . Don Juan, 4.5.

Then what I thought. . . Triumph of Life, 182ff.

On a battle-trumpet's blast. . . Prometheus Unbound, 1.694–701.

To suffer woes. . . Prometheus Unbound, 4. 570–4.

True love in this. . . Epipsychidion, 160–1, 149–53.

A vision like. . . Epipsychidion, 121–3 (earlier, not later).

Fly where the evening. . . Bussy D'Ambois, 5.3.

NOTES

dic sub Aurora. . . Hercules Œteus, 152ff. ('Tell the Sabaeans placed under Aurora, tell the Hibernians placed under the sunset, and those who suffer under the chariot of the Bear, and those who are oppressed by the burning axletree. . .').

sub ortu solis. . . Hercules Furens, 1140–1 ('Beneath the sun's rising, or beneath the course of the frozen Bear. . .').

lips only sing when they cannot kiss 'Art', section 3 (*Collected Poems*, 127).

p. 97 'Religion and Literature' (first published in *The Faith That Illuminates*, ed. V. A. Demant, 1935).

p. 107 'The Music of Poetry' (first published as the W. P. Ker Lecture for 1942 by the University of Glasgow Press).

p. 115 'What is a Classic?' (the Presidential Address to the Virgil Society, 1944; first published by Faber & Faber, 1945).

il temporal foco. . . Purgatorio, XXVII.

p. 132 'Poetry and Drama' (The first Theodore Spencer Memorial Lecture at Harvard University, published by Faber & Faber and Harvard University Press, 1951).

p. 149 *Ezra Pound: His Metric and Poetry* (first published anonymously in New York, 1917).

p. 151 'Henry James' (first published in *The Little Review*, January 1918).

p. 153 'Philip Massinger' (first published in *Times Literary Supplement*, 27 May 1920; a second part, here omitted, appeared in *Athenaeum*, 11 June 1920).

Can I call back. . . The Emperor of the East, 5.2.

Not poppy. . . Othello, 3.3.

Thou didst not borrow. . . The Duke of Milan, 3.1.

God knows, my son. . . II Henry IV, 4.5.

And now, in the evening. . . The Virgin Martyr, 5.2.

I shall fall. . . Henry VIII, 3.2.

What you deliver. . . The Great Duke of Florence, 3.1.

'Tis in my memory locked. . . Hamlet, 1.3.

Here he comes. . . The Roman Actor, 4.1.

the Cardinal lifts up. . . Duchess of Malfi, 3.4 ('he lifts up's nose').

as tann'd galley-slaves. . . The Roman Actor, 4.1. (The 'great lines' are in *Duchess of Malfi* 4.2.).

in her strong toil. . . Antony and Cleopatra, 5.2.

Does the silk worm. . . 'Tourneur', *Revenger's Tragedy*, 3.5.

Let the common sewer. . . Middleton, *The Changeling*, 5.3.

Lust and forgetfulness. . . Middleton, *Women Beware Women*, 5.1.

What though my father. . . Massinger, *The Fatal Dowry*, 1.2.

Why, 'tis impossible. . . The Changeling, 3.4.

309

p. 161 'Andrew Marvell' (first published *Times Literary Supplement*, 31 March 1921).

'It is such a king... 'The Statue in Stocks-Market' (not by Marvell).

'Men ... ought and might... Marvell, *The Rehearsal Transpros'd.*

Pallida Mors... Horace, *Odes* 1.4: 'Pale Death knocks impartially at pauper's hut and prince's palace.'

Nobis, cum semel... Catullus, *Carmina* 5 (*'Vivamus, mea Lesbia'*): 'When our brief light has faded, we must sleep an everlasting night.'

Le squelette... Théophile Gautier, 'Bûchers et tombeaux' (*Emaux et camées*, 1852).

Cannot we delude... The song in *Volpone*, 3.7.

Necessité faict... Villon, 'Le Testament', XXI.

The midwife... The Second Part of *Absalom and Achitophel*, 476–7.

A numerous host... *Absalom and Achitophel*, 529–30.

Oft he seems... *Samson Agonistes*, 1749ff.

Comely in thousand shapes... 'Of Wit', 6–8.

In a true piece... 'Of Wit', 57ff.

Art thou pale... 'To the Moon', 1–6.

p. 172 'Marie Lloyd' (first published *Dial*, December 1922 and as 'In Memoriam, Marie Lloyd', *Criterion* I, January 1923).

p. 175 *'Ulysses*, Order, and Myth' (first published *Dial*, November, 1923).

p. 179 'Lancelot Andrewes' (first published *Times Literary Supplement*, 23 September 1926, then in *For Lancelot Andrewes*, 1928).

che in questo mondo... Dante, *Paradiso*, 31, 110–11 ('Who in this world tasted, by means of meditation, the peace of that one').

Who is it... Nativity Sermon of 1622.

I know not how... ibid.

Christ is no wild-cat... ibid.

the word within a word... '*Verbum infans*, the Word without a word; the eternal Word not able to speak a word...' (Nativity Sermon of 1618). In this most curious of his misquotations Eliot is remembering his own *Gerontion* ('The word within a word, unable to speak a word'). In *Ash Wednesday* V there is a variant which restores the sense of Andrewes without altogether abandoning 'within': 'The Word without a word, the Word within / The world...'

It was no summer progress... Nativity Sermon of 1622.

I add yet farther... Nativity Sermon of 1611.

I am here speaking... *Fifty Sermons* (1649), Sermon 14.

A memory of yesterday's pleasures. . .   LXXX Sermons (1640),
Sermon LXXX.

p. 189 'Thomas Middleton' (first published *Times Literary Supplement*, 30 June 1927).

Why, 'tis impossible. . .   The Changeling, 3.4.

Can you weep. . .   The Changeling, 3.4.

A wondrous necessary man. . .   The Changeling, 5.1.

Beneath the stars. . .   The Changeling, 5.2.

I loved this woman. . .   The Changeling, 5.3.

Did I not say. . .   Women Beware Women, 2.2.

Troth, you speak. . .   Women Beware Women, 3.1.

'A fine journey. . .'   Michaelmas Term, 4.1.

I that am of your blood. . .   The Changeling, 5.3 (or, 'I am that of
your blood. . .').

p. 196 'Francis Herbert Bradley' (first published *Times Literary
Supplement*, 29 December 1927).

p. 205 *Dante* (first published 1929).

She looks like sleep. . .   Shakespeare, *Antony and Cleopatra*, 5.2.

Giustizia mosse. . .   Inferno, 3.

E come gli stornei. . .   Inferno, 5.

E come i gru. . .   Inferno, 5.

Noi leggevamo. . .   Inferno, 5.

se fosse amico. . .   Inferno, 5.

Amor, che a nullo. . .   Inferno, 5.

ed ei s'ergea. . .   Inferno, 6.

Poi si rivolse. . .   Inferno, 15.

Lo maggior corno. . .   Inferno, 26.

moans round. . .   'Ulysses', 55–6 ('The deep / Moans round. . .').

Put up your bright swords. . .   Othello, 1.2 ('Keep up your
bright swords. . .').

ov' Ercole. . .   Inferno, 26.

'O frati. . .'   Inferno, 26.

n'apparve una montagna. . .   Inferno, 26.

'Io fui di Montefeltro. . .'   Purgatorio, 5.

Non aspettar. . .   Purgatorio, 27.

una donna soletta. . .   Purgatorio, 28.

Nel suo aspetto. . .   Paradiso, 1.

Beatrice mi guardò. . .   Paradiso, 4.

Come in peschiera. . .   Paradiso, 5.

Quale allodetta. . .   Paradiso, 20.

Nel suo profondo. . .   Paradiso, 33.

O quanto è corto. . .   Paradiso, 33.

p. 231 'Baudelaire' (first published as Introduction to *The Intimate
Journals of Charles Baudelaire*, translated by Christopher
Isherwood, 1930).

ses ailes de géant. . . 'L'Albatros'.

Maint joyau. . . 'Le Guignon'.

Valse mélancolique. . . 'Harmonie du soir'.

Au coeur d'un vieux faubourg. . . 'Le vin des chiffoniers'.

p. 237 *'Pensées* of Pascal' (first published as Introduction to *Pascal's Pensées*, translated by W. F. Trotter, 1931).

p. 239 *'In Memoriam'* (first published as Introduction to *Poems of Tennyson*, 1936).

All day within. . . 'Mariana'.

Of love. . . 'Love and Duty'.

Dark house. . . *In Memoriam*, vii.

shall he. . . ibid., lvi.

No longer. . . ibid., Conclusion.

Dear as remember'd kisses. . . *The Princess*, 4.54.

And now no sacred. . . Swinburne, 'Ave atque Vale: In Memory of Charles Baudelaire'.

p. 248 'Yeats '(the first annual Yeats Lecture, delivered to the Friends of the Irish Academy at the Abbey Theatre, Dublin, in 1940; subsequently published in *Purpose*, July–December 1940, as 'The Poetry of W. B. Yeats').

You think it horrible. . . 'The Spur'.

p. 258 'Milton I' (first published *Essays and Studies* of the English Association, 1936).

O'er the smooth. . . *Arcades*, 84.

. . . paths of this drear wood. . . *Comus*, 37.

Shadowing more beauty. . . Marlowe, *Dr. Faustus*, 1.1.

While the ploughman. . . *L'Allegro*, 63ff.

The sun to me. . . *Samson Agonistes*, 86ff.

Thrones, dominations. . . *Paradise Lost*, 5.772.

Cambula, seat of. . . *Paradise Lost*, 11.388.

p. 265 'Milton II' (first published in *Proceedings of the British Academy*, 33 (1947).

'a dissociation of sensibility. . .' This passage occurs not in an essay on Dryden but in 'The Metaphysical Poets' (pp. 59–67 *supra*).

p. 277 'The Humanism of Irving Babbitt' (first published *Forum*, July 1928).

p. 285 *The Idea of a Christian Society* (first published 1939).

p. 292 *Notes Towards the Definition of Culture* (first published 1948).

NOTE ON THE PRINCIPAL COLLECTIONS OF T. S. ELIOT'S PROSE, AND ON SOME SECONDARY MATERIAL

The Sacred Wood, Eliot's first collection, appeared in 1920; the edition of 1928 has a Preface of importance, and the work is in print. *Homage to John Dryden* (1924) included three essays later reprinted in *Selected Essays*. *For Lancelot Andrewes* (1928) was similarly absorbed, and so was *Dante* (1929), and *Thoughts After Lambeth* (1931). *Selected Essays, 1917–1932* (1932) includes most, though not all, of the important essays up to that date. *The Use of Poetry and the Use of Criticism* (1933) continues in print, unlike *After Strange Gods* (1934). Later essays included in *Essays Ancient and Modern* (1936) were added to the third edition of *Selected Essays* (1951). Two further collections, *On Poetry and Poets* (1957) and *To Criticize the Critic* (1965) bring together the essays and lectures of the postwar years; the last also reprints Eliot's early essay 'Reflections on *Vers Libre*', and his first (anonymous) book, *Ezra Pound: his metric and poetry* (1917).

Much of the non-literary work is included in the general collections up to 1951, but *The Idea of a Christian Society* (1939) and *Notes Towards the Definition of Culture* (1948) were published as separate volumes. A considerable quantity of philosophical, social and religious writing has so far not been collected. Of several books on these aspects of Eliot's thought, the best is Roger Kojecky's *T. S. Eliot's Social Criticism* (1971). See also John D. Margolis, *T. S. Eliot's Intellectual Development, 1922–1939* (1971) and Herbert Howarth, *Notes on some Figures behind T. S. Eliot* (1965), especially Chapter 8. Raymond Williams, *Culture and Society* (1958) considers the ideas in a broader context, and from a leftwing position. Bernard Bergonzi's *T. S. Eliot* (1972) offers a useful conspectus. See also Stephen Spender, *Eliot* (1975). The standard bibliography is by D. Gallup (1952, revised and extended 1969).

INDEX

Page numbers in italics indicate that the reference includes a quotation. (?) after a title indicates that the authorship is in question.